QUAGMIRE

America
in the
Middle East

QUAGMIRE

America
in the
Middle East

Leon T. Hadar

CATO
INSTITUTE
Washington D.C.

Library of Congress Cataloging-in-Publication Data

Hadar, Leon T.
   Quagmire : America in the Middle East / Leon T. Hadar.
      p.   cm.
   Includes bibliographical references and index.
   ISBN 0–932790–94–1 : $24.95. — ISBN 0–932790–93–3
   (pbk.) : $14.95
   1. Middle East—Foreign relations—United States.
   2. United States—Foreign relations—Middle East.
   3. Israel-Arab conflicts.
   I. Title
   DS63.2.U5H34   1992   92–13488
   327.73056—dc20   CIP

Cover Design by Colin Moore.

Printed in the United States of America.

CATO INSTITUTE
224 Second Street, SE
Washington, D.C. 20003

Contents

Preface

This book is, in part, the outgrowth of an earlier discussion of the way the new American-Soviet relationship and the changing international system would affect U.S. policy in the Middle East. That study, entitled "Creating a U.S. Policy of Constructive Disengagement in the Middle East" (Cato Institute Policy Analysis no. 125, December 29, 1989), appeared when the Cold War was beginning to end and Europe was beginning to move toward unity.

In it I attempted to refute both the axiom of the neoconservatives and the Israeli lobby, that the interests of America and Israel are served by the extensive military and economic aid Washington provides Jerusalem, and the arguments of the liberals and the Arab lobby for intensive American diplomatic efforts to solve the Arab-Israeli conflict. Not surprisingly, that study alienated the Middle Eastern policy and scholarly community, which has always been divided into pro-Israeli and pro-Arab factions.

The thesis of the study was very simple: the end of the Soviet threat in the Middle East, the rise of the European Community as a political and economic force with close ties to the Middle East, and the continuing diplomatic intransigence and economic stagnation reflected in the policies of the Israeli government provided the United States with an opportunity to gradually disengage from the region and adopt a policy of indifference toward the Arab-Israeli conflict. I argued that by adopting a lower profile, Washington would provide Europe with incentives to accept more security and political responsibility for the Middle East and Israel with inducements to adopt a moderate diplomatic posture and reform its statist economic system.

At the beginning of 1990, when I began work on this book, developments in Washington and the Middle East seemed to confirm many of my arguments. The collapse of the Soviet empire and changes in other parts of the world were diverting attention from the Middle East, where there were very few signs of diplomatic breakthroughs or political or economic reform.

However, foreign policy paradigms die hard. Both Arabs and Israelis and their supporters in Washington were attempting to draw the United States back into active diplomatic and military involvement in the Middle East. Their efforts were seconded by those of frustrated Cold Warriors who hoped that perceived threats emanating from the Middle East would give rise to new calls for military expenditures and U.S. intervention.

In a July 1990 Cato Institute Policy Forum, I discussed the dangers inherent in those attempts. I pointed in particular to the way Saddam Hussein was being used by various members of the national security community and Congress as well as the Israeli and Arab lobbies and their clients to keep alive the decaying Middle Eastern paradigm. Two days before Saddam invaded Kuwait, I completed the written version of my remarks, which was subsequently published, with minor revisions, as "The Rise of the Middle Eastern Bogeyman: Sliding toward Post-Cold-War Interventionism" (Cato Institute Foreign Policy Briefing no. 2, September 5, 1990).

The war in the Persian Gulf gave me the opportunity to tie my historical and theoretical arguments to a concrete manifestation of what I believe is wrong and dangerous in the current American posture in the Middle East. Washington's adoption of a policy of benign neglect toward the region or engagement in new rounds of peace diplomacy will not change in any major respect the thrust of this book. It is in no way a historical study. It is an attempt to provide the reader with a framework for understanding U.S. policy in the Middle East—to explain not the what, where, and when but the why of America's involvement in the region—and to develop some policy recommendations based on that understanding.

Chapters 1 through 3 cover the evolution of the Middle Eastern paradigm from the early days of the Cold War to the Persian Gulf War. Chapters 4 and 5 analyze the American-Israeli relationship. Some of the material in those chapters appeared in "Reforming Israel—Before It's Too Late" (*Foreign Policy*, Winter 1990–91). Chapters 6 and 7, which discuss the rift between the United States and Europe over the Middle East, are based in part on "The United States, Europe, and the Middle East" (*World Policy Journal*, Summer 1991). Chapter 8 presents some ideas for establishing peace between Israel and her neighbors. Chapter 9 attempts to tie all those issues together against the backdrop of the post–gulf war international scene.

I would like to express my deep appreciation to members of the Cato Institute for their generous support and encouragement. In particular, I wish to thank Ted Galen Carpenter, director of foreign policy studies, whose hard work and unflagging interest were the driving force behind this book. The comments and advice of William A. Niskanen, chairman; Edward H. Crane, president; David Boaz, executive vice president; and Sheldon L. Richman, senior editor, are also deeply appreciated, as are the patience and attention to detail of my editor, Elizabeth W. Kaplan. Any remaining errors or inaccuracies are my own. Finally, I would like to express my thanks to my parents, Pnina and Baruch, and to my wife, Alyn, for supporting me in this work despite their strong disagreements with my ideas and views.

1. Introduction: Coping with the Post–Cold War Summer Blues

It was hot, humid, and boring on the shores of the Potomac in early July 1990. Very few of the movers and shakers of Washington stay in the city during the summer. Their power-lunch hangouts are deserted. Indeed, remaining in the nation's capital during July and August is a sign that you haven't made it yet. It suggests that a lack of political connections or serious cash-flow problems make it necessary for you to keep your law firm or consulting business open—or worse, to hang on to your dreary nine-to-five government job.

But that July the atmosphere was depressing not only for Washington's losers, sweating in their uniform summer suits, but for everyone, including the leaders of America's military-industrial complex and the foreign policy elite. True, the United States had won the Cold War. But instead of a mood of victory, a feeling of despair lingered in the air. Washington's governing elite was concerned that it was losing its raison d'être and becoming irrelevant to the flow of major international developments. Its members were worried that their city might cease to be the capital of the West.

A State Department official, Francis Fukuyama, had announced in a celebrated piece a few months earlier that we had reached the "end of history."[1] But no one, even in his worst nightmares, had thought that the end would look the way it did: The major television networks were gradually cutting their coverage of Washington and sending their crews to report on the collapse of communism in Europe. Foreign correspondents assigned to cover the United States were expressing envy of their colleagues who had been sent to Europe to report on the revolution in Romania or the aftermath of the fall of the Berlin Wall.

The city's pundits and experts were searching in vain for topics to discuss in their columns and television talk shows. Mundane

1

domestic problems, such as the budget deficit, education, and the environment, were pushing aside the foreign policy dilemmas that the self-appointed heirs to Walter Lippmann like to debate. Indeed, terrorism experts and Middle East analysts, the television news stars of the oil embargo dramas and the Arab-Israeli wars of the 1970s and 1980s, were no longer in demand on news programs. And their colleagues, the defense consultants and contractors, the so-called beltway bandits, were complaining that business with the Pentagon was drying up.

The Threat of American "Declinism"

On the other side of the Atlantic, a consensus was emerging that the disappearance of the Soviet threat and the reunification of Germany were making it necessary to alter the shape and purpose of the American-led Western alliance. European officials and analysts were calling for the restructuring of the North Atlantic Treaty Organization (NATO), if not for its elimination. Bonn asked Washington to remove its nuclear artillery from German soil, and Bonn and Paris began exploring closer coordination of their conventional and nuclear forces.[2]

When President Mikhail Gorbachev of the Soviet Union and Chancellor Helmut Kohl of West Germany met in Stavropol in July 1990 to discuss the shape of post–Cold War Europe, President Bush remained uninvited in Washington. There was a feeling on the Continent that the United States had become irrelevant to the new Europe. The media were full of stories about and analyses of the united Europe that would emerge in 1992 and the role Germany would play in that union. Brussels was suddenly competing with Washington for the services of international lobbying and public relations firms.

Indeed, when the leading industrial powers met in July 1990 in Houston, Germany and Japan acted with unprecedented assertiveness, staking out policies toward the Soviet Union and China, respectively, without the Bush administration's lead and often despite its reservations. President Bush, however, argued that now more than ever there was a need for a strong America. He insisted that other nations were too weak to fill a global power vacuum. Only the United States could assert world leadership, provided that it had the political will to remain a global power and that other

2

nations saw threats to their security or interests that gave them reason to follow the U.S. lead. As political scientist Joseph Nye put it, "If the strongest state does not lead, the prospects of instability increase."[3]

More specifically, the Bush administration stressed that the need to contain European "instability," a code word for German military resurgence, justified perpetuating NATO and maintaining an American military presence in Europe. Even that point, which reflected Lord Ismay's famous dictum that NATO's purpose in Europe was to "keep the Americans in, the Russians out, and the Germans down," did not sell very well in Europe.

Only Prime Minister Margaret Thatcher of Britain, a staunch opponent of European unity who was worried about the possible loss of Britain's power position vis-à-vis Germany, enthusiastically embraced continuing the American hegemony in the Western alliance. Bush, during his visit to Europe in early 1990, went out of his way to stress Washington's view of Germany as the rising European power. He downplayed America's "special relationship" with the British by not even stopping in London.

Questions were being raised about the need to maintain NATO and U.S. military leadership in the West, and Americans were beginning to seriously debate the need to perpetuate huge defense budgets in the post–Cold War era.[4] Bonn and Tokyo, as the conventional wisdom indicated in the dog days of the summer of 1990, were emerging as America's main international competitors. Economics was replacing the military as the main currency of international power; the trading state was supplanting the national security state.[5]

The realization that Europe and Japan were becoming less willing to accept American global leadership was slowly dawning on America's foreign policy elite. The notion of American "declinism" had been popularized by Paul Kennedy's historical study, *The Rise and Fall of the Great Powers*, that had occupied the *New York Times* and the *Washington Post* best-seller lists a year earlier. A debate was beginning among the country's political and financial leaders. As one analyst argued, two main rival groups were emerging.[6]

The first group included those who followed the "geo-economic" model. They called for a scaled-back U.S. military establishment and a greater investment of American resources in science, technology, education, and trade development. If the United States was to compete successfully with Japan and Germany, the geoeconomists held, it would have to spend less on military forces and more on economic revitalization.[7] The geoeconomic model, though popular on Wall Street, was not attractive to the political and corporate forces that had long associated U.S. power and prosperity with a strong defense and a significant military presence abroad.

The second group, those who advocated the "geo-strategic" model, called for a policy based on a U.S. role in guarding the Western world's principal trade routes and sources of raw materials against insurgency, sectarian violence, and regional adventurism or instability.[8]

The debate between the geoeconomists and the geostrategists, which cut across party and ideological lines, was not merely academic. Its outcome would entail extraordinary consequences for all concerned: it would determine who would control America's foreign policy establishment in the years ahead and how resources would be distributed domestically, which of the huge federal bureaucracies would prosper and which would fall into decline, and which giant corporations would receive lucrative contracts and which would not. "At issue in this contest, in other words," commented Michael Klare, "is the relative power, wealth and prestige of America's top movers and shakers."[9]

The geoeconomists included, on the left, proponents of a national industrial policy, who were interested in devising programs for government-led restructuring of the economy enhanced by protectionist policies, and black activists, who called for diverting military resources to domestic social programs. On the right, the geoeconomists included the paleoconservatives, heirs to the isolationist Old Right, such as Patrick Buchanan, who contended that the end of the Cold War should produce a less interventionist foreign policy and more focus on economic and social problems at home, and libertarians, who argued that international trade should be America's main activity in the international arena and that Washington should serve as a model for emerging democracies and free-market systems, a kind of a global "shining city on the hill."[10]

Despite their common denominator—support for a less interventionist foreign policy and a focus on international economic issues—there were major divisions among the members of the geoeconomic coalition. For example, while libertarians were committed to free trade, industrial policy buffs and paleoconservatives supported some level of protectionism and even Japan bashing. However, they all rallied around the come-home-America flag and agreed that, with the end of the Soviet threat, the United States should adopt a more cautious and disengaged foreign policy.

The geostrategists, on the other hand, contended that military threats to America, ranging from a new cold war to low- and mid-intensity conflicts in the Third World, still loomed. Although they were willing, of economic necessity, to accept modest cuts in nuclear and NATO-oriented forces, they insisted on the preservation and expansion of America's power projection forces—air, ground, and sea forces designed for rapid deployment to distant spots in the Third World.

In Search of a New Bogeyman

Some geostrategists warned that the Cold War was not yet over and that the Soviet Union could again rise as a global military threat. They conceded that the USSR might have lost its ideological drive but warned that a coalition of chauvinistic and anti-Semitic Russian nationalists and old-time KGB operatives, military generals, and party bosses might embroil Moscow in new military adventures.

Those warnings, sounded at a time when the Soviets were beginning to withdraw their military forces from Eastern Europe, were advanced by a declining coalition that included neoconservative proponents of global democracy (although some neoconservatives such as Irving Kristol and Jeane Kirkpatrick were beginning to exhibit isolationist symptoms), Republican Cold Warriors, lobbyists for the defense industry, the intelligence community, and the military establishment itself. In a way, they were a mirror image of the dark forces they saw, or hoped were, emerging on the enemy side. (That contention sometimes degenerated into a conspiracy theory according to which the entire collapse of communism was a brilliant ploy to lure the West to lay down its arms and then receive the ultimate hammer blow from the Soviets.)

Other geostrategists were publicizing the notion of international narcoterrorism and calling for a "drug war" as a justification for new domestic and international crusades. In addition to providing a new role for the military abroad, the drug war would strengthen internal security agencies to more effectively suppress civil liberties at home. The new crusade reached a peak in the first months of the Bush administration with the invasion of Panama and the imprisonment of former CIA "asset" and American ally Manuel Noriega for alleged involvement in drug trafficking.[11]

The debate between the geoeconomists and the geostrategists was reflected in the Bush administration's initial stated post–Cold War goal: containing instability abroad, especially in Europe. President Bush and his secretary of state, James A. Baker III, were clearly overtaken by the events in Europe, and some members of the administration were even mourning the end of the Cold War and the "order" it had brought to the international system—or to be more concrete, the elimination of the rationales for continued expansion of the U.S. national security establishment.

The Bush administration argued that, in addition to the perceived threat posed by the alleged military resurgence of Germany and its strengthening of ties with Moscow, there were other possible threats, such as the collapse of the Soviet empire or the emergence of a "Fortress Europe" after 1992. Those dangers and others made it necessary for the United States to maintain its forces in Europe and to continue to support NATO.

The president and his advisers were hoping for a gradual, evolutionary transition to democracy and free markets in the Soviet Union. A reformed and restructured Soviet Union could become a part of the civilized community of nations and might eventually join the United States, Europe, and Japan in maintaining a new international order with its underpinnings of political, economic, and military power: big government, big business, NATO, the United Nations, and other international organizations such as the World Bank. Some analysts even proposed that the Soviet Union join NATO.[12]

Although the administration seemed to be resigned to the possibility of an emerging multipolar system in the economic sphere, Bush, as a member of the internationalist Rockefeller wing of the Republican party and as a political figure whose major experience had been in foreign affairs and national security, was committed to American military superiority and maintenance of the geostrategic stance. Only by sustaining U.S. military power could Washington hope to reassert itself vis-à-vis Tokyo and Bonn, which lacked a serious defense apparatus. Hence, the fall of the Berlin Wall could be viewed as the beginning of a unipolar international system in which Europe and Japan would continue to play subordinate roles as junior partners.[13] The administration needed to find a way to refute the thesis of American declinism.

But the new bogeymen raised by the administration as a way of perpetuating American interventionism abroad—narcoterrorism, low- and mid-intensity conflicts, instability—did not elicit the kind of excitement that would produce public support for current defense budgets and continued intervention abroad, not to mention new international crusades. The threat of international terrorism, which the Reagan administration had used so effectively to mobilize public support for global commitment and national security expenditures, lost its popularity after the Iran-Contra affair, when the man we loved to hate, the Ayatollah Khomeini, was lying on his deathbed.

Political elites in democratic systems can play their foreign policy games as long as the public, which is usually not interested in international issues, tolerates the sport. Public tolerance is fostered by a legitimizing ideology and acceptable costs.[14] As the Cold War was ending and economic problems at home were mounting, the administration faced the threat that, with no Cold War ideology to justify its foreign policy and enormous defense expenditures and with critical domestic problems competing for limited economic resources, the views of the geoeconomists might prevail.

Then Saddam Hussein invaded Kuwait.

2. The Rise of the Middle Eastern Bogeyman: From a Cold War to a Middle Eastern War

A report issued in May 1990 by the Center for Strategic and International Studies reflected the geostrategic perspective. The report argued that, with the decline of the Soviet military threat to Europe, the potential for American involvement in the "dangerous form of conventional combat" in mid-intensity conflicts (MICs) in the Middle East and Moslem southwest Asia would "provide the key justification for military budgets during the 1990s and establish most of the threats against which U.S. forces [would be] sized, trained and equipped."[1]

"Growing domestic United States dependence on foreign oil resources," predicted the authors of the study, would lead to increasing American involvement in the Middle East. That, coupled with political instability in what Zbigniew Brzezinski once called the "arc of crisis," would force the United States into the center of high-intensity conflict there in the early 21st century. In the short run, the study recommended, Washington should plan for limited military involvement in regional MICs. One MIC discussed in the report was Washington's sending U.S. troops to Kuwait and Saudi Arabia to save those countries from an Iraqi invasion.[2] All the participants in a war-gaming exercise in early 1990 had similar expectations of U.S. involvement in the Middle East and concurred that there was at least a 30 percent chance of Washington's being drawn into a war involving Israel in the next decade.[3]

The success with which a variety of groups pressured the Bush administration to exert U.S. military might in the Persian Gulf a few months later suggested that such think tank studies and war games were not mere academic exercises undertaken by a group of frustrated Cold Warriors. They were part of an effort to condition the American elite and public for new military interventions in the Middle East.

Indeed, the geostrategists' efforts to refocus American attention on threats emanating from the Middle East as a way of prompting new American intervention abroad were not gratuitous. Nor was it a coincidence that the first serious post–Cold War U.S. military intervention abroad took place in the Middle East. After all, it is very doubtful that President Bush would have been able, even at that "defining moment in history," to use Secretary of State James A. Baker's term, to mobilize support in Congress, the bureaucracy, and the media for sending American troops to contain an invasion of Kashmir by Pakistan, even if Pakistan had been led by a ruthless dictator who controlled "weapons of mass destruction."

In many ways, the initial consensus that developed in Washington among policymakers and opinion makers of all persuasions about the need to reassert military and diplomatic power against Iraq was a knee-jerk reaction—the United States needed to "do something" about the political and military dangers developing in the Middle East.

That reaction was predicated on elements of the U.S. Cold War policy paradigm for the Middle East, which had had a major influence on American foreign policy since the late 1940s, and especially since the 1973 Yom Kippur War. That paradigm was dominated by the perception that any military escalation or political instability in the Middle East could produce one or more of the following effects: a confrontation between the Soviet Union and the United States, a cut in the oil supply from the Middle East, and a major threat to the existence of Israel.

To put it another way, Washington was programmed to expect that, without American military and diplomatic leadership, any Middle Eastern crisis might lead to a world war, an oil embargo, or the destruction of Israel. The Yom Kippur War clearly dramatized America's Middle Eastern paradigm. That war led to the anti-American Arab oil embargo, raised questions about Israel's survival, and produced a major superpower confrontation.

The American nuclear military alert during the Yom Kippur War and the subsequent U.S.-led Egyptian-Israeli peace process reflected the two sides—the military and the diplomatic—of America's Middle Eastern paradigm during the Cold War. The fear of a rerun of the Yom Kippur War scenario, on the one hand, and the hope of a new Arab-Israeli peace process, on the other, explain the American elite's continuing interest in the Middle East. The obsessive preoccupation with Middle Eastern issues on the part of the bureaucracy, Congress, and the media, coupled with the existence of powerful interest groups such as the oil and Israeli lobbies, helped to sustain support for American intervention in the area during the Cold War.

Hence, notwithstanding the debate over the strategy and tactics the United States should have employed to deal with Saddam Hussein's aggression (i.e., sanctions and diplomacy versus military options), very few observers questioned whether Washington, after the Iraqi invasion of Kuwait, should have activated its Cold War Middle Eastern paradigm and reasserted its hegemonic prerogatives in the area. Some members of Congress expressed dismay that Europe and Japan had contributed so little to the costs of the American military operation in the gulf. Others were concerned about the possibility that some members of the "coalition" might abandon the American bandwagon. However, almost no one seemed to doubt the assumptions underlying Bush's decision to contain Iraq's moves in the gulf or that Washington should be committed to a combination of hyperactive diplomacy and military engagement in the Middle East.[4]

On the contrary, new post–Cold War paradigms, ranging from containing Moslem fundamentalism and Arab radicalism to making the Middle East safe for democracy, were raised as a way of justifying new military and diplomatic commitments.[5] The Middle Eastern bogeyman also emerged as the most effective vehicle for mobilizing support for a permanent U.S. commitment to playing the role of global gendarme. Even staunch geoeconomists could be persuaded. Bush presented the new American geostrategic manifesto on August 2, 1990, in Aspen, Colorado, when he announced his tough stance vis-à-vis Saddam.

"Notwithstanding the alteration in the Soviet threat, the world remains a dangerous place with serious threats to important U.S. interests wholly unrelated to the earlier patterns of U.S.-Soviet relationship," explained Bush.[6] Because those threats included aggressive action by well-equipped regional powers, the United States had to retain its military forces at a high degree of strength and readiness. But it was only the perceived threat to the two most important components of the Middle Eastern paradigm—oil and

Israel—that enabled Bush to mobilize the necessary support for the first post–Cold War American intervention.

Sources of American Middle Eastern Interventionism Transformed

Ironically, the most dramatic and violent American intervention in the Middle East since 1945 took place at a time when the major elements of the American Middle Eastern paradigm, which had justified U.S. activism there during the Cold War, were becoming irrelevant.

There was little danger of a Soviet-American confrontation. The threat of Soviet expansionism or troublemaking was largely absent from the Middle Eastern equation. Since coming to power, Mikhail Gorbachev and his aides had transformed Soviet policy toward the region. The Soviet leader and his foreign minister Eduard Shevard-nadze had begun to try to solve regional conflicts, including those of the Middle East, through American-Soviet cooperation.[7]

Such cooperation was part of a grand strategy aimed at improving relations between the two superpowers and using the United Nations as a tool for dealing with various international problems. The new thinking in the Kremlin was that U.S.-Soviet cooperation and UN involvement would provide a basis for cutting the Soviet military budget, encouraging economic and financial aid from the West, and raising the international prestige of the USSR. More specifically, the Soviets, who were worried about the political stability of their Central Asian Moslem republics, had indicated an interest in achieving some stability in their geopolitical back yard. Stability would help to alleviate the sources of Arab radicalism and Moslem fundamentalism, which was acting as a magnet for the Moslem populations in central Asia and the Caucasus.

Moscow was also concerned about the spiraling arms race taking place a few miles from its borders—in particular the introduction of weapons of mass destruction, including nuclear arms, to the region. (Israeli Jericho missiles, armed with nuclear weapons, could theoretically reach Soviet territory.) The Kremlin was being very careful about supplying chemical, biological, and especially nuclear weapons to its Arab clients and had called for the establishment of a nuclear-free zone in the Middle East.

The Soviets had also expressed their impatience with irresponsible clients, such as Syria and Libya, who could draw them into a new confrontation with the United States and expose the USSR to all the inevitable associated political, military, and economic costs. In addition, arms exports to economically bankrupt clients, such as Syria and other Third World states, that lacked the hard cash and foreign currency to pay for them, were a major drag on the Soviet treasury.

As a result, Moscow was dramatically lessening its support for such clients as Syria, Iraq, and the Palestine Liberation Organization (PLO) and was improving its ties with Israel. Moscow made it clear to Syria that the Soviets were not going to support its plan to reach strategic parity with Israel and that Damascus should try to reach some sort of modus vivendi with Jerusalem. Moscow was also encouraging the PLO to take steps to recognize Israel and reach a political settlement. The steps the PLO had taken before the gulf crisis to accept UN Security Resolution 242 and to recognize Israel reflected that Soviet pressure.

Finally, the Soviets were improving their own relationship with Israel. In addition to raising the level of the diplomatic ties between the two countries, the Soviets, despite protests from the Arab world, opened their doors for a massive flow of Jewish emigrants who left for Israel. The expectation was that close to 1 million Soviet Jews would arrive in Israel in the following years. Although those people would create major social and economic challenges for the Jewish state, they would also provide it with a major human resource that could help energize the country's economy and strengthen its diplomatic and military resolve.

There were two major reasons for the Soviet opening to Israel. First, Gorbachev hoped that by improving ties with Jerusalem the Soviet Union could also strengthen its position in the American capital, especially among Israel's supporters on Capitol Hill and in the administration. Indeed, Washington's moves to repeal the Jackson-Vanik amendment and grant the Soviet Union most favored nation status were a direct result of Moscow's willingness to allow free Jewish emigration from the USSR.

Second, expanding diplomatic ties with Jerusalem increased Moscow's leverage over Israel and improved its chances of playing an active role in future Middle Eastern peace negotiations. Soviet officials indicated that they would be willing to establish full diplomatic relations with Israel if Jerusalem agreed to participate in an international conference on the Middle East and rejected efforts to exclude the Soviets from the Arab-Israeli peace process. The Soviets demanded, in short, to have a seat at any international peace conference.

On the eve of the Iraqi invasion of Kuwait, there was certainly no more Soviet "expansionism" to contain in the region. Apparently, Moscow was hoping to cooperate with Washington in solving major Middle Eastern conflicts, which ranged from the civil war in Afghanistan to the Palestinian problem. The opening of the dialogue between Washington and the PLO and the improving relationship between Moscow and Jerusalem were seen as two sides of the same coin: both superpowers were opening channels to their rival's client and creating a basis for recognizing each other's interests in the region.

Further questions about the rationale for American intervention in the Middle East were raised by the fact that, since the 1973 oil embargo, the United States had become less vulnerable to the Arab oil weapon. After oil prices were freed in 1981, markets could adjust quickly to supply and demand. All oil producers with excess capacity—including Iraq—had been cheating on their Organization of Oil Exporting States (OPEC) quotas and would probably have continued to do so.

Immediately after the Iraqi invasion of Kuwait, an internationally renowned oil expert suggested that even if Baghdad were to control all of the gulf oil, Saddam would "not be able to dominate the world oil market which today is large and diversified," especially with many interests, including those calling for environmental conservation and increased energy efficiency, "tending to hold down consumption."[8]

American foreign policymakers had always stressed that their Middle Eastern policy was dictated not by simple economic interest in continued safe access to oil but by concern that a threat to that access, especially by the Soviet Union or its surrogates, could weaken the political and economic resolve of Europe and tip the Cold War balance in favor of Moscow. Indeed, one major component of America's Middle Eastern paradigm had been the responsibility of Washington, as the hegemonic power in the Middle East during the Cold War, to secure access to Middle Eastern oil for its militarily and economically weak European and East Asian allies.

If the Iraqi invasion of Kuwait did indeed threaten access to Middle Eastern oil, that threat had little if anything to do with Cold War calculations. Rather, it had to do with regional problems, intra-Arab conflicts, and debates inside OPEC. Moreover, as it achieved greater economic unity through the 1992 process, Europe would become a new power center, which could be expected to compete with the United States in the international market. Perhaps the time had come for the Europeans to protect their own economic interests in the gulf.

One could have asked in August 1990 why a prosperous and powerful Europe did not pay the diplomatic, economic, and military costs of dealing with the Iraqi threat, especially since the Europeans, in particular the French and the Germans, had contributed so much to the building of the Iraqi war machine and were so dependent on Middle Eastern oil. If the Europeans (and the Japanese for that matter) showed so little willingness to defend their interests in the region and to stand up to Saddam, perhaps the Iraqi invasion of Kuwait was not such a great threat to their oil interests after all.

History may shed some light on the European attitude. In 1945 Washington inherited the job of securing Western interests in the Middle East from Great Britain and France, declining colonial powers that were suffering the ravages of World War II. France and Great Britain, along with the rest of Western Europe, have long since recovered from the war, but the United States has continued to be responsible for European interests in the Middle East. On the eve of the invasion of Kuwait, it looked as though Washington should consider returning that responsibility to Europe. Indeed, under the more cautious American foreign policy advocated by the economic strategists, the Middle East might well have been deemed a region from which Washington should gradually disengage by shifting more of its diplomatic and security responsibility to the Europeans (see Chapters 4 and 5).

Finally, the end of the Cold War spelled the end of Israel's role as America's anti-Soviet "strategic asset" in the region. After the fall of the Berlin Wall, the Jewish state found it more and more difficult to sell its strategic services to Washington, and a growing number of voices began to call for cutting the American entitlement program for Jerusalem. Moreover, Jerusalem's actions, ranging from the 1982 invasion of Lebanon to the brutal suppression of the *intifada* (violent Palestinian uprisings that began in 1987), had tarnished Israel's image as an endangered democratic entity. The results were loss of public support in the United States and increased doubts about America's moral commitment to the Jewish state (see Chapters 6 and 7).

If anything, the militant Likud government in Jerusalem— through its refusal to negotiate the future of the occupied Arab territories and its ideological commitment to a Greater Israel, manifested by the building of Jewish settlements in the West Bank— contributed to instability and radicalism in the Middle East.[9] Israel helped to create an environment that was hospitable to Saddam's radical agenda. Ironically, American aid and support for the Likud government helped to weaken Washington's position and prestige in the Arab world and produced anti-American sentiment in the area.

As the Cold War was winding down, more and more Americans were coming to the conclusion that the long-term threats to Israel's security did not lie in Baghdad, even a Baghdad that acquired nuclear weapons. In the long run, there was little Israel could do to prevent Iraq or other Arab countries from acquiring nuclear weapons. Jerusalem could only continue to maintain its existing (although officially denied) nuclear posture and hope that a balance of terror between it and its Arab neighbors would prevent an all-out war in the region. Indeed, several months before the gulf crisis, a top-ranking Israeli official met with several Iraqi leaders and reported that they were generally inclined to consider an agreement with Israel, which would have been tied to a solution to the Palestinian-Israeli conflict.[10]

Moreover, the possibility of Iraq's developing nuclear warheads could have contributed to the emergence of a balance of terror between Baghdad and Jerusalem, which in the long run could have actually led to greater regional stability. Israel, however, did not want to lose its regional nuclear monopoly. Hence, it conducted a campaign against Iraq's efforts to build nuclear devices.

The end of the Cold War accentuated the real long-term threats to the existence of the Jewish state: continued occupation of the West Bank and Gaza and perpetuation of Israel's bankrupt socialist economy. American aid and support tended to strengthen the forces in Israel that were opposed to a peaceful solution of the Palestinian-Israeli conflict and to reforming the Israeli economy.

A post–Cold War American policy that took into consideration both U.S. and Israeli interests could have been based on efforts to lessen Israel's economic dependence on Washington and encourage it to begin to solve its conflict with the Palestinians. Such a policy could have taken advantage of the new situation in which the Israeli-American relationship was returning to "basics." After all, Israel's position as the client of the United States, dependent on America's support and aid, was becoming a liability. Indeed, the new U.S.-Israeli relationship, coupled with continuation of Israeli settlement policies in the West Bank and suppression of the *intifada*, encouraged more voices in Washington to call, before August 2, 1990, for gradual diplomatic and military disengagement from Israel. The proposal of Sen. Robert Dole (R-Kans.) that the United States begin cutting its aid package to Israel (as well as to other recipients of American aid) reflected that mood.

At the same time, there was growing disillusionment in the American capital about Washington's ability to facilitate the Arab-Israeli peace process. U.S. diplomatic efforts to implement a peace plan, which had been suggested by Prime Minister Yitzhak Shamir of Israel, reached a stalemate as a result of Israeli intransigence, and the diplomatic dialogue between the PLO and Washington was terminated after that organization gave indications that its commitment to ending terrorism was not absolute. Without an Israeli de Klerk or a Palestinian Mandela to work with, and with no Middle Eastern Gorbachevs who were willing to take advantage of American assistance, there was a growing sense in the summer of 1990 among members of the American foreign policy community that Washington's ability to influence the outcome of the conflict was extremely limited.[11]

With more pressing international issues, such as the collapse of communism, competing for attention, and with other regional conflicts, such as those in southern Africa, promising more political dividends for a possible American diplomatic investment, the Middle East and its conflicts were gradually relegated to the bottom of the American foreign policy agenda. Americans were coming to the realization that the conflict between Zionism and Arab nationalism predated the Cold War and would continue long after the last brick of the Berlin Wall was removed. A kind of "plague on both your houses" attitude toward the Arab-Israeli conflict and a certain benign neglect of the problem were beginning to dominate American thinking. Baker's suggestion during testimony on Capitol Hill that the Israeli leaders telephone the White House when they were ready to make peace echoed the new tone. A combination of gradual cuts in aid to Israel and lower expectations of any new American activism on the Arab-Israel peace process front might have followed that statement.[12]

It looked for a while as though Washington might do the unthinkable, say farewell to the Middle East—which had provided so much action and excitement and so many jobs for policymakers and journalists, and whose terrorist acts and "peace processes" had supplied television news with so much good footage and so many colorful characters. It all was beginning to look like the summer reruns, and the urge was to switch channels, to Eastern Europe, to international trade problems, to economic crises at home.

Pressures from the Israeli and Arab Lobbies

However, several developments were converging to refocus American attention on the Middle East. Although many television crews in Israel were reassigned to cover developments in Eastern Europe, the bloody *intifada* continued to attract American television coverage. The growing tension between Iraq and Israel was reflected in stories in the Western press about Baghdad's nuclear military program and statements by the Iraqi dictator that he would destroy "half of Israel" with chemical weapons if attacked by the Jewish state. Those statements and developments began to stimulate calls for renewed American involvement in the Middle East.

Some Israelis were openly urging the United States to stop Saddam. The Western media reflected those Israeli concerns in "investigative" stories. Reporters quoted unidentified "sources" and pointed to the alleged Iraqi threat to regional and international security, especially Baghdad's development of its nuclear capability.[13] Such stories created the impression in Baghdad that the West, manipulated by Israel, was threatening Saddam's regime. The result was increased pressure on Saddam to adopt a more radical anti-Western posture.

At the same time, moderate Arab leaders were calling for renewed American leadership in the peace process, in particular for U.S. pressure on Israel to agree to negotiate to prevent radicalization of the Middle East. "The fanatical war, if unchecked, could extend from Cairo and Islamabad and beyond," warned the crown prince of Jordan, Hassan bin Talal, in a plea for new American activism. Unless the Bush administration intervened and "did something," he and other Middle Eastern players and experts argued, the area would descend into an Armageddon of chemical warfare and nuclear exchanges between the politico-religious fundamentalist regimes that might well come to power in both Israel and the Arab world.[14]

Interestingly enough, despite their differences and antagonisms, the Arab and Israeli lobbies, the rival twin engines of U.S. Middle Eastern policy, were united in their desire to see the United States engaged in the area, as it had been in the good old days of the Yom Kippur War or President Jimmy Carter's Camp David peace negotiations. The growing specter of American diplomatic and military disengagement and the possibility that Washington might view Middle Eastern affairs as less urgent created alarm in both Israel and the conservative Arab regimes.

The Arab and Israeli elites and their representatives in Washington have always been united in their desire to see America committed to the region. The debate, of course, has been about which side Washington should support. It was therefore not surprising that on the eve of the Iraqi invasion of Kuwait both the pro-Israeli and the pro-Arab constituencies in Washington were drumming up support for maintaining a high U.S. profile in the Middle East. One researcher affiliated with a pro-Israeli think tank argued that the Middle East would "still become the locus of crises demanding attention from Washington,"[15] while an analyst writing in a pro-Arab publication suggested that, despite the changes in the international system, "the U.S. cannot turn its back on the region."[16]

The spokesmen for the Israeli and Arab causes differed, of course, about whom the United States should back. The first scholar suggested that the Israeli military might serve in the post–Cold War era as "the best insurance" against radical players in the region, while his pro-Arab counterpart indicated his expectation that the "responsible regional states" in the gulf area would help defend American access to Middle Eastern oil. Both requested that Washington help militarily their favorite clients in the area. Deterring a radical Arab state, Iraq, and protecting the oil-rich pro-Western gulf states from the perceived threats of Saddam would become the common denominator uniting the coalition of the Israeli and the Arab lobbies that led the pack calling for war and the destruction of Saddam and Iraqi military capacity.

Saddam, even before his invasion of Kuwait and certainly after that event, emerged as the new bogeyman who could bring together two of the most powerful forces that have influenced American foreign policy since 1945, the Arab oil lobby and the Israeli lobby. Those two groups, which have been the driving force behind much of the U.S. intervention in the Middle East, had powerful allies inside the Republican party: the Rockefeller wing of the party with its extensive oil and business interests in the Middle East and the neoconservative wing with its close attachment to and support for Israel.

Indeed, after the Iraqi invasion of Kuwait, Washington saw a most dramatic development in the relationship between the Israeli and the Arab oil lobbies. Those two powerful foreign policy interest groups changed from bloody rivals into staunch allies trying to build support on Capitol Hill and in the media for a U.S. military move against Iraq. A think tank affiliated with the American Israel Public Affairs Committee (AIPAC) sent a group of journalists and other influential people to Jerusalem and Riyadh. The director of that think tank suggested that an informal alliance against Iraq was developing between the Israelis and the Saudis.[17] The Saudi ambassador to Washington, Prince Bandar bin-Sultan, who is the son of the Saudi defense minister and a nephew of King Fahd, met with Israel's supporters on Capitol Hill, including Reps. Stephen Solarz (D-N.Y.), Mel Levine (D-Calif.), and Tom Lantos (D-Calif.), and with various American Jewish leaders.[18]

Saudi and pro-Israeli activists also formed the Committee on Peace and Security in the Gulf, which supported the administration's bellicose moves against Baghdad. The committee was headed by Solarz and an interesting mix of Arabist figures with strong business contacts in the gulf, such as former secretary of defense Frank Carlucci, and spokesmen for Israeli causes, such as Jeane Kirkpatrick.[19] Solarz, previously an opponent of the war in Vietnam and an aid to the Contras in Nicaragua, became a leading House advocate of a firm military stand in the gulf. The *Wall Street Journal* reported that "critics . . . speculate that Mr. Solarz is championing the interests of Israel and the pro-Israeli forces in the U.S. who worry that if Saddam Hussein is left with his military machine intact after the crisis is resolved, he would pose a threat to the Jewish state."[20]

Before the congressional vote on the use of military force in the gulf, the AIPAC lobbied its friends in Congress to support the president. "Shortly before the vote many of [AIPAC's] major officers returned from Israel with a strong conviction that led them to contact legislators on an individual basis," wrote one reporter.[21] Similarly, the Conference of Presidents of Major Jewish Organizations supported the president's position on the use of force against Iraq and mobilized public and congressional support for doing so.[22]

Although Jewish legislators were divided over the war resolution, there is little doubt that the identification of Israel's interests with the decision to go to war played an important role in helping Bush to gain support for his position among leading liberal Democrats. "Often you have liberal Democrats, many of them Jewish Democrats, who are the more dovish elements of the Democratic party. That's not the case in this conflict because there is concern that if Iraq is allowed to stay strong, that would be dangerous to Israel."[23] While AIPAC and its affiliates were pressuring their supporters to give Bush a green light to go to war, the Arab oil coalition was financing a sophisticated public relations and lobbying campaign conducted through various front organizations.

The Kuwaiti government in exile, for example, hired the services of several high-powered public relations firms and indirectly funded the Coalition for America at Risk, which placed newspaper ads and television commercials calling on the United States to go to war to "liberate" Kuwait.[24]

The Israeli and Arab oil lobbies' efforts to facilitate American intervention in the Middle East exposed the real motives and interests behind their usual rationalization of U.S. commitments to their clients. Support for Israel as an anti-Soviet "strategic asset" and for securing access to Middle Eastern oil was becoming anachronistic, if not irrelevant, in the post–Cold War Middle East in which Soviet threats to American interests were improbable. A new U.S. engagement therefore meant nothing more than securing Israel's regional power, in particular its nuclear monopoly, against a local rival and supporting the local despots who ruled the oil-producing states and could continue to secure the interests of the American oil companies

21

and their allies in the national security establishment. Hence, there was a need to mask a naked projection of American power behind an international crusade to achieve moral goals.

As a result, what had started as an intra-Arab conflict over contested territory on the border of Iraq and Kuwait and an intra-OPEC struggle over oil prices turned into one of the major diplomatic and military events of this century, a "defining moment in history" whose outcome would supposedly determine the success or failure of the so-called new world order.

Other Players Pushing for War

The Israeli lobby–neoconservative axis and the Arab oil lobby–Rockefeller Republican alliance were not the only players urging Washington to go to war. Great Britain and Turkey, who like Israel were concerned about their international marginalization in the post–Cold War era, also encouraged Washington to intervene militarily. London was worried that it was being upstaged as America's principal European ally by the newly united Germany. A military confrontation in the gulf, in which Britain's value (as opposed to Germany's impotence) as a military player would be highlighted, might help to reverse a trend that suggested that Washington could base its Atlantic policy on ties with Bonn.

Ankara, like Jerusalem, was beginning to lose its position as an anti-Soviet strategic asset. In addition, Turkey's efforts to join the European Community had been rejected by the Europeans, who were worried about the possibility of a large influx of Moslem immigrants to their countries and critical of Turkey's human rights violations and its continuing occupation of northern Cyprus. Moreover, when a pro-American conservative government came to power in Athens, Ankara's main rival for American support, Turkey feared that it might lose U.S. financial and military aid. A military confrontation in the gulf, in which the Turks could once again prove their military value to Washington, was perceived by Turkish president Turgut Ozal as a way of turning the tide in favor of his country, a development that, he hoped, could be translated in the future into new American and Western European support.[25]

Finally, Soviet economic, diplomatic, and military weaknesses that became obvious in the summer of 1990 were clear signs of imperial decline. Gorbachev's willingness to accept the fall of the communist regimes in Eastern Europe and the reunification of Germany reflected that trend. So did the new Soviet policy toward the Third World and the Middle East, with its emphasis on cooperating with Washington and using the United Nations to resolve regional conflicts. That policy, which increased the international prestige of Moscow and Gorbachev, resulted in economic and financial aid from the West and in the freeing of economic resources to deal with urgent domestic issues.

The ruse orchestrated by Bush, a former ambassador to the United Nations and, unlike his predecessor Reagan, an enthusiastic supporter of that organization, to mask what was basically a unilateral American action in the gulf behind the facade of a collective security action could not have succeeded without the support of the Soviets, who had veto power in the UN Security Council. However, Moscow's decision to go along with Bush's international coalition gimmick and to abandon, in that context, its former military ally, Iraq, did not stem from a common ideological and political commitment to the building of a new international order and the containment of regional bullies.

It is true that Gorbachev, leading a declining military power, had shown interest in reasserting the importance of the UN Security Council, in which the USSR enjoyed power equal to that of the United States. However, Soviet support for the UN resolutions condemning the Iraqi invasion of Kuwait and calling for Iraq's withdrawal should have been recognized as part of a Soviet strategy for resuming an active role in Middle Eastern politics, especially in the Arab-Israeli peace process, and for preventing Washington from using its military might to impose a Pax Americana in the Soviet back yard.

The American-Soviet communiqué that was released after the September 1990 Helsinki summit and the statements made by Gorbachev in a press conference after his meetings with Bush reflected those Soviet ambitions. Moscow's last-minute diplomatic efforts at the United Nations and in the Middle East and its 11th-hour peace plan were designed to prevent a ground war and, by extension, a long-term U.S. military presence in the region. Hence, neither those who perceived the Soviet support for the American action in the gulf as acceptance of a U.S.-dominated unipolar system in which Moscow would be a second-rate power nor those who saw it as part of a grand conspiracy to embroil Washington in a bloody conflict that would tarnish its image in the Arab world, lead to a rise in the price of Soviet oil, and divert attention from brutal repressive moves in the Baltic states had put their finger on the real reasons for the Soviet policies.

Although all those factors and others may have played a part in Soviet calculations, it was primarily the effort to assert itself as Washington's equal in the Middle East, as its moves during the war's end-game would suggest, that led the Soviet Union to join Washington in the UN-led diplomatic efforts in the gulf.[26] That Soviet policy clearly had a major political value for Bush, since it helped him to mobilize support for his diplomatic and military actions against Iraq—specifically for sending the first wave of American troops and imposing an economic embargo against Iraq—among liberal Democrats who had usually been opposed to military interventionism abroad.

However, the perception that the American action was part of a UN-led effort, that it was supported by all the members of the international community including the Soviet Union, and that it was directed against an enemy of Israel (many liberal Democrats still feel a strong affinity with Israel as a result of Jewish political and financial support of Democratic candidates) made it almost inevitable that Democrats would back the initial American moves against Iraq. The UN-created collective security cover of the American military operation, which brought back memories of the anti-fascist World War II alliance with the Soviets, led even left-wing spokesmen such as Jesse Jackson and publications such as the *Nation* to give a cautious blessing to the initial American moves in the gulf. Only when the unilateral nature of the campaign became clear—especially when Bush doubled the number of troops in the gulf after the November 1990 election—did the left begin to have second thoughts about Bush's policies.[27]

From a Balance-of-Power Game to a Global Crusade

The Bush administration initially treated the Iraqi-Kuwaiti conflict as nothing more than a minor regional scuffle. The U.S. ambassador to Baghdad, April C. Glaspie, indicated in a meeting with Saddam on July 25, 1990, that Washington did not intend to intervene in the intra-Arab struggle. The administration, with its strong political ties to the oil-producing state of Texas, was probably not unsympathetic to Saddam's desire to be the "enforcer" who would pressure OPEC to raise the price of oil and bring some stability to the oil market.

Recent revisionist "who-lost-Kuwait" analysts, such as Jeane Kirkpatrick, have advanced the thesis that there was a direct connection between America's tilt toward Iraq during the Iran-Iraq War and Iraq's invasion of Kuwait.[28] They postulate that the allegedly ambiguous, if not positive, "signal" that Glaspie had given Saddam regarding his aggressive ambitions against Kuwait was a major incentive for him to send his troops to Kuwait.[29] The problem with that notion is that the tilt and the signal were both part of a balance-of-power policy that Washington had applied to the gulf for years.

The balancing act between Iran and Iraq was supposed to secure the interests of the Arab oil sheikdoms that were caught between the two antagonists and lacked the necessary military means to neutralize a threat from either Baghdad or Tehran. That policy was reflected in U.S. support for the shah of Iran when Iraq was a Soviet surrogate and a radical force in the region. It was later evidenced again by the American aid that was given to Iraq to enable that country to act as a counterweight to Iran, which, after the 1979 revolution, was regarded as a focus for expansionist Islamic fundamentalism in the Middle East.

The balance-of-power policy enjoyed bipartisan support in Congress and general backing in the media, even when Saddam was engaged in major human rights violations or aggressive policies toward his neighbors (e.g., Iraq's gassing of its own Kurdish citizens and its invasion of Iran). Moreover, that policy was backed enthusiastically by the conservative Arab regimes in the gulf and Egypt, which funded Iraq's war efforts against Iran. The U.S. tilt toward Iraq was also embraced by many Middle East experts and think tank analysts who considered it an example of sophisticated realpolitik. Some of those experts would later lead the crowd lashing out at that policy and calling for a war against Saddam.[30]

For example, in 1988 in an article published in *Orbis*, Middle East expert Laurie Mylroie attempted to sell Saddam and his regime to the American government and people. While it was true that Saddam ran a "tough regime," and while there was "considerable validity" to the charges of Iraqi brutality, those were "not reasons enough to prevent an improvement in U.S.-Iraqi relations," she wrote. Mylroie, who had visited Baghdad several times, asserted that there was a "rough and unrecognized congruence in American and Iraqi interests" and stressed that "American-Iraqi cooperation offers a potential source of mutual benefit." Iraq, she contended, was a de facto protector of American interests in the gulf from the real enemy, the "bellicose and ominous Islamic republic of Iran." Moreover, Saddam's "fervently secular and rationalistic" regime was "mellowing," and his commitment to Pan-Arabism was fading away. Saddam seemed to enjoy "genuine popularity" and was purportedly considering moving toward democracy for Iraq.[31]

That was an articulate presentation of the American administration's policy toward Iraq. However, after the invasion of Kuwait, Mylroie described Saddam in totally different terms in a series of articles in the *Wall Street Journal* and in an instant best seller she published with *New York Times* correspondent Judith Miller. He was now a brutal anti-American dictator, a threat to the region and the world, a fanatic and radical nationalist, a modern-day Hitler who should be destroyed by the United States.[32]

Interestingly enough, Mylroie, according to Israeli press reports, had served as an intermediary between Saddam's men and members of the Israeli leadership who were contemplating a settlement with Iraq. After one of those meetings, former Israeli defense minister Ezer Weizman indicated in a public address that there were "many signs that Saddam Hussein would like to join the Middle East peace process."[33] Weizman's statement reflected a debate taking place in Israel between the Arabists, who recommended that Israel try to open channels to Iraq as part of an effort to establish an alliance between Israel and the pro-Western Arab states against radical Iran, and most members of the Israeli foreign policy establishment, who still favored the traditional Israeli pro-Iranian orientation that was part of a policy intended to strengthen non-Arab players, such as Iran and Ethiopia, in the Middle East.

The pro-Iranian tilt of the U.S. administration during the Iran-Contra affair made it necessary for Washington to bend over backwards to pursue a pro-Iraqi policy during the last stages of the Iran-Iraq war so as not to antagonize Saudi Arabia and the other Arab oil states, including Kuwait. (The pro-Iranian tilt pursued by the main players in the Iran-Contra affair was very much influenced by the position of those Israelis and their American allies, such as Michael Ledeen of the American Enterprise Institute, who continued to advocate the more traditional affection for the anti-Arab Iran.)[34]

Moreover, the intransigent position of the Israeli government was contributing to increased support for Iraq in the Arab world. Jerusalem had threatened to turn Jordan into a Palestinian state; it was continuing its policy of settling the West Bank, buttressed by the rising flow of Soviet Jewish immigrants; and it had successfully sabotaged American-Egyptian peace efforts. The growing militancy of the Likud government and the continued support of the U.S. administration weakened the position of the more moderate Egypt and resulted in a genuine pro-Iraqi tilt by Jordan.

After the Iraqi invasion of Kuwait, Washington could have attempted to strengthen the position of Saudi Arabia and the other Arab oil states by calling assertively for Iraqi withdrawal from Kuwait, by passing resolutions in the UN Security Council, and by highlighting the presence of American naval forces in the area. Such actions, coupled with a more critical approach to the Likud government's policies, might have helped to turn the balance in the Arab arena in favor of Egypt and might eventually have helped to produce an intra-Arab solution that included Iraqi withdrawal from Kuwait in exchange for some minor changes in the disputed borders between the two countries. Instead, a marginal intra-Arab argument turned into a major global crisis that was supposedly going to define the nature of the post–Cold War international system.

Pressure from the Arab oil and Israeli lobbies, which were concerned about continued American backing for their regional clients, enhanced by support from the neoconservatives and Rockefeller Republicans, helped to activate the Cold War's Middle Eastern paradigm and energized Washington to launch its first campaign of post–Cold War interventionism.[35] An American effort to maintain the power of the Arab gulf monarchies and Israel's regional nuclear monopoly was now framed as a crusade to establish a new world order. That ploy was not new. America's entry into World War I, driven by British and French imperial interests in destroying Germany as a European and international threat, was described as part of a crusade to "make the world safe for democracy." To paraphrase Samuel Johnson, the Middle East had become the last refuge of the foreign policy activist.

3. The Sources of U.S. Intervention

The year was 1945 and the conversation took place in Washington, D.C., at the home of Sumner Welles, a respected American diplomat who had served as under secretary of state (1937–43). As a consequence of his anti-imperialist hostility toward Great Britain, Welles was one of the few supporters of Zionism in the foreign policy elite of Washington. His hostility was shared by many of the Zionist leaders in Palestine and in the United States, who were angry over what they saw as London's abandonment of its 1917 commitment, stipulated in the Balfour Declaration, to establish a Jewish homeland in Palestine. Welles was meeting with Eliahu (Epstein) Elath, at that time the senior representative of the Zionist movement in Washington (he later became the first Israeli ambassador to the United States). Elath complained about the growing power of the oil companies in Washington and their efforts to weaken public and elite support for the establishment of a Jewish state. He predicted that a coalition that would include the oil companies and the heads of the State Department and the Pentagon, who were at that time committed to the anti-Soviet containment strategy, would emerge as Zionism's main opponent in Washington.

Welles replied that Elath was wrong about the future Jewish state's long-term interests. To his listener's surprise, he suggested that one of the potential sources of Zionist success would be the power of no other than the pro-Arab oil companies and the administration's Cold War proponents. He explained that the oil companies and the new national security establishment had been instrumental in drawing attention to American strategic and economic interests in the Middle East and in increasing U.S. military and diplomatic involvement in the area. Otherwise, argued Welles, the Middle East would not have figured at the top of the American foreign policy agenda since the public, in the aftermath of World War II, was drifting back into its traditional isolationism.

Thus, contended Welles, the efforts of the anti-Zionists and the Cold Warriors in the administration and the oil lobby would in the

29

long run work to the advantage of a Jewish state. Support for that state would be rooted primarily in moral, historical, and domestic political considerations, and Israel would later be able to position itself as operating in the interests of Washington in the supposedly important Middle East, suggested Welles.

A Jewish state in the Middle East could benefit the Cold War strategists and their allies in the oil companies since it would provide moral and cultural justification for American involvement in a region that was otherwise populated by people whose background was alien to most Americans. Welles warned, however, that he did not expect the American people to support a long-term commitment to the region.[1]

The Rival Twins

Contrary to the conventional wisdom, the struggle between the pro-Israeli and the pro-Arab lobbies has not been a pure zero-sum game. Like the Social Security and national security lobbies that debate how to divide the American budget but agree on the need to increase expenditures, the Arabists in the State Department and members of Congress who represent Jewish constituencies have both supported increasing American involvement in the Middle East, although they have disagreed about the distribution of U.S. benefits and who the object of American affection should be.

Although support for increasing American financial and military commitments to the Middle Eastern players has been rationalized and sugar-coated with all kinds of national interest and moral arguments, the U.S. commitment is more a product of sophisticated pressures brought to bear by the Israeli and Arab lobbies and their clients, the political elites that manage the foreign policies of the Middle Eastern states. The costs of those policies are eventually paid in American taxes and lives.

During the gulf war, for example, we heard rationales for American involvement in the region that ranged from creating a new world order to safeguarding "our way of life" to containing a "new Hitler." In reality, American policy in the war was driven by the coalition of pro-Israeli figures and organizations and their backers on Capitol Hill and the representatives of the Arab oil states and their supporters in the administration—the very coalition of interest groups Welles had predicted 45 years earlier.

Welles had assumed that the coalition he saw emerging would be short-lived, mainly because of the unwillingness of the American public to pay the costs of interventionist policies in a region whose problems seemed to be only marginally related to those of the average citizen. Welles apparently underestimated the ability of interest groups and policy elites to advance their own particular agendas and perpetuate their issue-areas by waving the banner of public interest to mobilize presidential and public support.

As public choice theorists Nobel laureate James M. Buchanan and his coauthor Gordon Tullock stipulated, "Interest-group activity, measured in terms of organizational costs, is a direct function of the 'profits' expected from the political process by functional groups." Foreign policy decisions and outputs are "public goods" that provide such interest groups and their allies within the bureaucracy and Congress special "profits" and benefits.[2] Those benefits take the form of growing presidential and public attention that in turn leads to expansion of the bureaucracy; to increases in budgets; and to the provision of goods, such as economic aid and military assistance, to foreign clients. Hence, foreign policy elites make "increased investment[s] in organization[s] aimed at securing differential gains by political means."[3] The relationship between the foreign policy elites and the expansion of certain issue-areas in government, such as the defense budget and foreign aid, is not one-sided. "The organized pressure group thus arises because differential advantages are expected to be secured through the political process, and, in turn, differential advantages for particular groups are produced because of the existence of organized activity."[4]

A spiral effect comes into play: The success of foreign policy elites in pushing for certain bureaucratic measures and congressional legislation that protect and advance their interests and those of their clients produces an increase in total collective action in a given foreign policy issue-area. That success, in turn, produces incentives for other functional or interest groups to invest resources in political organizations. The various foreign policy groups rapidly become an integral part of the decisionmaking process. "Moreover, because of the activities of such groups, the range and the extent of collective action . . . tend to be increased," and "as more and more groups come to recognize the advantages to be secured by special political dispensation, this organizational process [continues.]"[5]

31

The spiral effect is manifested in the rise of foreign policy "iron triangles"—three-way interactions involving elected members of Congress, particularly key committee and subcommittee chairman and their staff members; career bureaucrats, particularly agency heads and senior staff members; and special interest lobbies. From that close triad of interests "involving small circles of participants who [succeed] in becoming largely autonomous," foreign policies emerge as Congress writes and passes favorable legislation, bureaucrats implement those congressional mandates in return for big budgets, and special interest groups back (with reelection moneys and other support) the helpful members of Congress.[6]

Although various struggles and coalitions develop among members of any foreign policy triangle, all of them have an interest in preserving and expanding the issue-area in which they operate. In a way, they are interested in perpetuating the problem that produced their issue-area and in focusing public attention on it. That creates an environment in which government is asked to do something to solve the problem. Solving the problem or diverting public attention from it by suggesting, for example, that it does not affect American interests, will remove the issue-area from the policy agenda and harm the interests of the members of the foreign policy triangle.

The Middle East issue-area has provided an opportunity for a foreign policy triangle to develop. Washington's Middle Eastern professionals, both the Arabists and the Zionists, derive obvious economic and political dividends from their services. Those dividends include decisions on oil prices and military procurement and election to seats in Congress; intellectual prizes in the form of positive scores in the popular Washington war of ideas, op-ed pieces, and television news bites; and personal rewards such as professional advancement in the bureaucracy, consulting jobs, and research grants. Middle Eastern terrorism, for example, has become a full-time industry for many experts and consultants.

One element of the Middle Eastern foreign policy triangle is the Israeli lobby that includes a network of American Jewish organizations headed by the American Israel Public Affairs Committee (AIPAC), which delivers favorable votes and financial support for members of Congress in exchange for their securing votes for financial aid and other benefits for Israel. The Israeli lobby also mobilizes congressional support for policies advanced by the bureaucracy in exchange for rewards (e.g., transfer of sophisticated arms) to Israel from the executive branch.[7] Another element of the Middle Eastern triangle, the Arab oil lobby, is a unique constellation of corporate and bureaucratic supporters, lobbyists, and special interest groups that back U.S. diplomatic and military commitment to the gulf oil states and receive in exchange rewards such as expanded military budgets, financial compensation, and high-powered jobs.[8]

The fragile political elites of both the Arab world and Israel, in turn, use American financial and military aid to perpetuate their domestic political power, which is usually unstable because of the lack of political legitimacy; to strengthen their regional power; or to support their inviable economic systems. In that context, external threats (Arab, Israeli, Persian, communist) and nationalistic ideologies (Zionism, Arab nationalism) serve both to mobilize domestic support and to justify American assistance.

In the same way policies advanced by managers of welfare programs tend to aggravate the condition of welfare recipients and increase their dependence on such programs, American support for the elites of Israeli and the Arab countries tends to perpetuate their bankrupt political and economic systems and produce disincentives for reform as well as create conditions conducive to continuing regional strife. That situation, of course, creates the need for more American aid for and commitment to the Middle Eastern players.

American aid to Israel tends to increase the power of Israeli elements that are opposed to economic reform and diplomatic solutions, which leads to growing economic problems for Israel and Arab-Israeli tensions, which lead to more American aid and involvement. American commitment to the Arab oil regimes tends to strengthen the power of their ruling monarchies.

Subsequent U.S. efforts to support Kuwait against Iraqi pressure before August 2, 1990, and the later decision to send American military forces to defend Saudi Arabia against Iraq produced disincentives for both the Kuwaitis and the Saudis to seek an intra-Arab solution to the conflict. That situation led, in turn, to the escalation of American commitments. Instead of encouraging the regional players to adopt a local balance-of-power system and to create their own security arrangements, American intervention in the gulf

33

increased the dependence of those players on Washington for both their external and their domestic security.[9]

Similarly, the American destruction of Iraqi military power produced disincentives for the Israeli leadership to work for a diplomatic solution to its conflict with the Palestinians; indeed, it made the Israeli government more intransigent. Even when Washington succeeded in mediating an Arab-Israeli conflict (the 1979 Egyptian-Israel peace treaty), it had to pay for its services by providing new American aid to Israel and Egypt and making new commitments to solve the Palestinian problem. As a result, Washington was forced to adopt Egypt as another permanent recipient of an annual American handout of economic and military aid.

As Welles had predicted, the efforts of the Arabists in the 1940s to focus American attention on the Middle East benefited Israel's long-term interests; the Jewish state eventually succeeded, in the 1970s and 1980s, in selling itself as an effective American "unsinkable aircraft carrier" in the eastern Mediterranean. Similarly, Israeli efforts to draw the U.S. elite and public into more involvement in the area played into the hands of the Palestinians by helping them to elevate their concerns to the top of Washington's foreign policy agenda in the 1970s.

The Israeli and the Arab oil lobbies and the Middle Eastern players have had an interest in keeping public attention focused on the Arab-Israeli conflict; its removal from the policy agenda could raise questions about the need to maintain the Middle Eastern issue-area. Public attention has strengthened the ability of the members of the Middle Eastern foreign policy triangle to continue to provide public goods for their regional clients. At some point, the various members of the triangle could lose their ability to provide those goods, if the American public loses interest in the Middle East or comes to the conclusion that the costs involved in maintaining U.S. commitments to that region are too high. As economist Robert Higgs suggested, although foreign policy elites are more successful than domestic policy elites in marketing ideologies and controlling information and, as a result, in manipulating public opinion, eventually "the burdens of death and taxes" can constrain even their advancement of their agendas.[10]

Issue networks, which are "shared-knowledge groups interested in some aspect or problem of public policy,"[11] help foreign policy triangles to disseminate ideologies that legitimize their policies and to dominate the policy discourse. Such networks include, for example, political activists, university professors, and media professionals who have an interest in or a commitment to the issue-area on which the members of the triangle thrive. The triangle spurs the network to write letters to the editor or the president, to provide academic advice, or to produce news stories to draw public attention to a particular issue-area.

The active pro-Israeli American Jewish community and the large media and academic communities that have been devoted to covering and studying the Middle East have been important components of the Middle Eastern information network. Many liberals supported pro-Israeli elements during the 1940s and 1950s, but many of them, especially in the black community, switched allegiance to the Arab-Palestinian cause in the 1960s and 1970s. Many conservatives, who had been regarded as part of the pro-Arab component of the Middle Eastern information network in the 1940s and 1950s, became supporters of Israel in the 1960s. Third Worldism provided the ideological glue that bound the members of the pro-Palestinian community on the left, and neoconservatism helped to cement ties within the pro-Israeli community on the right.[12]

International crises, especially wars, provide members of foreign policy triangles with opportunities to stir their information networks to action in support of a cause or crusade. As a matter of fact, wars and international crises can be used by the government to arouse the public, which then turns into a large network that supports the expansion of government expenditure and control. As Higgs pointed out in his study of American government, wars and crises have frequently been crucial in helping to legitimize the expansion of government programs.[13]

Since 1945 Middle Eastern wars and crises—post–World War II instability in the eastern Mediterranean, the 1956 Suez campaign, the 1967 Six-Day War, the 1973 Yom Kippur War, the Iranian revolution, the Soviet invasion of Afghanistan, the 1982 Lebanon war, and the Iran-Iraq war, as well as other dramatic developments such as the Egyptian-Israeli peace process—have been used by the Middle Eastern foreign policy triangle to maintain or increase American involvement in the region. Two ideologies—the historical and moral commitment to Israel and the Cold War ideology—have been used to activate information networks and mobilize public support for expanded diplomatic and military interventionism. Each regional war or crisis has marked another step in the growing American involvement in the region. Wars and crises have helped to create new constituencies in the bureaucracy and Congress and new interest groups that have acquired vested interests in American involvement in the region and joined the Middle Eastern foreign policy triangle. For example, each Arab-Israeli war was an important turning point in the evolution of AIPAC as a political force in Washington. As each war increased Israel's dependence on the United States, the attendant increase in demand for AIPAC's services was paralleled by an increase in the amount of aid and support Congress approved for the Jewish state.

Regional wars and crises expanded the Middle Eastern information network and mobilized public support for U.S. commitment to the region. Each Middle Eastern war provided opportunities for news organizations to expand their coverage of the region and to open new bureaus there, which produced growing public awareness of and interest in the region and led to even more news coverage. The result has been increased pressure on the administration to do something.[14] The Arab-Israeli wars, in particular the 1967 Six-Day War, also played a major role in spurring the American Jewish community to pro-Israeli political action. The 1967 war, as many historians suggest, "Zionized" the American Jewish community and helped to turn Israel into the "new religion" of its members.[15]

Most important, those regional wars and crises were usually followed by new presidential "doctrines" (Truman, Eisenhower, Carter). Those doctrines, which were supported by a bipartisan consensus in Congress and among the public, set new priorities for the U.S. foreign policy agenda and increased American diplomatic and military commitments to the Middle East—to the conservative Arab gulf states after 1956, to Israel after the 1967 and 1973 wars, to the Arab gulf states after the Iranian revolution and the Soviet invasion of Afghanistan. They also gave rise to new America aid packages—to Israel and Egypt after their peace treaty was signed. After each crisis, those doctrines, military commitments, and aid packages were institutionalized and became a permanent component of the American policymaking structure, and the new members of the foreign policy triangle that benefited from them and the new information networks that were mobilized to support them pushed for their expansion. There are few constituencies calling for their contraction. Members of the elite and the public take them for granted, as though commitments of billions of dollars to sustain the bankrupt economies of Israel and Egypt were guaranteed by the U.S. Bill of Rights.

However, as an ironic result of the extensive media coverage of the Middle Eastern issue-area, in early 1990 the public began to recognize the discrepancy between the costs of such commitments and the dividends they produce. Public discontent could eventually shoot down the automatic pilot that is fueled by the Middle Eastern triangle, especially if the ideology that provided the basis for the successful mobilization of the information networks disappears. Until 1967 moral support was the most important ideological factor in mobilizing support for Israel, and the Cold War ideology helped to maintain American commitment to the Arab gulf states. Since 1967 Israel has been able to use the Cold War ideology to its advantage by selling itself as a strategic asset, and the Arabs have begun using moral arguments more frequently to try to increase support for the Palestinians. By 1990 the end of the Cold War and the continuing *intifada,* as well as Palestinian terrorism, had begun to erode those two ideological components.[16]

The close ties that developed between the Israeli and the Arab lobbies during the gulf war in response to those changes seemed to prove Welles's thesis. After years of competing for control of the agenda of the Middle Eastern foreign policy triangle and its information networks, the rival twins finally joined hands as they confronted the possibility of American disengagement from the region at the end of the Cold War. Indeed, the end of the Cold War and the continuing unresolved Israeli-Palestinian conflict raised the specter that without a legitimizing ideology there could be a gradual erosion of the cohesiveness of the Middle Eastern information network and growing public recognition of the costs of America's Middle Eastern policy. Saddam emerged as a convenient substitute for the Soviet threat, and new ideologies and crusades were raised as a replacement for those that had served the triangle's interests during the Cold War. While the Arab oil lobby helped to establish a base of support for military and diplomatic intervention in the administration and the bureaucracy, the Israeli lobby helped to strengthen congressional backing.

After all, the only threat to the interests of the rival twins stemmed from their competition: The Israeli lobby, for example, had used its power in Congress to sabotage military aid to the Saudis and the Kuwaitis so as not to threaten Israel. The Arab oil constellation had blocked efforts by the bureaucracy to increase cooperation with Israel so as not to antagonize the Saudis and the Kuwaitis. Now, with Saddam as their mutual enemy, the members of the Middle Eastern triangle were united for the first time and able to bring together their different constituencies. As a result, they became unbeatable.

America Replaces Great Britain in the Middle East

In many ways, the post–World War II American involvement in the Middle East, in particular the complex alliances with Israel and the Arab oil powers of the region, can be seen as a continuation of the post–World War I British odyssey in that area. To put it differently, the increased American intervention in the Middle East after 1945, with its complex mix of political, economic, and military interests, was a kind of rerun of the previous British involvement in the region. Indeed, the notion of a set of common interests that could unite the Israeli and the Arab elites in the desire to draw America into the Middle East and perpetuate its commitment there, which Welles had predicted and which became so obvious during the recent gulf war, would not have come as a surprise to the British policymakers who were responsible for charting the empire's strategy in the region during and after the Great War.[17]

Both Zionism and Arab nationalism were at that time political forces that lacked any serious base of support among the Jewish masses of Eastern Europe or the Moslem people of the Middle East. Both "isms" were products of small political and intellectual elites who were in search of external supporters to advance their agendas of establishing, respectively, a Jewish commonwealth and an Arab empire in the Middle East. Those elites found a small group of British politicians, bureaucrats, and adventurers, both Arabists and pro-Zionists, such as Prime Minister Lloyd George, War Minister Lord Kitchener, and British agent T. E. Lawrence (Lawrence of Arabia), who were interested in their somewhat elusive ideas for Jewish and Arab political programs. The British imperial policymakers hoped to use the two movements to muster support in the

Moslem world and in the United States and Europe—and even in England where there was little enthusiasm for a new imperial adventure in the exotic Middle East—for a concentrated effort to destroy the declining Ottoman Empire and replace it with a Pax Britannica.

Those British politicians and operators, the predecessors of post-1945 American Arabists and Zionists, were motivated by a unique combination of political, strategic, bureaucratic, and economic interests: hostility toward the Ottoman Empire, which had for years been an obsessive preoccupation of some British leaders; friction between the officials responsible for Middle Eastern policy and those in charge of the India Office; prevention of German control of the region and, after 1917, of Bolshevist expansion into the Middle East in an attempt to sabotage French penetration of it; and, finally, continued British domination, through the government-controlled oil businesses, of the oil resources of Mesopotamia.

In the eyes of the British policymakers, there was no apparent incompatibility between support for Zionism and support for Arab nationalism. Zionism could help to mobilize backing for the new imperial project in the American Jewish community and, through it, in the general American public as well as among members of the British elite with their traditional fascination with the "people of the Book." A new and otherwise suspect British imperial drive could be justified by masking it behind an effort to realize a magnificent dream—Jewish independence in the biblical homeland. Arab nationalism could also help to build local support for the British strategy. After all, one could not have expected the region's Moslems to welcome a new wave of infidel crusaders. That could be achieved, however, by masking the crusaders' imperial goals behind a grand design for Arab independence. Great Britain, therefore, helped create Zionism and Pan-Arabism as regional forces while attempting unsuccessfully to reconcile the interests of the two.

After the fall of the Ottoman Empire, Great Britain, despite occasional power struggles with France, became the dominant imperial power in the region. The 1916 Sykes-Picot agreement gave Britain Mesopotamia (modern Iraq), and France got Syria (including present-day Lebanon). Palestine was to be placed under some form of international control. Those arrangements and the arbitrary territorial divisions they produced, defined officially in the Anglo-French mandates, were later formalized in the 1923 Treaty of Lausanne.[18]

As the price of Arab participation in the war against Turkey, however, Britain had guaranteed independence and territory to the two opposing dynasties on the Arabian Peninsula: the Wahhabis, under Emir Abdul Aziz ibn Saud, and the Hashemites, under Emir Hussein ibn Ali. Not only were Great Britain's promises to those dynasties conflicting, but its commitment that Hussein's son Feisal would rule an Arab state from Damascus clashed with the Sykes-Picot provision that Syria be within the French sphere. In 1917, further undermining its promises to the Arabs, the British government proposed the Balfour Declaration, which viewed with favor the establishment in Palestine of "a national home for the Jewish people" on the condition that nothing be done that would "prejudice the civil and religious rights and political status of existing non-Jewish communities or the rights and political status enjoyed by Jews in any other country."[19]

The United States was not a serious player in the Anglo-French game of musical chairs in the post–World War I Middle East. Not having declared war on the Ottoman Empire, the United States was not a participant in the 1920 San Remo conference that decided on peace terms with Turkey. Nor was it either a negotiator of or a signatory to the peace treaty of Lausanne between the Allies and Turkey in 1923.

President Woodrow Wilson's Middle Eastern policy reflected the contradiction between U.S. support for British interests in the Great War and the idealistic American commitments to establish a new world order, make the world safe for democracy, and help national groups to achieve self-determination. Wilson assured the people of the Middle East that, free after 400 years of Turkish subjugation, they could look forward to political independence, which Washington promised to guarantee. In a July 4, 1918, speech, responding to the British and French machinations in the region and denouncing their secret agreements, he promised the Middle Eastern nations "an undoubted security of life and an absolutely unmolested opportunity for autonomous development."[20]

Wilson's statement reflected the Soviet-American rivalry that developed after the new Bolshevik government of Russia made public the secret agreements of America's allies and exposed the British-French plans to partition the Middle East. To counter Arab outrage at those revelations, Wilson renewed pledges to support Arab independence and put pressure on Great Britain to reiterate them. The King-Crane report, based on a study conducted by two of Wilson's advisers, echoed the president's call for self-determination for the peoples of Arab Asia and an awareness of the Syrian opposition to French rule or the detachment of Lebanon or Palestine to form a separate state. The report recommended the establishment of a united Syrian state to be given independence and ruled by Hussein's son Feisal.[21]

However, Wilson's idealistic project fell victim to British and French intrigues. Even the King-Crane report, which was eventually consigned to oblivion in the State Department, recommended a British mandate in Mesopotamia. Meanwhile, Great Britain and France had arbitrarily divided Palestine from the rest of Syria and enlarged the areas over which they had assumed provisional mandates. First, the nominee for ruling a united Syria, Feisal, was ousted by British forces, which also annexed parts of Turkey to Syria. Then, despite local opposition, France enlarged the Christian section of Syria (Mount Lebanon) and created an expanded state called Lebanon. The Britain annexed oil-rich Turkish territory (Mosul and Kurdistan) to Mesopotamia and made Iraq an independent state with Feisal as its king. Still beholden to the Hashemite dynasty of Arabia for leading the Arab revolt against Turkey, however, the British divided Palestine east of the Jordan River and created Transjordan, with another of Hussein's sons, Abdullah, on its throne.[22]

The 1917 Balfour Declaration reflected the sympathy of many members of the British elite for Jewish aspirations, the power of Zionist lobbying in Whitehall, and the hope that a Jewish homeland in Palestine would help to weaken support for socialism and communism among the Jews of Eastern and Central Europe (dramatized by the large number of Jews among the leaders of those movements). In addition, the British, recognizing the rising political power of the American Jewish community, hoped to enlist that power on their side (most American Jews at that time were of German descent and had supported Berlin during the European war) and thereby muster support in Washington for Britain's Middle Eastern imperial designs.[23]

Washington's failure to advance its idealistic projects in the Middle East exposed the fallacies on which American intervention in the Great War had been based. The sense of betrayal that Wilson felt when he learned that London and Paris had exploited the "liberation" of the Middle East from Turkish rule to advance their own national interest objectives, not to build a new order in the Middle East, is echoed today by the surprise and anguish expressed by many Americans over what seems to be a cynical and realpolitik basis for implementation of American policy in the Middle East after the Desert Storm victory. Indeed, the prewar idealistic rhetoric about democracy, peace, and stability gave way to a postwar alliance between Washington and the annexationist Likud government of Israel and the pro–status quo regimes of the gulf that wish to deny the Palestinians and the Kurds democracy and self-determination. America's policies in the gulf today remind one of a remark one of Wilson's advisers made about British policy in the Middle East after the fall of the Ottoman Empire, "They are making it a breeding ground for future war."[24]

No order or stability came to the Middle East after 1918. Between that year and 1949, there were 18 revolts in Syria, and the promised Syrian independence was not granted by France until 1945. The French mandate over Lebanon ended in 1941, but only after World War II did France agree to Lebanese independence. American diplomatic pressure was necessary to force French troops to leave in 1946. In 1942 British troops were sent from India and Transjordan to overthrow a nationalistic (and pro-German) Iraqi government, illustrating that Iraq's "independence" existed in name only.[25]

British policy in the Middle East was based on complex and, as British officials were to find out, incompatible alliances with the Zionist leadership and the Arab puppets London put in charge of the state system it had created. However, the costs of managing the region's Pax Britannica, including those of dealing with the growing conflict between Arabs and Jews, resulted in Britain's gradual withdrawal. Between the two world wars Britain began to hand over its responsibilities in the Middle East to the United States. It was at during that time that Washington's Middle Eastern policy started to take shape. Although it continued to present itself as a champion of independence and freedom for the region's people, the United States was starting to follow in the more self-interested footsteps of Great Britain and to stake its claim on oil and influence. Post–World War I U.S. administrations, which were worried about the penetration of the American market by cheap British-produced Middle Eastern oil that might threaten the oil monopoly of the Rockefeller family, warned against a possible oil shortage and encouraged American expansion into the Middle Eastern oil market.[26]

As the sun set on their empire, the British decided to cut the U.S. companies in on the oil business. In 1928 a conference, arranged by the British Royal Dutch-Shell Company, was held to settle conflicts between American and British oil companies over international oil fields. It produced the Red Line Agreement that set the rules for competition between the British and the American oil companies and under which two American firms, Standard Oil of New York and Standard Oil of New Jersey, would jointly hold (through the Iraq Petroleum Company) a quarter share of the Iraqi oil exploration. That venture was the predecessor of the Seven Sisters cartel— a consortium of one British, one Anglo-Dutch, and five American companies—that would dominate the oil trade until the 1973 war, when their power began to shift from production to distribution.[27]

British-American oil competition reached its climax during World War II and its aftermath. American leaders recognized that Washington's bargaining power in the post–World War II international arrangement would depend on its ability to control the Middle East, to which the center of oil production had shifted during the war.[28] Middle Eastern leaders, including the rulers of the Arabian Peninsula where large new reserves of oil had been found, resented the machinations of the British and began to look to the United States and its military and economic might as the new external power that would defend their strategic interests and help them to turn their oil into wealth and power.

The intertwining of U.S. foreign policy goals and the political and economic interests of America's national security and business elites was manifested in the close relationship that developed during and after the war among the State Department, the Pentagon, and the Aramco Company. In 1944 major U.S. oil firms (Texaco, Standard Oil of New Jersey, and Socony Vacuum) formed Aramco, an American–Saudi Arabian oil company, and President Harry S Truman created a committee of bankers and businessmen, headed by the president of Chase National Bank, to enlarge the U.S. share of Middle Eastern oil production.[29]

Although the United States had maintained and expanded oil holdings in the Middle East since the 1920s, Middle Eastern oil did not become particularly significant until after World War II. Its appeal lay in its low production costs. American success in weakening British domination of the Middle Eastern oil market was reflected in the dramatic changes that took place after the war. British-owned companies had accounted for four-fifths of Middle Eastern oil output during the war. By 1953 the British share had dropped to 31 percent, and the U.S. share had jumped to 60 percent.[30]

The almost total economic bankruptcy of Great Britain after the war and its reliance, along with the rest of Europe, on the Marshall Plan for economic recovery helped to speed U.S. penetration of the Middle East. The United States took over British commitments to support Greece and Turkey against perceived Soviet and other communist threats. It furnished assistance to those countries under the Truman Doctrine. Strong U.S. pressure also induced Moscow to withdraw Soviet troops that had been stationed on Iranian soil since the end of the war. Interestingly enough, more than 10 percent of Marshall Plan aid to Europe between 1948 and 1952 was spent on petroleum products. American oil companies helped to build major British refineries and thereby undercut independent U.S. oil refineries in the European market. One analyst argued that the "Aramco oil destined for Europe [during the Marshall Plan period] was priced at the inflated Texas price, with the difference being absorbed by the U.S. taxpayers."[31] And of course, American taxpayers began to pay indirectly for the "cheap" Middle Eastern oil by subsidizing the huge defense system that was maintained to protect the oil sources of the Middle East.

In that context, Saudi Arabia became one of the most important elements of American policy in the region. That country's importance to the United States dated from the early 1930s, when Standard Oil of California and Texaco produced the first barrels of Arabian crude. Saudi Arabia became a quasi-American colony; President Franklin D. Roosevelt's secretary of the interior, Harold Ickes, even suggested building U.S. government–owned refineries there.[32]

Not only did Washington inherit from London the job of protecting Middle Eastern oil; it also began to integrate the other component of British policy in the Middle East, Zionism, into the American foreign policy agenda. During World War II the Zionist leaders—disappointed with what they perceived as Britain's betrayal of its commitment to a Jewish state and aware of both the weakening global position of Britain and the growing political power of the American Jewish community—had begun to shift their diplomatic and lobbying efforts to the United States. Domestic political pressure from the Jewish community and its supporters, a sense of obligation to help European Jews in the aftermath of the Holocaust, and an interest in sabotaging Soviet plans to use the new Jewish state as a base from which to weaken Western interests in the region all contributed to Truman's decision to support the 1947 UN plan to partition Palestine and later to recognize Israel. As a result, Washington became one of Israel's midwives.[33]

As had Great Britain after World War I, Washington found itself with new and sometimes incompatible commitments to the Zionist and Arab elites who were in control of the new state system in the Middle East. Guilt about Western anti-Semitism and the demand for oil helped produce, as historian Paul Johnson suggested, the U.S. commitments to Israel and to the defense of the oil resources in the Middle East. Those two commitments, which were similar to the considerations that had earlier influenced British policy, and the Cold War project became the building blocks of American policy in the region.[34]

Interventionist Cold War Assumptions

The Cold War provided the Israeli and Arab rival twins with their major intellectual leverage over U.S. policy in the Middle East for the next four decades. The framework for American interventionism in the region after World War II was the following: Because of its strategic location and its massive oil reserves, on which Western Europe, Japan, and, to some extent, the United States depended, the Middle East would inevitably become a focus of Soviet-American military and diplomatic competition. That assumption was the core of the argument that Washington should strive to contain Soviet expansionism in the Middle East through a mixture of direct military involvement and support for its clients.

Those clients included Israel and the Middle Eastern oil states. American support for Israel, framed in moral and historical terms, was largely the result of domestic political considerations, in particular the need to court the Jewish vote. The "moderate" Arab states (and Iran) enjoyed powerful domestic allies in the oil companies whose political and economic interests were intertwined with those of America's Cold War managers.

Hence, from the outset, an interesting pattern of influence, exerted by the domestic patrons of the two U.S. clients, was apparent. Whereas Israel enjoyed the backing of the public, who felt a moral commitment to the Jewish state, and of members of Congress, to whom it could deliver the votes of its supporters, the Middle Eastern oil states' base of support was concentrated in the executive branch and the national security and business elites. Only in the late 1960s did that pattern begin to change as Israel gained more support from the executive branch because its strategic value was thought to be rising and, somewhat later, the Palestinians began to gain the moral support of the more liberal segments of the American public.

Since America's clients included both Israel and the Arabs, a consensus developed among American policymakers that Washington should try to bridge the differences between them so that they could develop a strategic consensus to contain Soviet expansionism with U.S. help. Because the Soviets had been able to widen their influence by exploiting anti-Western attitudes and the Arab-Israeli conflict, reducing the level of that conflict, it was argued, would deprive Moscow of a valuable asset. Reconciliation of America's interests in the Persian Gulf and its commitment to Israel, as well as its relationship with its European allies, was one of the major dilemmas confronting American policymakers. Those issues have resurfaced again and again, as they did during the 1973 Yom Kippur War and the 1991 gulf war. Washington's policy began to take final shape between the 1967 and 1973 wars and became more concrete after Secretary of State Henry Kissinger's Middle Eastern diplomatic initiative, which ultimately led to the Egyptian-Israeli peace treaty of 1979. Middle Eastern interventionism and its rationales—containing Soviet threats, maintaining access to oil, supporting Israeli and Arab clients, and trying to settle the conflicts between them—remained one of the few foreign policy areas that, even at the height of the post-Vietnam debate, enjoyed a public consensus and bipartisan congressional support.

Superpower Intervention in the Middle East and Its Limits

Most analysts agree that concern over Soviet expansionism in the Middle East was one of the main factors that drew Washington into the area after 1945 and one of the major building blocks of the Cold War strategy. The United States, having replaced Great Britain and France as the major Western power in the area, undertook the defense of the interests and the assets of the free world against the Communist bloc, especially oil resources, global communication, and important links in the "containment chain" around the Soviet Union. The assumption was that orderly decolonization would induce independent Middle Eastern states to remain in the Western camp and help to maintain American influence in the region.

The most explicit enunciation of that strategy was the 1957 Eisenhower Doctrine, which was announced after the Suez crisis. Suggesting that a power vacuum existed in the Middle East, which was likely to be filled by Soviet infiltration unless effective counteraction was taken, the Eisenhower Doctrine offered economic and military support to Middle Eastern states threatened by "international communism."[35] To some extent, that has been the stated policy of the United States since 1957 under both Democratic and Republican administrations. Historians will debate whether that policy was inevitable and whether U.S. policymakers could have avoided such a major commitment to defend what were thought to be American interests in the area. However, it would be misleading to examine the issue in isolation from the development of the containment policy and the extension of American commitments worldwide.

Suffice it to say that the U.S. Middle Eastern strategy was an outgrowth of America's commitment to Western Europe, the principal Cold War prize, and that the dilemmas Washington faced in the Middle East were not substantially different from those it faced in other parts of the world. For example, the mix of diplomatic and military tools Washington should use to effect its policies (e.g., American moves during the 1973 war); how Washington should balance its commitments to clients involved in intraregional conflicts (Israel versus Saudi Arabia); how it should distinguish between global factors (Soviet expansionism) and local problems (the Palestinian problem); and how a commitment to a strategic ally could be coupled with an effort to reform its political and economic system (Iran under the shah).

American performance during the Cold War was probably no worse and no better in the Middle East than it was in Latin America or Africa. Washington encountered diplomatic and military failures (e.g., in its relationship with Egypt under Gamal Abdel Nasser) as well as successes (e.g., in its relationship with Egypt under Anwar Sadat). It has been argued that Washington was able to secure the flow of Middle Eastern oil to the industrialized West and prevent Soviet domination. However, it is possible to suggest that even without the massive American commitment to U.S. clients, the oil-exporting states would have continued to sell their valuable resource to the West (what else could they have done with it?) and that, even assuming that the Soviets were planning to dominate the area (a questionable assumption), regional and domestic constraints would have prevented them from pursuing that goal to the limit. After all, the Arab and Moslem cultures have never been hospitable to communist ideas, and most of the Arab regimes, including those that allied themselves with the Soviet Union, such as Egypt and Iraq, had outlawed domestic communist parties for long periods and jailed or even executed communist leaders.[36]

Some analysts have suggested that Moscow's goals in the region reflected less an effort to expand the communist empire than an attempt to preserve the traditional interest of Russia in its own geographic back yard and to gain access to warm-water ports. As a result, as diplomat and historian George Kennan put it, Soviet policy was motivated by "apprehension of potential foreign penetration in that area."[37] The primary goal of the Soviets "was to prevent the region from becoming a safe asset for the West in its policy of encircling the Soviet Union. That meant that western political and economic influence should be challenged when feasible."[38] With the exception of the 1979 invasion of Afghanistan, the Soviet Union took no overt military action in the Middle East after World War II. Indeed, it attempted to discourage its Arab clients from going to war against Israel and actually called upon them to recognize the Jewish state.[39]

Whereas American policy in the region reflected some clear imperialist tendencies, in particular political-economic interests in Middle Eastern oil, Soviet policy tended to be reactive, taking advantage of American losses and exploiting anti-American sentiment. That sentiment resulted from, among other things, Washington's support of Israel and of the traditional Arab monarchies; its hostility to nationalist Arab leaders such as Nasser; its efforts, especially during the Eisenhower era, to establish security arrangements such as the Central Treaty Organization; and its identification with British interests. In many ways, American policy was a continuation of more than 100 years of British efforts to prevent the Russians, and after 1917 the Soviets, from gaining a foothold in the Persian Gulf.

However, both the United States and the Soviet Union discovered that it is impossible for an outside actor to impose its agenda on the Middle East. In the Middle East everything is related to everything else; the boundaries between local, national, regional, and international issues are blurred. Therefore, any attempt by an outside power to impose a solution results in counterefforts by unsatisfied players to form an opposing regional alliance and to secure the support of other local players and international actors. As Middle East scholar L. Carl Brown suggested, just as "with the tilt of the kaleidoscope the many tiny pieces of colored glass all move to form a new configuration, so any diplomatic initiative in the Middle East sets in motion a realignment of the players."[40]

As the Soviets and the Americans found, the safest policy for outside powers is to avoid moving beyond the point at which easy victories cease, to resist the temptation to try to eject great power rivals, and to settle instead for an implicit balance of power. The efforts of Secretary of State John Foster Dulles to foster the pro-Western Baghdad Treaty, which excluded Cairo, resulted in the Egyptian-Czech arms agreement and the beginning of a major Soviet presence in the area. The Eisenhower Doctrine failed to impose a Pax Americana on the Middle East since it did not accord with clearly expressed regional interests. The American policies that facilitated the Egyptian-Israeli peace treaty repeated the error. They attempted to exclude the Soviet Union from the peace process and the Palestinians from the peace agreement. Those moves resulted in the 1982 Israeli-Palestinian war in Lebanon and the success with which a Soviet client, Syria, sabotaged other American peace efforts after that war.

The Soviets realized immediate gains from their 1955 arms agreement with Egypt because it reflected major Egyptian and regional interests. But they did not succeed in using Egypt as the vanguard of a more assertive policy in later years because their interests did not jibe with those of Egypt's leaders. The result was Sadat's expulsion of the Soviet advisers and his opening to the United States after the 1973 war.

Perhaps the best illustration of the constraints on an outside power is the U.S.-brokered Egyptian-Israeli peace treaty of 1979. That treaty was not the result of an American initiative but a response to a regional move on the part of Sadat. Cairo and Jerusalem, in their own self-interest, could have reached a similar formal or informal agreement without U.S. help. U.S. policymakers initially regarded Washington's role as a diplomatic victory, but it proved to be costly in both financial and diplomatic terms. Washington claimed exclusive sponsorship of the negotiations without having enough control over either Egypt or Israel to make the claim stick, thus ensuring that, although the initiative would remain largely with the regional parties, the responsibility for any failure would be borne largely by the United States.[41]

Thus, Washington was unable to enlarge the scope of the peace process to include the Palestinian question. Differences between Cairo and Jerusalem on the Palestinian problem were unbridgeable, and Washington lacked the resources to pressure either of them to moderate their positions. The lack of progress on the Israeli-Palestinian front, which eventually led to the 1982 war between Israel and the Palestine Liberation Organization (PLO) in Lebanon, was perceived throughout the region as an American diplomatic failure. Consequently, Washington felt a need to project its leadership and political visibility during the Israeli invasion of Lebanon, which in turn led to a major and costly diplomatic debacle. Washington's initial commitment to help solve the Palestinian problem at Camp David also prompted the *intifada*'s efforts to induce Washington to play a more active role in the area.

Hence, Washington's attempts to dominate the politics of the Middle East, to exclude Moscow and its clients, and to manipulate regional actors have tended to backfire. Better results have ensued when Washington has adopted a less grandiose approach and taken the interests of the Soviets and the regional actors into consideration. One example of the more fruitful approach was Kissinger's shuttle diplomacy immediately after the 1973 Yom Kippur War.

Such lessons should be heeded before Washington is drawn into yet another round of unilateral intervention. For example, attempting to exclude Iran from the regional security arrangement Washington is contemplating for the gulf is bound to backfire in the long run. Iran could emerge as a major anti–status quo country and could threaten the Arab gulf states. Indeed, after the Madrid peace conference was convened on October 30, 1991, Iran's leaders expressed strong opposition to the American-led initiative and stated their intention to mobilize the Arab and the Moslem worlds against the "peace conspiracy with the Zionist enemy" and to form an anti-American "rejectionist front" in the region.[42]

The Tail Wagging the Dog: Clients and the Dangers They Pose

The Middle East is probably the most internationalist, or what political scientists call "penetrated," area of the world. Numerous national, regional, and extraregional political players combine and divide in shifting patterns of alliance. Applying Brown's kaleidoscope model to the Middle East, one can see why diplomacy in the region is characterized by a mishmash of local and global issues, never-ending conflicts, and unsolved problems. Chaos and instability have indeed been the rule, not the exception, since the fall of the Ottoman Empire. Outsiders who want to play the Middle Eastern game should expect to become part of the chaotic system, not vehicles to stabilize it.

Indeed, the politics of a thoroughly penetrated system such as the Middle East is not adequately explained—even at the local level—"without reference to the influence of the intrusive outside system."[43] Yet, as American and Soviet experience in the region suggests, the outside actor can rarely control the politics of such a system and frequently becomes involved in issues that have nothing to do with its original interests in the region. A major power's ability to impose policies on local players or exclude other major powers is limited. Even a superpower sometimes falls hostage to local powers.

The Middle Eastern elites use outside powers, including the United States, to advance their domestic and regional interests. Those elites lack either stable and legitimate political systems or economic structures capable of sustaining their bottomless budgets, or both. It is external, especially American, support that allows the political elites to perpetuate their control. Washington's sponsorship of the negotiations that culminated in the Egyptian-Israeli peace accords enabled Cairo and Jerusalem to mobilize domestic and regional support for the accord. Their political elites could justify concessions that would not otherwise have been acceptable to either their rivals or their supporters ("The United States forced us to evacuate the Sinai; we had no choice"). The Egyptian and Israeli elites could also cite the alleged political commitments ("The United States will force Israel to give up the West Bank") and lucrative economic and military aid packages that Washington offered in exchange for concessions.

Clearly, the role of the United States was not merely that of a mediator. Both Israel and Egypt had definite political and economic motives for reaching a peace agreement. Although giving up the Sinai was a major financial sacrifice for Jerusalem, doing so removed the largest and militarily strongest Arab country from Israel's list of enemies. Likewise, making peace with Israel not only returned the Sinai to Egyptian control but ended Egypt's involvement in a devastating military conflict, which was not directly related to its interests, and enabled it to reconstruct its economy. Even under such favorable conditions for the negotiation of a peace treaty, both President Sadat of Egypt and Prime Minister Menachem Begin of Israel insisted on involving the United States in order to strengthen their domestic support, justify their actions, and receive compensation for their concessions.

Although Washington certainly enhanced its international prestige as a result of the Egyptian-Israeli peace agreement, that accord did not compensate the United States for the "loss" of Iran by creating, as some had hoped it would, a pro-American Arab-Israeli axis. The peace agreement may have actually contributed to instability by freeing Israeli military forces to invade Lebanon in 1982 and creating more hostility among the Palestinians and other Arabs who were angered by America's inability to "deliver" Israeli concessions on the West Bank problem. Moreover, the peace agreement resulted in increased American financial and military commitments, especially the new obligation to supply Egypt with a level of aid similar to that given to Israel.

Washington thus became part of the Middle East's political and diplomatic kaleidoscope. An American political move can bring about a realignment of the other players that initially seems to be a gain for the United States but later turns out to be a major loss. For example, Washington's intervention in Lebanese politics after the 1982 Israeli invasion brought about not only the 1983 bombing of the Marine barracks in Beirut but a major confrontation with Lebanon's previously quiescent Shi'ite community. That confrontation brought Syria and Iran into the picture and led to other anti-American terrorist acts, such as the 1985 hijacking of TWA Flight 847. The spiral of violence prompted the Reagan administration's misguided arms-for-hostages formulation, which contributed to the policy calculations that led to American intervention on the side of Iraq in its war with Iran in 1988.[44] That move contributed, in turn, to the chain of events that eventually produced the 1991 Persian Gulf War.[45]

Supporting a local elite makes an outside power such as the United States a symbol of evil in the eyes of opposition forces. It creates political and economic expectations that cannot be fulfilled, thereby causing the outside power to be derided by those who originally sought its aid. For every friend an outside power wins, it is liable to gain 10 enemies.

American support for Israel has been one of the factors that have created so much hostility toward the United States in the Arab and Moslem worlds. U.S. backing of the dictatorial regime of the shah of Iran, whom Washington helped to restore to power in 1953, turned America into an object of hatred in the eyes of most Iranians and helped to accelerate developments that led to the 1979 Iranian revolution. The United States has still not recovered from that experience, and it will probably take years to mend its relationship with Iran. Similarly, the alliance between Washington and the Christian Maronite minority in Lebanon after the 1982 Israeli invasion of that country, and its embroilment in the Maronite-Shi'ite civil war, resulted in the bloody Shi'ite campaign to evict the United States from Beirut.[46]

Alliances with outside powers are often less costly and more beneficial for the regional actors than for the outside powers. Outside sponsorship provides the regional players with prestige, power, and money that would otherwise not be available. If a regional actor reaches the conclusion that the returns on an alliance with an outside patron are diminishing, it can always reverse its orientation (as did Egypt and Iraq) or even use its benefactor as a scapegoat.

Tempting Washington to assume an active role is often the main objective of a regional player's diplomatic and military incursions. Egypt's surprise attack on Israel in 1973, for example, was intended to involve a reluctant United States in the stalemated peace process. Similarly, one of the goals of the *intifada* was to elicit a response from the American public and Washington—which had become wary of the consequences of such escapades as the 1982 intervention in Lebanon, the failure of the Reagan plan for Middle Eastern peace, and the intervention in the Iran-Iraq war. The *intifada*, precisely as its planners had intended, tilted the kaleidoscope, and Washington soon found itself conducting a dialogue with the PLO. The Iraqi invasion of Kuwait, as has been noted, was used to pressure the United States to recommit itself to Israel and the Arab gulf monarchies.

Such are the basic realities of foreign intervention in the Middle East. Those realities have been borne out by the experience of the United States (and of the Soviet Union) in its relationships with Egypt, Iran, Lebanon, and the Horn of Africa.

When it comes to Arab-Israeli issues, the kaleidoscope model becomes even more complex and politically costly because of the interjection of the Middle Eastern iron triangle and information networks described earlier. Decisions to either sell arms to Arab countries or take unfriendly steps against Jerusalem create a political backlash among supporters of Israel, which produces major costs for an American president. For example, President Reagan's decision to sell AWACS planes to Saudi Arabia in 1981 led to a nasty fight with supporters of Israel on Capitol Hill.[47] President Carter's decision to allow the UN Security Council to condemn Israel for its policies in the occupied territories probably cost him the 1980 New York Democratic primary. Similarly, arguments over policies toward the Palestinians have produced tensions between American blacks and Jews. For example, after former U.S. ambassador to the United Nations Andrew Young met with a PLO representative, American Jewish leaders successfully pushed for his resignation. Many activists in the black community felt they had been betrayed.[48]

Domestic repercussions of Middle Eastern policies tend to poison the political debate at home and create more problems for U.S.

policy in the region. The success with which Israel's supporters pressured Washington to end its dialogue with the PLO in 1990 contributed to feelings of despair in and radicalization of the Palestinian community. That despair and radicalization helped to mobilize support for Saddam among Palestinians living in Jordan and the West Bank during the gulf war.

Washington's commitments to its clients in the Middle East and pressure from their domestic lobbies helped to produce the dangerous situation in which the United States finds itself today. U.S. alliances with the oil-producing states, the Arab gulf states, and (until 1979) Iran resulted in the so-called petro-military complex of the 1970s and the 1980s. For years Washington based its policy in the gulf on building the military might of Iran and supporting more modestly the regimes in the Arab gulf states. After the United States succeeded in pressuring the Soviets to leave northern Iran, the CIA overthrew the centrist anti-communist regime led by Mohammed Mossedegh and restored the authoritarian shah to the throne. Billions of dollars were spent on arms for Iran. "Nixon and Kissinger had established a 'blank check' policy, giving the Shah a free hand to buy as many American weapons systems as he wanted, even the most technologically advanced, so long as they were not nuclear," noted historian Daniel Yergin. In the mid-1970s Iran was responsible for half of all American arms sales abroad.[49]

The blank-check policy was part of the "twin pillar strategy," established for regional security in the gulf in the wake of Britain's withdrawal. Iran and Saudi Arabia were the two pillars. To strengthen its gulf allies, Washington refrained from working aggressively to force oil prices down. The concern was that successful pressure on Saudi Arabia and Iran to lower the price of oil "could risk their political stability and maybe their security," since they might be perceived as surrendering to outside pressures, according to Kissinger.[50] Moreover, the rise in oil prices in the early 1970s helped the Iranians and the Saudis to purchase huge quantities of American military equipment and increased the profits of the major American-controlled oil companies. Higher oil prices were, in a way, a form of taxation through which Americans helped to subsidize the gulf oil states—and through them the military-industrial complex in this country. Indeed, the higher oil prices enabled the gulf states to increase their military spending from less than $800

million a year before the 1973 war to more than $4 billion a year by
1975.

Washington thus helped to promote the rise of the Organization
of Petroleum Exporting Countries (OPEC), the political and economic power of which led to the Arab oil embargo of 1973 and to
the international oil shocks of the 1970s. The American taxpayers
helped to support the petro-military complex through which the
oil-producing states, the oil companies, and the American banks
and arms industry were washing each other's hands—an interesting international partnership of industry and government.

The Saudi profits (petrodollars) were recycled. They were depos-
ited in American banks and spent to support weak and usually
corrupt regimes in non-oil-producing Third World ("Fourth
World") states that had suffered from the oil shocks. Indeed, the
oil shocks of the 1970s were a most devastating blow to the economic
development of those countries. "Not only were those developing
nations hit by the same recessionary and inflationary shocks, but
the price increases also crippled their balance of payments, con-
straining their ability to grow, or preventing their growth alto-
gether."[51] The way out for some was to borrow, and therefore a
number of surplus petrodollars were recycled through the Western
banking system to those developing countries.

To get out of debt, the Fourth World nations were then instructed
by the American-financed World Bank and other multilateral aid
organizations to follow statist economic policies, which aggravated
their economic situation. At the end of the day, American taxpayers
were asked to bail out both the debt-ridden banks and the poor
Fourth World states.

Petrodollars were also used to help stabilize the weak dollar in
financial markets and to purchase billions of dollars worth of military equipment, another form of recycling. "Transactions in armaments became a huge business" as a result of the oil boom in the
Middle East, explained an oil analyst.[52] The 1973 disruption of
Middle Eastern oil supplies caused the Western industrialized
nations that were highly dependent on that oil to view security of
access to oil as a strategic concern of the first order. "Weapons
sales, aggressively pursued, were a way to enhance that security
and maintain and gain influence," while the "countries in the
region were just as eager to buy."[53]

The build-up of the petro-military complex helped to create the instability that led eventually to military conflicts such as the one between Iran and Iraq or the 1991 gulf war. Among the products of the build-up were the dictatorial regimes of Libya and Iraq, which were able to use their oil to build ruthless domestic dictatorships and expansionist military regimes. Another result was the anti-American and anti-Western backlash that the alliance between Washington and its local clients, such as the shah of Iran, helped to ignite. The corrupt and decaying regimes in the oil-producing states have become a symbol of American influence in the eyes of have-not segments of the population in the region, and new revolutionary elites are directing their anger and frustration not only against the American government but also against the American people.

The average American citizen is the main loser under the present system. Not only is he asked to subsidize, through higher oil prices, the petro-military complex; he is also expected to pay the costs of the problems it produces: debt-ridden American banks, bankrupt developing nations, and Middle Eastern regional wars and domestic crises. Those costs have taken the form of higher taxes, terrorist acts, and, more recently in the gulf, a risky war.

The Road to War

America's policies in the gulf have revolved since the 1950s around the dilemma of whom to use as the regional policeman to defend the power of the regimes that control the oil resources of the area. Under the shah, Iran had played that role throughout the 1950s, 1960s, and most of the 1970s. Iran was replaced by Saudi Arabia after the 1979 Iranian revolution that brought to power a radical anti-Western government that threatened to export its brand of Islamic fundamentalism to other countries in the region. Indeed, Washington pinned its hopes for the region quite openly on the Saudis. Reagan's secretary of defense, Caspar Weinberger, supported increasing American military aid to the Saudis, including the controversial sale of AWACS planes, which was only narrowly approved by the Senate.[54]

Saudi Arabia, like Israel, was integrated into Washington's anti-Soviet global crusade. The Saudis agreed to underwrite anti-Soviet covert operations around the world and financed, among other things, the Afghan rebels and Jonas Savimbi's rebels in Angola. "Throughout the 1980's, Saudi Arabia operated as a member of the secret team, the hidden government that advanced American foreign policy outside the scrutiny of Congress according to the political designs of the Reagan and Bush administrations," observed one analyst.[55]

The extent to which the Middle Eastern foreign policy triangle had integrated the Saudi kingdom into domestic American politics was made apparent by Vice President George Bush's visit to that country in April 1986. Bush, a former oil man, had maintained close political and business ties with the heads of the oil companies in Texas. He requested that the Saudis reduce production and increase the price of oil to help the recovery of the U.S. domestic oil business, and indirectly the political fortune of the Republicans in the 1986 Senate races, especially in the farm belt and oil-producing states. Indeed, Bush's request produced for the Saudis "an incentive to restore the stability of prices."[56]

That incident pointed to the danger in which American policy-makers have placed themselves. Both the Israeli and the Saudi leadership, through their extensive behind-the-scenes relationships with America's national security managers in the Middle Eastern iron triangle, have gained enormous power to influence American foreign policy. In other words, the Saudi and Israeli tails could, if they wished, wag the American dog. Both Israeli and American sources have suggested that the involvement of Israeli government officials and agents as middlemen between the radical Iranian leadership and Reagan's advisers, as part of the so-called October Surprise and the Iran-Contra affair, allowed the government in Jerusalem to blackmail both the Reagan and Bush administrations and reduced the latter's incentives to pressure Israel to make diplomatic concessions. Similarly, Saudi involvement in America's "secret wars" and in Washington's efforts to manipulate the international oil market made the United States feel obligated to cash the IOUs Riyadh was holding.[57]

The Iran-Contra affair was remarkable in the way in which groups in the Israeli and Saudi leadership, along with elements of the American foreign policy establishment, were able to manipulate U.S. foreign policy in the gulf. Their manipulations led to policies that harmed U.S. interests in addition to eroding the ability of

58

Congress to monitor the activities of the executive branch. That affair also reflected the problematic and dangerous cross-pressures that had operated in American foreign policy since the fall of the shah and the beginning of the Iran-Iraq war at the end of 1980, events that were largely a result of American policy toward the region during the preceding three decades.

On the one hand, following Israeli and Saudi advice, Washington had attempted to encourage, through the sale of arms and other inducements, the rise of reputed moderates in Tehran. On the other hand, it had tried to strengthen the military forces of the Saudis and the other Arab gulf states and to find ways to curry favor with Saddam Hussein's Iraq as a counterweight to fundamentalist Iran. The American "tilt" toward Iraq was evident in the 1983 removal of that country from Washington's "terrorist list," the opening of the door for U.S. government–guaranteed agricultural loans, the establishment in 1984 of diplomatic relations with Baghdad, and the sale of up-to-date weaponry to Iraq through third parties. However, when the tide in the war in the gulf began to turn against Iraq in late 1986 and Iran started attacking Baghdad's Arab allies' ships, including those of Kuwait, Washington found it necessary to intervene directly, by protecting Kuwaiti ships with U.S. naval forces.[58]

That American move was necessary to counter the impression that had prevailed in Kuwait and other Arab gulf states, as a result of the Iran-Contra affair, that Washington was actually tilting toward Tehran. If the United States did not intervene directly, there was a risk that the Kuwaitis might seek Soviet protection or even make separate deals with the Iranians. The American intervention, including the accidental shooting down of an Iranian Airbus in July 1988 by the U.S. destroyer *Vincennes*, led eventually to the Iranian decision to seek a cease-fire with Iraq.

The cease-fire left Iraq as the major military power in the gulf, and other major players in the region felt threatened. Saudi Arabia, Kuwait, and the other Arab oil sheikdoms were concerned that, with the military and political power Saddam exerted in the region and no Iranian power as a counterweight, Iraq would become the hegemonic power in the gulf. Baghdad also demanded that the Arab oil-rich states channel billions of dollars to it to help rebuild its war-torn economy. In addition, Iraq's interest in raising OPEC's oil prices collided with that of Kuwait and the United Arab Emirates, which refused to reduce production and raise prices.

Egypt was worried that Saddam might eventually wrest leadership of the Arab world from Cairo, especially since Israeli intransigence, encouraged by American aid and support, was playing into the Iraqi leaders' hands by radicalizing the Arab world, particularly the Palestinian community. The Ba'ath regime in Damascus watched with suspicion as Saddam, ruling over a rival Ba'ath government in Baghdad, gained power in the region and supported the Christian forces in Lebanon that were opposed to Syrian domination of that country. Israel used military moves and propaganda efforts to express its opposition to Iraqi attempts to question Jerusalem's regional nuclear monopoly.

Hence, the Iraqi invasion of Kuwait exposed the bankruptcy of America's balance-of-power games in the region. On the one hand, U.S. policies had strengthened Saddam's power and even suggested to him that Washington would not be opposed to his acting as an "enforcer" in OPEC and forcing oil prices up to the satisfaction of Bush's adopted state of Texas. On the other hand, America's moves encouraged the Kuwaitis not to succumb to Iraqi demands and later helped persuade the Saudis not to move toward an Arab solution to the crisis but instead to count on direct American military involvement to contain Saddam.

Washington's policies both prepared the way for the Iraqi aggression and helped to activate a constellation of regional forces headed by the Saudi and Israeli rival twins and their supporters in Washington. That constellation added weight to the arguments of elements of the administration that were pushing for American military intervention in the region as a way of keeping alive America's outdated Middle Eastern paradigm.

4. The Special Relationship between America and Israel

One of the many ironies of the gulf war is that, within a week after the start of hostilities, it looked as though Saddam Hussein had contrived to restore the American-Israeli "strategic alliance," which had seemed to be on a decline since the fall of the Berlin Wall, and to restore the special relationship between the two counties after two years of mounting tensions between the Bush administration and the government of Prime Minister Yitzhak Shamir.[1]

Less than a year earlier, in June 1990, during testimony on Capitol Hill, Secretary of State James A. Baker III had voiced frustration over Israel's failure to cooperate in the Middle East peace process. Baker was particularly annoyed by the clear lack of a serious response on the part of the Shamir government to American diplomatic initiatives aimed at solving the Israeli-Palestinian conflict, even though the U.S. effort was an attempt to implement the Israeli prime minister's own plan for elections in the occupied territories.

Not content to leave it at that, Baker gave out the White House telephone number and said that the Israeli government knew where to call when it got serious about peace.[2] President Bush himself privately expressed irritation with Shamir. He accused Shamir of deceiving the administration about the Jewish settlements in the West Bank and postponed meetings with him.[3] But on the eve of the war, the two leaders met in the White House where Bush apparently told a satisfied Shamir about his plans to destroy Iraq's military machine.[4] Deputy Secretary of State Lawrence Eagleburger spent several days in Israel attempting to establish strategic coordination between Washington and Jerusalem, and the American president and the Israeli prime minister talked on the telephone more frequently during the first week of the war than during the previous 23 months that Bush had occupied the White House. Baker promised to respond positively to any Israeli request for military and economic aid.[5]

Enduring Missiles and Accumulating Brownie Points

The dramatic developments occasioned by the gulf war were evidenced by several U.S. actions. The U.S. aircraft carrier *Forrestal* was ordered to the eastern Mediterranean so its contingent of combat and reconnaissance planes could help to defend Israeli airspace. (An irony not lost on some Americans and Israelis: the carrier was named after a former secretary of defense who had been a fierce anti-Zionist and an opponent of American support for the establishment of Israel.) Thirty Galaxy transport planes ferried batteries of U.S. Patriot surface-to-air missiles to Israel in the most massive airlift of American military hardware to reach that country since the 1973 war.

Unloaded and rendered operational within hours, the protective umbrella of anti-missile missiles was welcomed as a tangible expression of American support for an Israel virtually paralyzed by Iraqi missile attacks. Despite the relatively minimal casualties and physical damage, the Iraqi Scud missile attacks on Israel stunned many Israelis. Thousands fled from Tel Aviv to Jerusalem before nightfall each evening, and others moved to the southern coastal city of Eilat. Tel Aviv's mayor, Shlomo Lahat, characterized those people as "deserters."[6]

Across the country, Israelis clung to their gas masks day and night as they waited for the sirens to sound. The threat of an Iraqi poison gas attack was especially traumatic for a civilian population that included many Holocaust survivors and their families. But despite the deepening national trauma and several deaths caused by the Scud attacks, the country's leaders continued to heed the international requests for restraint, especially those from Washington.

For 40 years Israel's leaders had espoused the doctrine that deterrence could be maintained only if Israel's neighbors were convinced that any attack would entail inexorable retaliations. Indeed, when the Scuds began to fall on Israel, the commander in chief of the armed forces, Dan Shomron, declared that the Iraqi attack would not be allowed to pass without response. However, Israel's military men with their "automatic response" view were overridden by the civilian leaders. The latter responded to pressure from Washington, which, because it was scrambling to fend off the looming threat to the fragile anti-Iraqi coalition, refused to give the green light to an

Israeli retaliation.[7] In addition to rushing to Israel Patriot missiles manned by American crews, the United States switched a considerable portion of its bombing to western Iraq, for a thorough search-and-destroy campaign against Scud battery sites.[8]

The growing military coordination between the two countries was also buttressed by increasing public support for Israel in the United States. The dramatic television coverage of the terror suffered by Israel's population during the Scud attacks seemed to neutralize the effect of three years of broadcasts from the West Bank, which had featured Israel's brutal suppression of the *intifada* (Palestinian uprising).

Israeli officials hoped to translate the brownie points they accumulated during the war into a postwar political victory.[9] In particular, they believed there would be reduced pressure for an Israeli withdrawal from the West Bank and Gaza. Israeli spokesmen argued that the Palestine Liberation Organization (PLO) should be denied any role in future Middle Eastern peace talks because of its support for Saddam.[10]

The Postwar Scenario Unfolds

American officials were stunned by a request made by the Israeli minister of finance, Yitzhak Modai, for an American aid package worth $13 billion to "compensate" Israel for the costs of the war and to finance the absorption, through the bankrupt state-controlled economic system, of the huge wave of Soviet Jewish immigrants that was arriving in Israel. Although the Israelis withdrew their aid request, they continued to express hope that, by doing nothing to punish the Iraqis, they would gain American public support and would thus later be able to call upon a debt of gratitude from Washington in the form of more financial aid, in addition to the $3 billion or more Israel received from Washington during fiscal year 1991.[11]

Indeed, after arduous negotiations with Israel and its supporters on Capitol Hill, the Bush administration decided to reward Israel with $650 million as compensation for the costs of the war. In addition, after initial hesitation, the administration signed a guarantee of $400 million in loans to Israel to be used to pay some of the costs of the absorption of the immigrants. The administration

guaranteed the loan after it received written promises from Jerusalem that Israel was not sending the new immigrants to settle in the
occupied Arab territories.[12]

Although those developments were "good news" for Israel, there
was also some bad news for the nationalist government in Jerusalem. Notwithstanding the Israeli government's commitment not to
settle the immigrants in the occupied territories, the continued
building and expansion of Jewish settlements there were expected
to undermine Israeli-American ties.[13] Only a small percentage of
the Soviet Jews are settling in the occupied territories, but the rise
in the price of housing in Israel proper is driving many Israelis and
some of the new immigrants to move to the West Bank where
they can enjoy cheap housing, subsidized indirectly by American
taxpayers.

Indeed, almost a year after he had given the Israeli government
the White House telephone number, Baker, during testimony on
Capitol Hill, blasted Jerusalem for obstructing postwar Arab-Israel
peace efforts by establishing new Jewish settlements and said, "I
don't think that there is any bigger obstacle to peace than the
settlement activity that continues not only unabated but at an
enhanced pace."[14] Baker's testimony reflected the frustration of the
Bush administration with its inability to take advantage of what
U.S. officials characterized as the "window of opportunity" for
Arab-Israeli peace that supposedly opened as a result of the American military victory in the gulf. By the end of January 1991 both
Bush and Baker had stated that, in the aftermath of the gulf war,
Washington would pursue efforts to bring peace and stability to
the Middle East and would propose a solution to the Palestinian-
Israeli conflict.[15]

Highlighting that point was a Soviet-American declaration published in Washington in late May 1991 that suggested that the Arab-
Israeli peace process would be led by Moscow and Washington.
The expectation was that the two would chair an international
peace conference at which the region's problems, in particular the
Palestinian-Israeli conflict, would be addressed. Other American
and Soviet statements also indicated a willingness to try to get rid
of the region's weapons of mass destruction, including Israel's
nuclear arsenal.[16]

On March 7, 1991, in a victory address before Congress, President
Bush promised "to create new opportunities" for peace and stability

in the Middle East. "Our commitment to peace in the Middle East does not end with the liberation of Kuwait," Bush stated, adding that he would lead the way to a "comprehensive peace" based on the principle of land for peace and on guaranteed security for Israel and "legitimate Palestinian political rights." Sending a message to the Likud government, Bush stressed that "we have learned in the modern age, geography cannot guarantee security [which] does not come from military power alone."[17] After the president's speech, the conventional wisdom in Washington was that the bulldozer of the new international order would roll from Kuwait toward Jerusalem, that the same level of American power that had been exerted by Bush in the military arena to push Saddam out of Kuwait would be applied on the diplomatic front to pressure Shamir to withdraw from the West Bank.

Some forces were already pushing in that direction. The Palestinians had lost the moral high ground during the war because they had bet on the wrong horse. However, the Palestinian problem was still perceived as serious. The radicalization of Jordan, reflected in television news bites emanating from Amman, had reinforced that impression. More important, argued the pundits in Washington, the linkage that Saddam had promised the Palestinians would be delivered after the war by the Arab members of the anti-Saddam coalition. Israel had perhaps earned some brownie points by the restraint it had exhibited during the war. However, the fighting Arab forces had scored higher in the overall American strategic calculations and might therefore have greater influence on Washington's view of the postwar scenario.

That perceived leverage was enhanced by pressure from the Soviets, the Europeans, and the United Nations, as well as from the media that were creating a momentum for continuing the Middle Eastern peace show. As President Bush's popularity reached an all-time high, the feeling in Washington was that he had the necessary political clout to push for an Arab-Israeli peace.[18] To thwart such efforts, the members of the Israeli lobby suffused Washington's diplomatic discourse with their new line of the day. Forget the Palestinian problem, they argued, using again and again the news bite of Palestinians cheering Scuds falling on Tel Aviv. Instead of pursuing an international peace conference oriented toward an Israeli-Palestinian agreement, the Israeli lobby recommended that the administration focus its energies on making peace between Israel and individual Arab states, such as Saudi Arabia.[19]

Attempting to find a compromise between the pressures coming from Israel's supporters on Capitol Hill and America's war allies, who had wanted to assign priority to the Israeli occupation of the West Bank, Bush devised the so-called dual strategy: parallel talks between Israel and the Palestinians and between Israel and the Arab states at a regional conference sponsored by Washington and Moscow. Secretary Baker was sent to the Middle East to try to bring all the sides together. In addition to meeting with Israeli and Arab leaders, the secretary of state also conferred with Palestinian leaders in the West Bank. After several rounds of shuttle diplomacy aimed at implementing the American strategy, it looked for a while as though the Bush peace bulldozer was losing speed and might get stuck somewhere on the roads between Jerusalem, Cairo, and Damascus. The window of opportunity began to look like a very narrow peephole that might quickly close.[20]

However, on October 30, 1991, Washington succeeded in convening, under its auspices and those of Moscow, a peace conference that brought together Israel, Syria, and a Palestinian-Jordanian delegation as well as a group of observers from the United Nations and the European Community. Washington was able to drag Shamir kicking and screaming to the conference only after Bush made it clear that the United States would link approval of a $10 billion loan guarantee, which Israel had requested to help it to absorb the flow of Soviet Jews, to the willingness of the Likud government to adopt a more accommodating position on the Arab-Israeli issue, including freezing the settlement drive in the occupied territories.[21]

Bush's tough stand led to a major power struggle in September between the administration and Israel and its lobby in Washington. The president was able to defeat the pro-Israeli forces on Capitol Hill and win the necessary support in Congress for delaying the decision on the loan guarantees for four months. With the Israeli economy on the verge of total bankruptcy and with the Israeli public supporting the American-led peace efforts, Shamir, despite his reservations about U.S. diplomacy and in particular about the presence of Palestinians affiliated with the PLO at the conference, realized that if he wanted to maintain American support for and aid to his country, he had no choice but to go to Madrid and later to attend the bilateral negotiations in Washington.[22]

By the beginning of 1992, there was a growing sense in Washington and Jerusalem that the special relationship between the two countries was not so special anymore. Bush's position seemed to reflect the American public's increasingly negative attitude toward the Jewish state. The end of the Cold War and economic problems at home were making the American people unwilling to continue to support the annual entitlement program for Israel, not to mention a $10 billion loan guarantee.

Indeed, Americans, by a margin of three to one according to a late 1991 poll, supported Bush's hard line on Israel. More Americans (58 percent) supported aid to the former Cold War enemy, the Soviet Union, than supported aid to Israel (46 percent), and more Americans regarded Israel as an obstacle to peace (41 percent) than regarded the Arabs as such (29 percent).[23]

The Likud government, however, seemed to be intent on its efforts to settle the West Bank and to close the door on any possibility that Israel would agree to exchange the territories for peace with the Palestinians. The Israeli policies produced growing anger and frustration at the White House and the State Department as the relations between the two countries continued to deteriorate.[24]

Israel: No Glasnost, No Perestroika

The cause of Bush and Baker's frustration is closely related to the reason Shamir did not follow Baker's advice and call the White House in June 1990. It was not because the lines were busy. The narrowly based Likud government in Jerusalem is the most nationalistic and militant in Israel's history, and it will continue to resist American efforts to deal with Israel's occupation of the West Bank and Gaza. Led by the former anti-British underground leader Shamir, the government is committed to the long-term goal of annexing the Palestinian territories to the Jewish state. It had taken no step before the gulf war to exploit the new chapter in U.S.-Soviet relations and to enter into negotiations about the future of the West Bank and Gaza with a Palestinian leadership that in December 1988 had finally recognized Israel and renounced terrorism.[25]

The Likud government is willing to continue indefinitely its violent suppression of the three-year-old *intifada*, which has resulted in the deaths of more than 800 Arabs. Sharon, who is a serious contender for prime minister after Shamir, has supported the idea of converting the Hashemite kingdom of Jordan into a Palestinian state. Sharon's position and the perception that the Likud intends to destabilize Jordan were two of the important factors that convinced King Hussein of Jordan to strengthen his military and political ties with his namesake to the east, hoping that Saddam would help to neutralize the Israeli threat to his regime.

Unfortunately, the rising global tides of political liberalization and free-market economics have not produced Israeli versions of glasnost or perestroika. The current government has opposed calls from large segments of the population to reform the electoral system so that the bargaining power of small parties, especially that of the Orthodox religious groups, will reflect their true strength in Israeli society, which is small. Those religious groups have used the Israeli electoral system to gain disproportionate influence over policymaking and unfair access to the state's treasury, which they use to finance their narrow political interests.

Moreover, 42 years after its establishment, Israel has yet to adopt a constitution or a bill of rights, and there is no chance that the hard-line Likud majority in the Knesset, or for that matter the socialist Labor opposition that ruled Israel until 1977, would support the adoption of either. Contrary to the claims of Israeli propagandists, who like to play up the supposed cultural affinity between Israel and America, religion and state are not separate in the Jewish state. Religious groups spend government (and indirectly American taxpayers') money to support their educational and other programs and to force local and national authorities to impose religious rules (such as forbidding the showing of films in private movie theaters on the Sabbath).

Immediately after the state of Israel was established, the government, which controls elementary and high school education, made a political deal with two Orthodox political parties. That deal gave those parties the right to operate separate educational systems that are subsidized by the taxpayers of Israel and the United States (whose constitution, ironically, prohibits government subsidies to religious schools).[26]

Israel's citizens are required to carry identity cards that give their religious affiliation, which is determined by the heads of the various religious sects, and by extension their "national" identity. Jews are identified as belonging to the Jewish nation, and Arabic-speaking

Christians and Moslems are identified as Arabs. (Imagine the outcry among pro-Israeli American Jews if such a system were proposed in this country.) Although the Christian and Moslem Arab populations theoretically enjoy the same civil rights as does the Jewish community, in reality they are discriminated against in education and government employment. Since most Arabs, with the exception of the Bedouins and those who belong to the Druze sect, are not drafted into the military, they are automatically excluded from the benefits given to veterans of the Israeli Defense Forces. And Arab municipalities receive far less government financial support than do Jewish municipalities.

As Israelis watch on television the dramatic transformation of statist economies in Eastern Europe, their own economic system remains the most statist in the Western world. A massive influx of Soviet Jews makes the anomaly all the more glaring. Leaving behind the ruins of a planned economy, the immigrants may have imagined they were escaping to the capitalist West. But with the changes taking place in Eastern Europe, it is quite likely that the nations there will soon have economic systems that are more favorable to free enterprise than is Israel's. As Daniel Doron, head of a Tel Aviv think tank, has suggested half seriously, "After the fall of the regime in Albania, we might remain the last outpost of socialism in the world."[27]

Founded by East European Zionists and led by a powerful socialist elite, Israel adopted many of the attributes of a Western democratic system—in particular, a strong and independent judiciary. But it also retained some of the elements of East European political culture: a huge bureaucracy, a centralized economy, political fragmentation, respect for political authority, an intellectual class with a decided anti-business bias, and a national identity that is closely tied to ethnicity and religion. Notwithstanding all the talk about robust cultural and ideological ties between Israel and the United States, Israel's is a political culture whose sources are Hegel, Marx, and Heinrich von Treitschke (the philosopher who developed the idea of organic nationalism), not Smith, Mill, and Locke.[28] In Israel, as the popular saying puts it, the state does not belong to the people; the people belong to the state. And that state is a collection of political parties whose ideological origins go back to early 20th-century Moscow, Warsaw, and Vienna. It controls everything from

the large government agencies and public corporations to the educational system, the health services, and the soccer teams, as well as wages and prices—and the weight and shape of doughnuts.[29]
Some indications of the government's reach and influence follow.

- Israel's tax system is probably the most oppressive in the Western world; the income tax rate reaches 45 percent for salaries of $19,748. In fiscal year 1988–89, tax revenues and fees soaked up more than 50 percent of the country's gross national product.[30]
- The public sector employs about 500,000 workers—some 40 percent of the workforce—about 200,000 of whom work for the national government.[31]
- Ninety-three percent of Israel's land is in the hands of governmental authorities. Through its construction ministry and its land policy, along with the high taxes it imposes, the government has made it almost impossible for a young middle-class family to own or rent an average-sized home.[32]
- Transportation is controlled by government agencies or monopolistic cooperatives; the state discourages private ownership of vehicles by imposing burdensome taxes. As a result, Israel has fewer motor vehicles per capita than either Spain or Greece.[33]
- The state controls the communication system. There are no privately owned telephone companies or broadcasting operations, and the government has been known to keep politically controversial material off the air.[34]

Israel's huge government apparatus enables the ruling political parties to control the economy and to award benefits to their leaders and supporters, the state's *nomenklatura* (bureaucratic elite). Benefits include jobs, tax exemptions, budget increases, and perquisites such as free flights on Israel's national airline and speedy installation of telephones. (It can take the average Israeli more than a year to have a phone installed in his home.)

The Israeli welfare system has been disastrous for the state's economy. As a 1988 study noted, "Israel suffers from a socialist drag: growth rates are lower than they would be if the economy were organized along capitalist lines."[35] The socialist system has given rise to a huge bureaucracy, enormous domestic spending, and low productivity. Israel's labor costs are the highest in the West.[36] Thus, despite its human resources, Israel cannot compete in international markets or raise the standard of living of the average citizen. As one study pointed out, Israel's standard of living has failed to increase for more than a decade, whereas the standards of living of several East Asian nations, which started their post–World II development at lower levels of income and output, have soared.

Of course, Israel's statist, anti-market economic system and its parallel theocratic and discriminatory political structure could not survive without reform were it not for massive U.S. assistance, which has created disincentives for economic changes. Nor would the Likud government be able to continue the occupation of the West Bank and Gaza and to build new Jewish settlements in those territories were it not for American military and diplomatic support.

Questioning the Foundation of American-Israeli Ties

Despite the temporary improvement in American-Israeli relations that followed the U.S. military operation in the gulf, the tensions between the two countries have returned to the surface in the postwar period. Those tensions are to a large extent the result of new forces in the international system that were produced by the collapse of the Soviet empire and the changes in the relationship between the two superpowers. The diplomatic and strategic fallout of the Persian Gulf War may pose new and more difficult questions about the nature of the special relationship between Israel and the United States, raise more doubts about a strategic alliance between Washington and Jerusalem, and undermine the axiom that Israel's acting as America's military surrogate in the Middle East has bene-fited both countries.[37]

Even before the gulf war, the dramatic events of the end of the Cold War had begun to shatter the intellectual and political marriage between American neoconservatives, with their messianic Cold War agenda, and the Likud government, with its vision of a Greater Israel. During the Reagan years, those two groups had developed an anti-Soviet strategic alliance that they successfully pressed upon Washington and Jerusalem. Although many neoconservatives have attempted to take advantage of the Persian Gulf War to once again position Israel as a strategic asset, this time against Arab radicalism, their efforts are probably doomed to fail—particularly since countries such as Argentina and Romania contributed more than Israel did to the American war effort. In addition to airfields in the gulf states, the United States used airfields in England, thousands of miles from the gulf, not airfields in the geographically closer Jewish state.

During the height of the Cold War, neoconservatives typically described America's alliance with Israel as part of a grand anti-Soviet strategy. But America's support for the establishment of Israel, which produced the supposedly special relationship between the two countries, stemmed from entirely different factors. One of those factors was the American Jewish community's lobbying; another was the moral appeal of both a homeland for Jewish refugees after the Holocaust and a democratic state in the mostly undemocratic Middle East.

Most of the grand strategists who managed the early stages of the Cold War decried America's recognition of and support for the new Jewish state because they believed that it would damage U.S. relations with the Arab nations and as a result threaten American access to the strategically significant and oil-rich Middle East.[38] "It is likely, indeed, that if the crisis [the 1948 war of independence] had come a year later, after the Cold War had really gotten into its stride, the anti-Communist pressures of the Truman administration would have been too strong," noted one analyst, who added that "American backing for Israel in 1947–48 was the last idealistic luxury Americans permitted themselves before the Realpolitik of global confrontation descended."[39]

Ironically, the Soviet Union, which wished to push the British imperialists out of the Middle East, backed the creation of Israel in the late 1940s. The Soviets, although ideologically opposed to the idea of Jewish nationalism embodied in Zionism, fantasized about an anti-imperialist alliance that would include Israel and the newly independent Arab states. But the continued hostility between Zionism and Arab nationalism (which years later doomed President Ronald Reagan's similar attempt to establish an anti-Soviet strategic consensus between Israelis and moderate Arabs), coupled with the Israeli leadership's decision to join the Western camp, made it impossible to implement those plans.

Before 1967 the idea of Israel's playing a NATO-type strategic role in the region would have seemed ridiculous to U.S. policymakers. Actually, many of them regarded Israel as a drag on America's efforts to establish military bases in Arab countries and to secure access to the oil fields. In those days America's economic aid to Israel was justified on the basis of moral, not strategic, considerations, and Israeli policymakers were divided over whether Israel should join the Western camp or adopt a more neutral approach to world affairs and attempt to resolve its conflicts with the Arab states. That debate was won by Prime Minister David Ben-Gurion and his allies in Mapai, the ruling party, who persuaded their opponents that it was necessary to adopt a hawkish approach to national security—essentially an Israeli version of containment—because the Arab states were not ready to make peace with Israel. The Mapai also contended that the refusal of the Eastern bloc nations to allow most of their Jewish population to move to Israel made a confrontation with them almost inevitable.

Moreover, Ben-Gurion and his allies argued, adopting a pro-Western stance might enable Israel to win Western support, especially U.S. economic and military aid, that would help subsidize the country's socialist economy. They also suggested that the political power of American Jews would help to produce that aid.[40]

It is often forgotten that Israel did not receive direct military aid from the United States until 1962, when President John F. Kennedy agreed to sell Hawk anti-aircraft missiles to Jerusalem. Previously, Israel had played a very marginal role in America's strategic calculations. For example, President Dwight D. Eisenhower did not hesitate to force Israel (as well as Britain and France) to withdraw from Egyptian territory during the 1956 Suez crisis.[41]

The 1967 Six-Day War was the turning point in the relationship between Israel and the United States. To the administration of President Lyndon B. Johnson, which was embroiled in Vietnam, the Israeli victory suggested that America's moral commitment to Israel could serve U.S. strategic interests. Israel could be a regional "balancer" that would reduce Gamal Abdel Nasser's ability to expand Egypt's radical policies. Hence, for the first time, the United States agreed to sell Israel offensive weapons, including tanks and Skyhawk fighter-bombers.[42]

Johnson's support for Israel's strategic role in the Middle East was intertwined with his domestic problems, especially with his failure to gain support from liberals for his policy in Southeast Asia. The president's advisers hoped that, by drawing parallels between the strategic roles of Israel and South Vietnam and by stressing the need for a strong American defense posture and interventionist policies abroad as a way of securing Israel's interests in the Middle East, the administration would be able to mobilize support from the significant pro-Israeli segments of the liberal anti–Vietnam War community.[43]

Attempts to use Israel to mobilize support among liberals for militant pro–Cold War policies would become more obvious during the Reagan administration. Israel was also used to gain the backing of conservative Republicans for large foreign aid programs.

The message to the liberal Democrats was: There is a certain inconsistency between your strong support for military aid to Israel and Israeli efforts to contain communist expansion in the Middle East and your overall rejection of a strong American military posture to stop the global Soviet threat. Resolve it by supporting the latter. The message to conservative Republicans was: There is an inconsistency between your strong support for economic aid to Israel and your overall rejection of a large foreign aid program for other parts of the world. Resolve it by supporting the latter. In short, Israel became an important factor in mobilizing domestic support for interventionist Cold War policies.

Although the strategic alliance was not formalized until Reagan became president, Israel gradually emerged as a major element in U.S. diplomacy and strategy. The tremendous amount of U.S. military and economic aid that was given to Israel reflected the strategic role assigned to that country: containing Egypt and other Soviet clients in the Middle East. Israel's role was constrained, however, by America's need to maintain friendly relations with the moderate Arab states. In an effort to resolve that dilemma, Washington (especially the Arabists in the State Department) entertained and devised various plans for peace between Israel and the Arab world (including the 1969 Rogers plan).[44]

With the emergence of Henry Kissinger as the dominant player in American foreign policy, Israel's role as a pawn in the U.S.-Soviet rivalry became more significant. In September 1970 Kissinger used Israel as a deterrent to Syria, a Soviet client that was supposedly trying to topple the pro-American regime in Jordan. And although the 1973 Yom Kippur War was traumatic for both Israel and the United States, Kissinger skillfully capitalized on the outcome of that struggle to persuade Egypt to finally switch alliances.[45]

Although the policies of the administrations of Presidents Richard M. Nixon and Jimmy Carter assigned to Israel an anti-Soviet strategic role, each administration balanced its approach somewhat by assuming the role of mediator between the Israelis and the Arabs. Under the Reagan administration, American policy assumed that key Arab states would find the Soviet threat so menacing that they would work with Israel and the United States to combat it. The Palestinian problem was relegated to the bottom of both the American and the regional foreign policy agendas.

The Legacy of the Reagan Era

During the Reagan years Israel was gradually elevated in U.S. policy to the functional equivalent of a NATO member. A memorandum of understanding on strategic cooperation was signed by Secretary of Defense Caspar Weinberger and Defense Minister Ariel Sharon in 1981. In 1983 Reagan and Shamir announced the establishment of a joint political-military group to examine, as Reagan put it, "ways in which we can enhance U.S.-Israeli cooperation" with special attention "to the threat to our mutual interest posed by increased Soviet involvement in the Middle East."[46] And in 1988 Reagan and Shamir signed a memorandum of agreement that, the White House noted, "formalizes and perpetuates the bilateral . . . consultative groups that meet periodically to discuss joint military, security assistance, and economic development questions."[47]

For neoconservative intellectuals such as Jeane Kirkpatrick and Norman Podhoretz, and for more traditional anti-Soviet officials such as Robert McFarlane and Oliver North, Israel was a country that could combat Soviet mischief by a realistic, no-nonsense foreign policy unbound by domestic legal constraints. Israel therefore was central to the Reagan administration's efforts to help Washington to recover from the so-called post-Vietnam syndrome. Israel was a model to inspire decadent political and intellectual elites in the United States to renew American energy, drive, and intervention abroad. The unilateral nature of American intervention in places such as Grenada and Libya resembled Israel's iron-fisted approach to Middle Eastern issues. Washington and Jerusalem found themselves increasingly alone in international organizations. A man from Mars landing at UN headquarters in 1985 would have found it difficult to decide, after listening to U.S. Ambassador Kirkpatrick and Israeli representative Benjamin Netanyahu, which of the two represented the United States and which Israel.[48]

To the Likud party, the policies of the Reagan administration seemed to offer Israel time to consolidate its hold on the West Bank and Gaza. Israeli officials therefore encouraged Washington to view the Arab-Israeli conflict through Cold War lenses and to identify Palestinian nationalism as an extension of Soviet-induced international terrorism. In that context, Washington could view Israel's occupation of Palestinian lands with indifference. Indeed, in his first news conference, Reagan took issue with four preceding administrations on the status of the Israeli settlements in the occupied territories; he declared them "not illegal" and responded with a flat "no" to a question about whether he felt any sympathy for the Palestinians.[49] Taking Reagan's remarks as a cue, the Likud government greatly expanded Jewish settlements in the occupied territories and engaged in massive air and land attacks on PLO bases in Lebanon.

Soon, however, the neoconservative-Likud alliance led both Israel and the United States into serious difficulties. Israel's invasion of Lebanon in 1982 and its attempt to impose a new political order on the Levant, to which Washington gave a green light, ended in a humiliating Israeli military withdrawal.[50] Washington then found itself performing a difficult peacekeeping role in Lebanon, where its actions to assist the Christian minority soon brought it into conflict with Lebanon's Shi'ite community. The results included the greatest American bloodshed since the Vietnam War, increasing waves of anti-American terrorism, and loss of U.S. prestige.

In other parts of the world, the neoconservative-Likud alliance encouraged U.S.-Israeli cooperation in the era's "secret wars." Implementation of the Reagan Doctrine to roll back communism brought the two countries together in such faraway places as Central America and Zaire. Israel assisted both the Contras and President Mobutu Sese Seko's regime with financial and military aid; its lobbyists also drummed up support among pro-Israeli liberal members of Congress for those causes.[51] The liberals were bombarded with propaganda linking the PLO-Soviet terrorist network with the Sandinistas, the communist regimes in black Africa, and other subversive forces in the Third World. The implication was, of course, that by not supporting the Cold Warrior policies of the

Reagan administration, in particular the Reagan Doctrine, dovish liberals were undercutting support for Israel.

The American-Israeli adventures ultimately culminated in the disastrous Iran-Contra affair in which the Jewish state's spies and operatives were used (ironically, to circumvent constraints imposed by a pro-Israeli Congress) as part of an effort to make American foreign policy more pro-Iranian. That adventure, and the perception it created throughout the Arab world of a pro-Iranian American tilt, was an important factor in the U.S. decision to intervene militarily on the side of Iraq in its war with Iran by reflagging Kuwaiti ships and protecting those vessels with an enhanced U.S. naval presence. That development, of course, eventually helped to strengthen Iraq's position in the gulf and its ties with Washington. And Iraq's position ultimately produced a regional environment hospitable to Saddam's decision to invade Kuwait.[52]

However, the development that has highlighted more than anything else the destructive consequences of the strategic alliance has been the *intifada;* it points to the error of skirting the Israeli-Palestinian issue. The Palestinian uprising and the Israeli reaction to it eroded American support for Israel and created deep divisions in the body politic of both countries. Even before the changes in the superpower relationship and the fall of the Berlin Wall, Israelis and Americans were confronting what might be termed the "strategic asset paradox."

The Strategic Asset Paradox

American and Israeli proponents of the strategic alliance have argued that bringing America's "real" strategic interests into almost complete harmony with its moral incentive to support Israel had benefits for both countries: On the one hand, it supposedly provided the United States with a strong ally that helped to check or roll back the influence of Moscow and its allies and promote a pro-American order in the Middle East. Israel's supporters in Washington also helped to mobilize backing for U.S. global Cold War policies. On the other hand, it enabled Israel to counterbalance the Arab world's quantitative military advantage and acquire a margin of security that allowed it to take risks in the pursuit of peace. Unfortunately, since 1967, especially during the Reagan era, U.S.

military and diplomatic support has weakened instead of strengthened Israel, undermined the interests of both countries, and created the strategic asset paradox.

As U.S. aid to Israel has increased, so has Israel's reluctance to pursue a more moderate foreign policy that might result in an Arab-Israeli peace agreement. Instead of providing Israel with a margin of security, U.S. aid has given it a margin of inflexibility and strengthened the political forces in Israel who are opposed to a diplomatic solution, including withdrawal from the occupied territories. Those intransigent elements have been able to argue that Israel will not have to pay a price for clinging to the occupied territories because America's support for its "unsinkable aircraft carrier" in the Mediterranean region is guaranteed.

However, perpetuating the status quo in the territories, by establishing settlements in the West Bank and suppressing the Palestinian population, caused Israel to become ever more isolated from the international community and more dependent on the United States. Israel was increasingly perceived as an American dependent committed to the suppression of an alien population; its relations with the Eastern bloc and many Third World countries were severed; and its ties with West European countries were strained. Israel's policy toward the territories also necessitated channeling more and more of its resources into the military sector, which weakened its economy and increased its dependence on the United States. Those developments were coupled with domestic political and social tensions as well as dissension over the future of Israel and its policy toward the territories.

Moreover, ever-increasing American economic aid to Israel helped to perpetuate a bankrupt socialist economy and to strengthen the domestic constituencies that were opposed to economic reform along free-market lines. It helped to keep in place a corrupt political elite that has a vested interest in maintaining what has become the American entitlement program for Israel.

The strategic asset paradox started to become evident as early as 1973. Instead of proving that Israel was a strategic asset to the United States, as it claimed to be when selling itself to the American people and its leaders, the Yom Kippur War revealed Israel's military and diplomatic weaknesses. Israel was unable to launch a preemptive strike against Egypt for fear of antagonizing Washington; its defense posture (which was based on the assumption that

78

the occupied territories and the huge Israeli military machine would either deter any Arab attack or provide the necessary margin of security in case of such an attack) was shown to be flawed; and it was becoming almost totally isolated from the international community. The 1973 war also discredited the assumption that Israel's American connection would deter the leaders of the Arab states from trying to disrupt the status quo. The American connection had actually encouraged Egyptian president Anwar Sadat to do exactly that in the hope of bringing Washington over to his side (which he ultimately did).[53]

The manifestations of the paradox during the Reagan presidency were more dramatic. The green light given the Israeli invasion of Lebanon in 1982 did not result only in a humiliating Israeli withdrawal; it also helped to produce an Israeli version of the Vietnam syndrome, which increased the strain on Israel's social fabric. And of course, by playing down a solution to the Arab-Israeli conflict and focusing almost exclusively on the strategic alliance as the basis for the relationship between their two countries, Washington and Jerusalem contributed to the continuation of the occupation of the West Bank and Gaza and to the growing resentment among the Palestinians, which eventually led to the *intifada*. That uprising has, indeed, been the most striking manifestation of the paradox. Deep domestic divisions over whether Israel should continue to occupy the territories have created a policy paralysis. Unable to absorb the territories and unwilling to leave them, Israel has been increasingly viewed as a repressive regime and mentioned in the same breath as South Africa.

The occupation, as military historian Martin van Creveld has noted,[54] also had disastrous effects on the Israeli Defense Forces; it damped their motivation to fight. Ironically, the policy of promoting Israel as a strategic asset has weakened that country both politically and militarily, turning it into a liability instead of an asset in the eyes of American policymakers. That policy has also helped to enhance the power of radical anti-American forces in the Arab world.

Another irony: the Reagan administration, which tried to put the Palestinian issue on the back burner and highlight the strategic alliance with Israel, found itself, as a result of the *intifada*, negotiating with the PLO, a move that most Israelis have regarded as detrimental to their interests. Jerusalem's policy toward the *intifada* has also been eroding American support for Israel, especially within the two traditional bastions of pro-Israeli sentiment, Congress and the Jewish community, and tarnishing its image as a democratic country. As a result, two important bases for the special relationship between the two countries have been weakened.

The End of the Cold War: Time for a Change?

With the end of the Cold War and Moscow cooperating with Washington in addressing various Middle Eastern issues, Israel was increasingly unable to sell itself, on the eve of the gulf crisis, as America's anti-Soviet strategic asset in the Middle East. With the anti-Soviet glue that had helped to keep the strategic alliance in place beginning to melt, officials in Washington began to realize that the interests of Israel and the United States diverge on such issues as Lebanon, the West Bank, and the peace process. Israel's bargaining power was weakened, and serious calls for reassessing the special relationship between the two countries were heard in the American capital.

Indeed, as the concept of Israel as America's unsinkable aircraft carrier seemed less and less buoyant, policymakers started to question the need for continuing what is currently America's largest foreign assistance program—some $3 billion in military and economic aid to Israel every year. The proposal by Sen. Robert Dole (R-Kans.) to cut by 5 percent the aid package to Israel and other major recipients in order to free money for Eastern Europe reflected the new trend. In May 1990 a major supporter of Israel, Sen. Howard Metzenbaum (D-Ohio), warned Shamir that congressional "support for Israel is in jeopardy."[55] An official in the Israeli embassy in Washington reportedly cabled to Jerusalem that Israel had become "an object of ridicule" on Capitol Hill.[56]

Those warnings also reflected a growing disenchantment with Israel's policies in the occupied territories on the part of the American Jewish community in particular and the American public in general. A study prepared by the Israeli-Diaspora Institute at Tel Aviv University of 780 officials and leaders of American Jewish organizations found 74 percent in favor of talks between Israel and the PLO and 76 percent in favor of territorial compromise.[57] A July 1990 *New York Times*/CBS poll detected a serious erosion of public support for aid to Israel. Forty-seven percent of respondents backed a Palestinian homeland in the West Bank and Gaza.[58] Those and other polls suggested that Israel's policies, ranging from the 1982 invasion of Lebanon to the suppression of the *intifada*—as well as Jerusalem's ties with the apartheid government in Pretoria and cooperation with other unsavory regimes in the Third World—were gradually eroding support for Israel even among important pro-Israeli constituencies.

Although repudiated by the Israeli government, former Mossad agent Victor Ostrovsky's revelations of Israeli intelligence activities that were harmful to U.S. interests added to the deepening sense of unease.[59] Israel seemed to be losing not only its strategic value in the eyes of some of its conservative supporters but also the moral high ground it had been accorded by the liberal community. (In 1985 the news that the Israeli government had persuaded an American Jew, Jonathan Pollard, to use his position in the U.S. government to spy for Israel had had a similar, albeit temporary, effect on the U.S.-Israeli relationship.)[60] On the political left, powerful constituencies, in particular black groups in the Democratic party, whose views were articulated by Rev. Jesse Jackson, were challenging the knee-jerk support for Israel. Those groups were not only sympathetic to the plight of the Palestinians and critical of Israel's ties with South Africa; they also thought that the major entitlement program for Israel should be cut and its costs diverted to pay for domestic social programs and aid projects for black Africa. The growing tensions between the American Jewish leaders and Jackson and other members of the black leadership during the 1984 presidential election campaign reflected those problems.[61]

On the political right, a new, more cautious, and more selective approach to foreign policy intervention emerged at the end of the Cold War. Characterized by some as the "new isolationism," that approach was taken by conservative thinkers such as Patrick Buchanan, who challenged the neoconservative paradigm with its emphasis on a perpetual crusade for global democracy and the alliance with Israel. Buchanan and his colleagues argued that the alliance was a prescription for a long-term conflict between the United States and the Arab world and that Washington should gradually disengage itself from the Middle East.[62]

Moreover, with the econostrategists beginning to win the day in the foreign policy debate, Israel's militarist posture seemed to be out of sync with their increasingly popular views on economic interdependence, the anachronism of armed conflict, and a more peaceful international system. Indeed, in an international system in which economic power could replace military might as the main currency in relations among states, Israeli military power might have gradually become irrelevant to American interests. The erosion of support for Israel was also evident in the American Jewish community. When Israel campaigned to cut off the U.S.-PLO talks in 1989, three Jewish organizations—the American Jewish Congress, the American Jewish Committee, and the Union of American Hebrew Congregations—refrained from supporting Israel.[63]

Those developments sent shock waves through the Israeli establishment. Academics, columnists, and foreign policy practitioners started to debate a reorientation of Israel's foreign policy. Some suggested a focus on Israel's new neighboring superpower, the post-1991 European Community, and others expressed their belief that a reunited Germany, which had a moral commitment to Israel and was not dependent on Arab oil, could replace Washington as a rainy-day protector. Israel's ambassador to Spain proposed integration of Israel into a "Mediterranean alliance" led by France. One Israeli professor, Paul Eidelberg of Bar-Ilan University, even raised the idea of an alliance between Israel and the Soviet Union to contain the rise of Islamic fundamentalism, which obviously threatened Israel and could jeopardize Moscow's control over its Moslem republics.[64] Another interesting development was the growing ties between Israel and the Serbian republic in Yugoslavia, as well as between Israel and Armenia and Georgia in the USSR. Like Israel, those countries are located on the periphery of the Moslem world and fear Moslem domination.

Those new ideas for Israeli foreign policy, however, all faced a major catch. Earlier, candidates for new alliances might have seriously considered a proposal from Israel because they could have hoped that Jerusalem would provide a valuable prize: a closer connection with Washington. The erosion of the U.S.-Israeli relationship, however, made Israeli proposals less attractive. Moreover, both Brussels and Moscow would also demand major Israeli concessions on the Palestinian issue in exchange for close cooperation.

Most Likud leaders did not even try to confront the new diplomatic realities. They argued, instead, for business as usual with

Washington. Such wishful thinking recalled the refusal of the Israeli leadership after the end of the Algerian War in 1962 to recognize that the convergence of strategic interests between Paris and Jerusalem, raised almost to the level of a formal alliance during the French confrontation with the forces of Pan-Arabism in North Africa, had disappeared after Algeria won independence. Several years passed before the changes that had taken place at the strategic level were finally reflected in the transformation of Israeli-French relations. Then in 1967 President Charles de Gaulle of France suddenly imposed an arms embargo against Israel during the Six-Day War.[65]

Replacing the Cold War Threat with the Global *Intifada* Bogeyman

As had been the case for Great Britain and Turkey, the crisis in the gulf and the war that followed seemed to play into the hands of Israel by reversing the post–Cold War trends that the econostrategists had cited as reasons for the United States to adopt a less militarily interventionist posture. In the context of a revival of the neoconservative paradigm with its stress on a renewed American international military role, Israel could once again emerge as America's strategic asset. As Washington resumed its role as global policeman, Israel could reemerge as its Middle Eastern cop.

Indeed, even before the crisis in the gulf erupted, some supporters of Israel insisted that the concept of Israel as a strategic asset was still alive and well. Washington, they argued, could store in Israel military equipment that was withdrawn from Europe and could be used in future mid- and low-intensity conflicts in the Middle East. The new line of reasoning was that the removal of the Soviet factor from any Middle Eastern calculations actually increased the value of the special relationship between the United States and Israel since the military strength of the Jewish state could serve as a deterrent to radical Arab regimes and help to shore up shaky moderate ones.[66] Israel could thus become the contemporary crusader nation, a bastion of the West in the struggle against a new transnational enemy, radical nationalism and Islamic fundamentalism.

Neoconservative and pro-Likud columnist Charles Krauthammer termed the new enemy the "global intifada."[67] The operational implication of that type of reasoning was that the original *intifada,* still bubbling in the West Bank, could and should be forgotten and Israel should be elevated again to the status of an American ally. Indeed, neoconservative columnists played a crucial role in producing the Zeitgeist in which the new enemy, the Middle Eastern bogeyman symbolized by Saddam Hussein, replaced the Soviet Union as America's arch-rival. Publications sympathetic to the Likud government, such as *U.S. News & World Report*, whose cover story characterized Saddam as "the most dangerous man in the world," carried stories focusing on Iraq's nuclear military program.[68]

The Likud government was worried that if Iraq acquired a nuclear capability it would endanger Israel's regional nuclear monopoly. Israel, which apparently had no military option for dealing with the Iraqi threat (it was impossible to repeat the daring 1981 attack on the Iraqi nuclear reactor because the element of surprise would have been missing), was hoping to ignite an anti-Iraqi campaign in the West that might weaken the Baghdad regime and isolate Saddam internationally. In that context, it was not a coincidence that writers such as Krauthammer also supplied the ideological "Saddam-is-Hitler" formula that was so conducive to mobilizing elite and public support for sending American troops to the gulf to deal with the Iraqi invasion of Kuwait. That formulation was also intended to help Israel to revive its strategic role.

However, in spite of those hopes, Israel did not reemerge as Washington's strategic ally during the gulf war. Ironically, according to Israeli press reports, on the eve of the Iraqi invasion Shamir received a memorandum outlining the prospects for growing American-Israeli strategic cooperation; among other things it suggested that "the American interest [in] cooperation with Israel stems from the need to secure the energy sources and the regular supply of oil to the U.S. and Japan." The memorandum also predicted that the partnership between the two countries would help the United States to "contain aggression by regional powers" and that Israel would serve as a "maintenance base for [American] forces that might operate in the area."[69]

But Israel's exclusion from the U.S.-led military and economic campaign against Iraq and America's reliance on military and political cooperation with the moderate Arab nations pointed out the weakness of America's strategic cooperation with Israel. The decision to base the American strategy in the gulf on an American-Arab alliance also reflected the fact that, unlike the neoconservative elements with their strong emotional ties to Israel, the Bush-Baker team represents the Rockefeller wing of the Republican party as well as Texas interests. Those two constituencies have strong oil business ties to the Arab world and limited sentimental ties to the Jewish state.

As a matter of fact, Washington made a special effort during the crisis to play down any suggestion that it was coordinating its moves in the area with Israel and asked Jerusalem to keep a low profile. "We are not a strategic asset," announced Israel's largest circulation daily, *Yediot Aharonot*, in an editorial referring to the cold shoulder Israel was receiving from Washington. "The war in the Persian Gulf threatens to destroy the legend of Israel's existence as a front-line base for the United States against half-crazy oil pirates," wrote commentator Akiva Eldar in the newspaper *Ha'aretz*. "On the face of it, the American taxpayer [has] the right to ask his representatives why they are shelling out $3 billion to a country that, in the moment of truth, turns out to be nothing but an empty vessel."[70]

Israel was exposed as a liability during the war. Not only could it not perform any effective military role in the crisis because of political constraints, but Washington found itself expending military resources to defend Israel from Iraqi Scud attacks. Washington also focused diplomatic attention on preventing Israel from entering the war. Israeli participation in the war might have endangered the American-Arab coalition and played into Saddam's hands by creating the perception of a conflict between an American-Zionist alliance and the Arab and Moslem worlds.

The Persian Gulf War thus demonstrated the dangers of the militant Likud policies supported by Washington. Although the gulf crisis might have diverted attention from the *intifada* for a while, the October 1990 confrontation in Jerusalem's Old City between Palestinian demonstrators and Israeli security forces, which resulted in 21 reported Arab deaths, suggested that the continued status quo in the territories was working against cementing the American-Arab alliance and was instead playing into the hands of the Iraqi leader as well as other radical forces in the region.

While Jewish members of Congress were divided over the resolution authorizing the president to use force in the gulf, the Likud government and its neoconservative supporters, such as Krauthammer, William Safire, and A. M. Rosenthal, did not hide their enthusiasm for a full-scale American attack on Iraq. Their arguments helped to strengthen AIPAC's fierce campaign among pro-Israeli members of Congress, who were less inclined to support Bush's war strategy, to convince them that only a military move against Iraq would secure Israel's interests in the region.[71]

At the same time, pro-Israeli figures on Capitol Hill, in particular Reps. Stephen J. Solarz (D-N.Y.) and Tom Lantos (D-Calif.), were mobilizing support for the administration's gulf policy.[72] While its effects are difficult to measure, it is conceivable that the "Israeli factor" played a role in deciding the votes of wavering senators and representatives.

After the war started, the pro-Likud and neoconservative columnists, following the Israeli line, called on Washington to set war aims that went beyond the stated U.S. and UN goal: the removal of Iraqi forces from Kuwait and a return to the status quo ante. Krauthammer, for example, suggested that the United States should not stop bombing Iraq until "the air war is doing nothing more than making the rubble bounce."[73] Norman Podhoretz suggested that "by holding the Israelis back, we are squandering a precious strategic asset. . . . Surely then, it is time . . . to start unleashing them."[74]

During the war the Israeli government, through Foreign Minister David Levy, stated that it would not agree to participate in a peace process unless the Americans produced the defeat and the downfall of Saddam.[75] The best-case scenario, from the Likud government's point of view, was that the war would create violent anti-American feelings in the Arab and Moslem regions, lead to the fall or the weakening of the moderate pro-Western Arab regimes, and leave Washington no option but to put all its Middle Eastern eggs in the Israeli basket.

The realization of that scenario, or a variation of it, clearly could have played into Shamir's hands. However, Bush's decision not to invade Baghdad reflected the more limited nature of the administration's agenda in the region, in particular its interest in shoring up the power of the pro-American monarchies and its rejection of the wider goals propagated by the neoconservatives. Predictably, the decision not to go all the way to Baghdad elicited hostility from the neoconservatives, and the Kurdish tragedy was used by commentators such as Rosenthal and Safire and by pro-Israeli congressmen such as Solarz as an excuse to call for renewing the war against Iraq.[76] The administration turned a deaf ear to those arguments.

5. Transforming the American-Israeli Connection: Helping Israel to Help Itself

The end of the gulf war and Washington's efforts to establish a new Middle Eastern order will inevitably lead to growing strains on the American-Israeli relationship. In the aftermath of the war, the Bush administration has found it difficult to maintain its position that American interests in the gulf and in the Palestinian-Israeli conflict can be separated. The administration has tried to link continuing support for Israeli security needs with real progress on peace negotiations. Egypt and Saudi Arabia, in exchange for their active diplomatic and military support for Washington during the gulf war and for their participation in a future Arab anti-radical alliance, are demanding that Bush pressure Israel for a settlement of the Palestinian problem.

Why Disengagement from Israel Is Difficult

However, there is little chance that Prime Minister Yitzhak Shamir's Israel will accommodate itself to the changes in the international and regional environment. Instead, it seems determined to occupy a position comparable to that of Fidel Castro's Cuba, resisting suggestions from its superpower patron that it reformulate its foreign policy and reform its bankrupt economy. That stance will make it difficult to absorb the hundreds of thousands of highly educated professionals who are immigrating to Israel from the former Soviet Union.

Israel's renewal of diplomatic relations with the East European countries and the massive immigration of Jews, expected to reach more than 1 million people in the next several years, on the one hand, and the adoption by Syria, under pressure from the Kremlin, of a more moderate posture, on the other hand, were the results of a radical change in Soviet Middle Eastern policy. Moscow drastically cut military aid to Syria, its ally in the Middle East, and reduced the number of Soviet advisers in that country. It made clear its rejection of Syrian president Hafez al-Assad's grand design for achieving strategic parity with Israel.[1]

Unfortunately, the response of Israel's Likud government has been to stall the peace process and to shirk domestic reforms. It has avoided a historic opportunity to move toward peace so the country can concentrate on absorbing the refugees. The Likud hopes that the new masses of Jews from the former Soviet Union will tip the demographic balance in historical Palestine in favor of Israeli Jews and make permanent Israeli control of the occupied territories more likely, a prospect that worries the Palestinian leaders and the Jordanian regime.

Instead of dismantling statist structures and adopting free-market solutions that could provide jobs for the hundreds of thousands of highly educated Jews arriving in Israel, the government is attempting to absorb them through a government-controlled system—in the end subsidized by the United States—that tends to aggravate social tensions between native Israelis and the newcomers as a result of competition for limited state resources.

An American policy of disengagement from Israel would send a clear signal to the Likud government about the need to start facing the diplomatic and economic music and would enable the United States to devise a Middle Eastern policy based on its own national interest, independent of that of the militant government in Jerusalem. Such a signal would finally sink the concept of Israel as America's strategic asset in the eastern Mediterranean. In addition, disengagement from Israel would mean a massive cut in American entitlement programs for the Jewish state and would send to Jerusalem the message that the United States has neither the desire nor the resources to bankroll a Middle Eastern version of 1970s Poland.

Since 1976 Israel has received more U.S. aid, both annually and cumulatively, than any other country. From 1949 through 1965 American aid to Israel, over 95 percent of which was economic development and food aid, averaged about $63 million a year. A modest military loan program began in 1959. From 1971 to the present, the period during which Israel rose as a strategic asset, U.S. aid to Israel, 66 percent of which has been military assistance, has averaged over $2 billion a year. In fiscal year 1990 U.S. aid to Israel came to $3 billion.[2] Since 1967 U.S. aid to Israel has amounted to about $77 billion.[3]

U.S. aid has allowed Israel's leaders to avoid paying the political and economic costs of clinging to the occupied territories and to refrain from making decisions that might lead to an Israeli-Palestinian peace agreement. It has also allowed them to avoid the costs of perpetuating a welfare state system. Moreover, U.S. aid helps to secure the power of the existing Ashkenazi (Central and East European Jewish) political elite and prevents major reform of the Israeli political and economic systems.

However, the idea of an immediate and total disengagement from Israel would encounter enormous domestic obstacles. The American Jewish community cares passionately about the security and welfare of Israel. American Jews, through their votes and financial contributions, provide support for key members of Congress in exchange for their backing of Israel. And the Jewish state, despite recent setbacks, still enjoys considerable support among many other segments of the American public, such as Christian evangelicals, who are influenced by the historical and moral legacy, in particular the Holocaust, that binds the two nations.

Therefore, as a practical matter, any attempt to transform the relationship between the two countries would have to be gradual. What is needed is a policy of constructive disengagement from Israel, one that would reduce that country's dependence on the United States and remove the disincentives for diplomatic and economic change that American aid to and support for Israel produce.

This is not a call for a hyperactivist policy. Washington cannot produce an Israeli reformist regime or impose a perestroika on the promised land. But it can use its leverage over Israel to help that country to help itself, and it can create conditions that are conducive to diplomatic initiatives and economic reform by devising and implementing policies vis-à-vis Israel that fit with American interests and values.[4]

The Web of the American-Israeli Connection

American policy toward Israel has always been driven by the notion that Washington could not and should not attempt to encourage changes in the positions of the Israeli public and elites. The argument has been that Israel's domestic and foreign policies are developed without reference to one another, as though each were in its own watertight compartment. Israelis, according to the conventional wisdom, debate their domestic and foreign policies among themselves with little input from the outside world, reach consensus about what constitutes their national interest, and then make their choices through the ballot box. According to that view, Washington's only task is to negotiate with Israel's elected officials over their respective foreign policy agendas, while refraining from "interfering" in the domestic affairs of a democratic ally.

That approach reflects a diplomatic version of affirmative action toward the Jewish state, which is thus protected from the kind of U.S. diplomatic pressure that countries in other parts of the world experience regularly. In Europe, for example, the Reagan administration made its preference for the policies of Margaret Thatcher and Helmut Kohl known during key elections in Great Britain and West Germany. Voters in those countries, and the results of those elections, may have been influenced by the U.S. position.

More recently, the Bush administration was reluctant to assist the new democracies in Eastern Europe and the Soviet Union with massive financial support because it argued that such aid might discourage the people and leaders of those countries from taking bold steps to adopt free-market economies. In light of its desire to instill capitalist values in other countries, why should Washington, in its own national interest, not "interfere" in some appropriate way in Israeli politics—especially since that interference would take the form of withdrawing an unjustified subsidy?

There are several explanations of America's diplomatic timidity. One is that other segments of the American public are influenced by the guilt-ridden reluctance of American Jews to criticize Israel's political choices. Many American Jews accept the argument, advanced by members of the Israeli right and their supporters, that by not moving to Israel, American Jews "forfeit the moral right to pass public judgment on matters which for Israelis—but not for us—are questions of life and death," as historian Gertrude Himmelfarb has put it.[5]

Closely intertwined with that argument is the influence of the Holocaust. Israel receives special diplomatic and economic treatment from the West because it is perceived as a refuge for survivors of the Nazi horror and anti-Semitism in other countries, including the United States.

For years, certainly until 1967, a clear consensus on Israel's national security interests united the majority of that country's political parties. Until 1967 the Israeli leadership's view of the Jewish state's national interest was also supported by the vast majority of Israeli citizens. Hence, any American attempt to put pressure on or weaken the political fortunes of a stubborn government, it was argued in Washington, would have boomeranged. Israelis would have circled the wagons and rallied behind their leaders and the flag.

It is time to sweep those arguments aside. Israel's domestic and foreign policies should never have been treated as separate entities. The international system, especially ties with the United States, has always constrained or expanded Israel's concrete options and influenced its most sensitive national security moves. An American nod helped to produce Israel's June 1967 decision to launch a preemptive attack on Egypt, for example, and potential U.S. opposition prevented a similar move in 1973.[6]

More important, Israel's ties with other international actors, especially with the United States, have always been a very powerful influence on the public choices of Israelis and, consequently, have influenced the political fortunes of the country's leading parties and personalities. The rise and fall of Israeli leaders has been closely connected with debates about and consequences of foreign policy orientations. The ability of Israeli leaders to deliver the foreign support needed to counter the Arab threat and to provide financial backing for the country's socialist system has always affected their personal and political fortunes at home.

Israel's first prime minister, David Ben-Gurion, successfully strengthened his domestic political base in the early 1950s by orienting Israel's foreign policy away from neutrality and nonalignment between the two superpowers toward an alliance with the West. That policy culminated in the decision to support the United States in the Korean War. His centrist social democratic Mapai party gained position at the expense of the more popular (especially among the young voters) pro-Soviet Mapam movement, which along with other political parties and groups called for a "neutralist" Israeli foreign policy designed to establish a nonaligned Middle East based on an "anti-imperialist" Arab-Israeli alliance.[7]

Ben-Gurion's pro-American orientation, which he had begun to formulate as a policy option in the midst of World War II when most Zionist leaders still expected Great Britain to help establish a

Jewish state in Palestine, was the first step in an Israeli effort to produce a Western, in particular an American, commitment to militarily defend Israel in exchange for Israeli support for U.S. Cold War goals. Moreover, that pro-American orientation also helped to gain the financial aid needed to support a state-controlled economic system through which Mapai was able to retain the political allegiance of hundreds of thousands of new immigrants—Holocaust survivors and refugees from Arab countries—and, as a result, to maintain its position as the country's ruling party until 1977.

That arrangement, which has helped to make it possible for Israel to perpetuate an inviable economic system at America's expense, goes back to the early 1920s, when the Zionist leaders in what was then Palestine were already conceding that their socialist economic institutions would never be profitable and would always need support from outside sources. Some American Zionist leaders were not willing to accept that idea, and one of them, the prominent jurist Louis Brandeis, asserted that the Jewish pioneers in Palestine should "develop a system that will allow them to earn their living. . . . This should not be done with subsidies." Brandeis also argued that the economic system should be "depoliticized" because "without economic democracy the political freedoms might be endangered."[8] Brandeis and his allies lost the battle. Jewish Palestine, and later Israel, became quite literally a welfare state. Initially, most of the financial support for the Zionist socialist experiments in Israel came from the Jewish communities abroad; later American taxpayers assumed the burden.[9]

American aid still keeps afloat Israel's huge public sector, which is controlled by the members of the country's Ashkenazic *nomenklatura* who rule over a majority of Sephardim (Jews from Moslem countries) and Arabs and control their access to the state's political and economic resources. The Ashkenazim, mostly descendants of the founding families of Israel, dominate the country's political and economic system through the large public sector and the political parties that maintain it. The public sector includes, in addition to the huge government bureaucracy, the Histadrut (the national trade union affiliated with the Labor movement), the banking system, and the military-industrial complex responsible for producing and importing Israel's military equipment.

The leaders of the Israeli *nomenklatura,* who rule over both Labor and Likud, have been able to co-opt leading members of the Sephardic community by awarding benefits—political positions, jobs, budget increases, and other perquisites—to Sephardim who support them. (For example, there are currently 26 cabinet ministries, which means, of course, 26 bureaucracies, each of which is a fiefdom of a political party.) The elite also maintains a dominant anti-Arab ideology and perpetuates a siege mentality that helps to mobilize public support for its domestic and foreign policies among the lower-middle-class Sephardim.

The American-subsidized statist economic system helps to preserve the economic and social inequalities between the Ashkenazic elite and the Sephardic majority. Economic reform along free-market lines could benefit the Sephardim. A recent study by a sociologist at Tel Aviv University found that while the income gap between the Ashkenazic and the Sephardic population has been widening in government and publicly owned enterprises, where the former tend to be managers and the latter mid- and low-level bureaucrats, it has been closing in the small private sector, where many Sephardim are succeeding.[10]

American support and aid for Israel have been channeled through the system that Ben-Gurion established in the early 1950s, aided by the lobbying and fundraising efforts of organized American Jewry, especially the United Jewish Appeal and the American Israel Public Affairs Committee (AIPAC). By using the Israeli cause to gain financial and political support from the American Jewish community and to stifle dissent (by raising the specter of the Holocaust and playing on American Jewish guilt for not moving to Israel), the self-appointed American Jewish leaders can maintain their own huge organizations and powerful positions as middlemen between the Israeli and the American governments.

Members of the Israeli elite who travel to the United States, where they stay at expensive hotels, address Jewish audiences, and meet American politicians at the expense of the American Jewish organizations, and American Jewish leaders who fly to Israel, where they meet for "closed briefings" with the Israeli prime minister and are accorded VIP treatment, are the two sides of the "American-Israeli complex." Its main driving force is the self-interest of Israeli politicians, American Jewish activists, and key members of Congress and the administration. The American taxpayer finances that complex through grants and loans to Israel.

The Interaction between Israel's Domestic and Foreign Policies

Foreign policy orientations played a major role in the bitter political struggle in Mapai in the 1950s and 1960s. The conflict pitted the old guard of the party, with its more cautious foreign policy approach, against Ben-Gurion and Mapai's activist "young Turks," who, after Washington turned a cold shoulder on their proposals for strategic cooperation between the United States and Israel, advocated a European orientation based on close military ties with the defense establishments of France and West Germany and a confrontational national security posture. (Just as Washington's European allies resented the way they were treated during the 1956 Suez incident and were later concerned by President John F. Kennedy's efforts to reach accommodations with the Soviets, Israelis were concerned that Washington's opening to Gamal Abdel Nasser's Egypt would be at their expense.)[11]

The old guard advocated a close relationship with Washington even if it constrained Israel's defense effort, including the nuclear option. Ben-Gurion's success in forming a clear alliance with Paris resulted, among other things, in the 1956 Suez campaign in which Israel found itself aiding the two declining imperial powers' last efforts to maintain their position in the Middle East. The domestic consequence was the political fall of Ben-Gurion's main rival in Mapai, moderate Prime Minister Moshe Sharett.[12] The demise of the European orientation, including the severance of strong defense ties with France, and the reorientation of Israel's foreign policy toward Washington by Ben-Gurion's successor, Levi Eshkol, weakened the power of the "Old Man" and his clique. A split in Mapai followed.

Later, American policy toward Israel helped to tip the balance in the political struggles inside the Labor party over the occupied territories, and after that between Labor and Likud. Secretary of State Henry Kissinger's successful efforts before the 1973 Yom Kippur War to neutralize any serious pressure on Israel from within the Nixon administration to respond to the peace overtures of President Anwar Sadat of Egypt and Jordan's King Hussein helped to consolidate the power of hawkish Laborites Moshe Dayan and

Yigal Allon. The lack of any American pressure for accommodation made it possible for those two rivals, who represented minority wings in Labor, to force the party's moderate majority, which was interested in maintaining party unity, to expand Jewish settlement efforts in the West Bank and Sinai. They were also able to block each other's initiatives, the Allon plan for the West Bank and Dayan's 1970 proposal for limited withdrawal from the Suez Canal.[13]

In the 1980s President Ronald Reagan's Middle Eastern policies played into the hands of the right-wing forces in the policy debates between Labor and Likud, especially during the administration of the national unity government. Secretary of State George Shultz's decision at the end of 1987 to discontinue American efforts to facilitate the initiative of Israeli foreign minister Shimon Peres to start negotiations between Jordan and Israel released diplomatic pressure on Shamir and helped to create the policy gridlock that led to the *intifada*. The argument that "even America" did not take seriously the Peres peace initiatives did not go unnoticed by most Israelis. The Reagan team's lack of effort to relate continuing American support to more diplomatic flexibility on Israel's part helped to convince at least Likud voters that Israel could have its cake—U.S. aid—and eat it too—continue to settle the West Bank.[14]

American aid continued to finance the socialist system that the Likud government had inherited. There were early expectations that the right-wing Likud coalition that came to power in 1977 would replace the corrupt Labor party machine, which was suffocating Israel's economy, and attempt to reform the economy. But after toying for a while with some market-oriented steps—inviting Milton Friedman to give advice, freeing the rate of exchange—the Likud adopted the statist and populist agenda of the Herut wing of the party and rejected the more free-enterprise orientations of the Liberal wing.

Like Labor, Likud used the government budget to reward its political supporters and to placate its large Sephardic constituency with welfare money. The government expanded, and Likud's political corruption simply replaced Labor's. Washington was asked to pay (and did) the costs of that economic mismanagement as well as those of Likud's settlement of the West Bank and its military campaign in Lebanon. There is little doubt that without an American bailout, Israel's economy would have been bankrupt in the early 1980s.

It would be a mistake to analyze the impact of the American connection on Israeli political choices only in the context of intra-party or government debates. For most Israelis the relationship with America is more than just $3 billion in annual economic and military aid. The ties with Washington transcend even such important elements as family connections, cultural influence, business relationships, and the strategic alliance. For most Israelis, isolated in a hostile region of an unfriendly world, the United States represents a lifeline to international society. Psychologically, the American tie is a protective shield that encourages them to continue building the third Jewish commonwealth.

Hence, an Israeli leader who failed to maintain the American connection—or worse, one who harmed ties with the United States—would eventually suffer at the polls. Nothing raises the popularity of an Israeli prime minister like a photograph with a smiling American president on the eve of a Knesset election. Israelis follow very closely every American move or gesture toward their country, ranging from statements by the president to the body language of the State Department's spokesperson, from the writings of a Washington columnist to the results of public opinion polls. The overt and covert messages the American leadership and public send to the Jewish state are decoded by Israeli opinion makers and voters and then used to evaluate their government's performance.

America's messages to Israel, of course, can influence public choices only if they interact with political reality. The decline of the Labor party stems from long-term demographic changes in Israeli society; no amount of American influence can reverse that trend.[15] Also, any American pressure on Israel to take steps that most Israelis oppose, such as dividing Jerusalem, clearly will backfire. American messages can have an impact, however, when they touch upon issues that split the Israeli polity. Examples include the Likud settlement policy in the West Bank or even the kind of economic system the country should adopt.

What Should Washington Do?

One of the major problems with the thesis that rejects the propriety of American interference is that U.S. military and economic aid to Israel has always constituted interference in Israeli politics. Beginning in the late 1960s, and especially with the rise of Israel as a strategic asset in the 1980s, American aid began to suffer from the law of diminishing returns. Instead of supplying Israel with a security margin and an economic safety net, American support began to strengthen the forces in Israel that were opposed to a diplomatic solution to the Palestinian problem as well as to economic reform.

American aid and support send the Israeli public a dangerous message: clinging to the occupied territories will not involve any serious costs in terms of the relationship with the United States, and regardless of economic setbacks, Washington will continue to bail out Israel's bankrupt economy. As a result, barring a military disaster like that of 1973 or a major economic crisis like the one Israel faced in the late 1980s, there are no public pressures on the leadership to change the status quo.

To put the matter another way, American support for Israel has provided the Israeli public and its leaders with disincentives and deterrents. There is no reason Washington should not use its existing connection with Jerusalem to try to remove those disincentives in a way that will strengthen the forces within Israel whose vision of their country's future converges with American interests and values. Americans who reject such moves while continuing to support "business as usual" between Washington and Jerusalem help to maintain the status quo, including the power of the more extreme members of Likud.

Friends of Israel in the administration and Congress who understand the long-term threats to the American-Israeli relationship posed by continuing Likud policies should be in the vanguard of those who seek to create a new set of incentives for Israel. Those incentives should encourage political change without endangering Israel's national security. No one, after all, is calling for a military coup or using National Endowment for Democracy funds to support particular political parties in Israel. Instead, true friends of Israel should want the United States to provide Israeli voters with the information they need on the constraints and limits of American-Israeli relations so that they can make rational decisions on election day.

The strong forces in Israel that support some kind of territorial compromise, aided by clear messages from Washington, might help shatter the status quo in the occupied territories. Thus, the administration and Congress should start developing strategies to promote more constructive Israeli policies. During a June 1990 debate in the House, Rep. David Obey (D-Wis.) suggested that Congress use aid as a political tool to send a "very friendly warning" to the Israeli government. More specifically, Obey and other members of the House Appropriations Committee proposed that in future budgets aid to Israel be reduced by the amount it spends to build or expand settlements in the West Bank and Gaza.[16]

Today, although the United States has stipulated that aid cannot be used in the occupied territories, no accounting is required, and therefore Washington has no way of knowing where its dollars are going. The Israeli government can argue that it is not diverting U.S. aid to the territories. However, one does not have to hold a degree in accounting to understand that the American financial infusion can release funds, which could have been used for other purposes, to build new Jewish settlements in the West Bank and Gaza.

Indeed, at a time when Jerusalem was requesting $10 billion in loan guarantees, the Israeli press reported that the Likud government was planning to build new Jewish settlements in the occupied territories.[17] The building of new Jewish settlements and the expansion of old ones continued as Washington revived the Israeli-Arab peace process after the gulf war. Particularly unfortunate for American policy is the fact that those settlements have been a breeding ground for the most nationalistic Israeli groups, whose leaders have emphasized time and again that their main goals are to use the settlements as a tool for annexing the territories to Israel and to sabotage any possible Israeli withdrawal from them.

By not following Obey's recommendation, American policymakers are spending U.S. tax dollars to increase the power of forces in Israel whose interests run counter to American values and interests. It is as though American funding were being used by the anti-Semitic Russian Pamyat movement to establish settlements in the Ukraine.

As a first step, the United States should cut aid to Israel by the amount Jerusalem spends on new Jewish settlements in the territories. That would not damage any real Israeli security interest, and it would send a clear message to the Likud government. Other options and messages are also available to the United States. Several analysts in Washington have urged an end to the special payment arrangements that Israel now enjoys. The Jewish state receives all its U.S. aid up front. (The normal practice is to give aid recipients quarterly allotments so as to deny them the opportunity to invest U.S. funds and earn commercial interest.) Those may be minor changes, but they would be useful initial steps. The ultimate goal, of course, should be to end the subsidy entirely, even though that step is unlikely, given the realities of U.S. domestic policy.

At a time when even Peronists in Argentina and erstwhile Communists in the former Soviet Union are taking major political risks by attempting to dismantle statist structures, the United States should encourage economic reform in Israel by gradually but inexorably cutting back its $1.2 billion economic aid allotment. Such a large sum fosters big government both by feeding it directly and by obscuring the drag that an excessively large public sector exerts on the economy. The losers are the young American-style Israeli entrepreneurs, who sometimes need more than 10 licenses to open a business, and the professionals who fled the Kafkaesque Soviet system only to be repelled by Israel's own enormous bureaucracy.

Yet another instrument for change is U.S. immigration law. It is no secret that the reason hundreds of thousands of Jews are leaving the former Soviet Union for Israel and not America is that the Bush administration, under pressure from the Israeli government (and ironically American Jewish organizations that have always strongly supported free immigration policies), decided at the end of 1989 to place an annual ceiling of 40,000 on the number of Soviet Jews who could enter the United States as refugees. At the same time, the United States announced that it would no longer allow Soviet Jews to use Israeli visas to immigrate to this country.[18]

Without a diplomatic solution to the Palestinian problem and economic reform, the massive tide of immigrants will be used to advance the dream of Greater Israel and bolster a socialist economy. The security and well-being of the new immigrants could actually be endangered. The suggestion of possible liberalization of U.S. immigration quotas for Jewish immigrants from the former Soviet Union could link the continuation of immigration to Israel to greater diplomatic moderation and economic reform and force some clear choices on the Israeli public and government. (Supporters of free and open immigration to this country, including members of the

American Jewish community, should in any case be in favor of allowing talented Soviet professionals to come to the United States.)

In one dramatic instance Washington was able to effectively use its ties with Jerusalem to encourage changes in Israeli policies that in the long run had a positive impact on both American and Israeli interests. After the 1956 Suez campaign, President Dwight D. Eisenhower forced Israel to withdraw from Sinai and the Gaza Strip. Jerusalem and many of its supporters criticized that move. However, instead of becoming embroiled in policing refugee camps in Gaza and being subjected to international condemnation and isolation, as a result of the American pressure, Israel was able, after the withdrawal, to devote its resources to economic and social development and forge friendships in Europe and Africa. In many ways, thanks to Eisenhower, 1957–67 turned out to be the "golden age" of Israel's development.[19]

The American-Israeli Relationship: The Need to Return to Basics

After the Six-Day War, Israeli prime minister Eshkol visited the United States and met with President Lyndon B. Johnson at his ranch in Texas. At the end of their discussion, Johnson called the Israeli leader aside and asked, "As you look to the future, Mr. Prime Minister, what kind of Israel do you expect us, the American people, to support?" No Israeli leader, including Eshkol, has ever responded to that question. The time has come for the leaders of Israel—the country that receives the most U.S. aid and whose survival depends very heavily on American military support—to answer Johnson's question by stating their willingness to give up control over 1.7 million Palestinians in exchange for peace and to reform Israel's political and economic systems.

It is doubtful that the American public and elites will continue to support a repressive mini-empire and a socialist mummy. In the long run, the power of the Israeli lobby to elicit such support is limited, especially given the increase in the political power of blacks in the Democratic party and the more isolationist trends among Republicans. Also, congressional redistricting, which will weaken the power of the northeastern states, in particular New York, with their large Jewish populations, could neutralize the power of Israel's supporters.

Moreover, the Israeli lobby, like any other interest group, can succeed only in an atmosphere conducive to the spread of its message. (An American Albanian lobby, for example, could not help mobilize support for Albania even with the best lobbying and public relations firms at its disposal.) For many years, Israel's supporters in this country were able to muster financial and military support for the Jewish state because Israel enjoyed the genuine sympathy of the majority of the American people. It was perceived as a Western democratic state, which shared American values and provided a safe heaven for Jewish refugees, courageously fighting for its life amid hostile and primitive Arabs supported by the Soviet Union.

Those images, which the movie *Exodus* helped to produce, were magnified and probably exaggerated, but they have been quite effective. As they are eroded and replaced by television coverage of the suffering in the West Bank, and as the post-Holocaust generation comes to power in Washington, the Israeli lobby will find it more and more difficult to achieve its goals. There may, however, be some lag between changes in American public support for Israel and changes in its lobby's power in this country. Like any other interest group, AIPAC may continue to fly on automatic pilot until it recognizes that the fuel needed for its operation, general public support, is leaking.

Even though the United States seems today to be expanding its military and diplomatic presence in the Middle East, most Israelis should recognize that the growing U.S. budget crunch and the costs of military intervention are bound to put pressure on this administration or future ones to disengage. Without the global Soviet threat, no future administration will be willing or able to commit permanently the kind of economic and military resources (to contain Arab and Moslem radicalism) that were committed during the Cold War.

As its role as an anti-Soviet strategic asset vanishes, Israel will find it difficult to sell it services as an ally in the containment of the "global *intifada*." In recent years, even when the United States has taken it upon itself, as it did in the gulf war, to deal with a fuzzy threat, it has preferred to use the military aid of Arab states. Israel has been perceived as a liability. In the post–Cold War and post–gulf war era, and certainly if Israel fails to reach a modus vivendi with its neighbors, more Americans may consider the alliance with Israel a prescription for entanglement in the never-ending conflicts of the Middle East. To avoid such a shift in American public opinion, Washington should reject the idea of using Israel as a base from which to contain Arab radicalism and Moslem fundamentalism.

Israel has an alternative. As part of an agreement with the Palestinians and Jordan, it can withdraw from the West Bank and Gaza while retaining a few military outposts along the Jordan River and perhaps in certain strategic areas in the West Bank. That move would allow Israel to finally concentrate on the things that are really critical to its survival: reconstructing its economy along free-market lines; reforming its political system (including adoption of a constitution); restructuring its military as a "lean and mean" force that could deal effectively with real external threats instead of fighting stone-throwing kids; developing a national political consensus; strengthening its relationship with the democratic West, including the United States and the European Community; and forging new regional and global economic and diplomatic links. More important, withdrawing from the occupied Arab territories would enable Israel to retain its democratic character and moral standing.

The possibility would then exist that Israel might form a federation with a Palestinian state and an economic confederation with Jordan, Lebanon, and Syria. It might even apply for associate membership in the European Community. As an associate member of the European Community and a vigorous trading state, Israel could become a Middle Eastern Singapore, a successful member of the new global economic market. It could become an economic partner of the United States instead of being its regional Cuba, continually draining U.S. resources.

The establishment of the U.S.-Israeli free-trade area in September 1985 was a step in the right direction. However, as economist Joseph Pelzman explained, the value of the free-trade area is primarily political; it demonstrates America's special relationship with Israel but does not force Israel to liberalize its economy. As he put it, Israel will realize major economic benefits from the free-trade area only "if and when the Israeli private sector is allowed to flourish."[20]

Washington can do nothing more than send the right messages to Israel. Even then it is possible that the Israeli public and elite will refuse to reformulate their domestic and foreign policies to build a new basis for the American-Israeli relationship. Israel's domestic and foreign policy problems will be exacerbated if radicalism spreads in the Arab world, especially among the Palestinians. If Washington and Jerusalem fail to bridge their short-term differences, we will probably see growing tensions between them as each pursues its own interests.

The United States should certainly not become hostage to the policies of a militant and isolated Israel. Unable to retain American support, Israel might attempt to find, and even succeed in finding, new regional and global partners. Israel's nuclear military arsenal would work to its advantage even if it were totally isolated internationally, an improbable scenario. That arsenal would deter, at least in the short and medium run, any combination of Arab states from attempting to liquidate the Jewish state. And Israel's strong educational and technological base would provide some sort of economic independence. However, without a political solution to the Arab-Israeli conflict, some Arab states will eventually acquire nuclear military capability and pose a serious threat to Israel's survival.

In the long run, Israel can ensure its survival only by entering a "post-Zionist" phase and becoming a "normal" state. After adopting a secular identity and a constitution that guarantees the civil rights of all citizens and separates state from religion, Israel would become a pluralistic liberal society that absorbed Jews and non-Jews alike. Its ties with the Jewish world would be more cultural and less political, and it could merge with an independent Palestinian state (which would maintain its own cultural ties with the Arab world) through a confederal or federal system that would lay the foundation for a secular and democratic Israeli-Palestinian entity.

6. Between American Hegemony and European Free Riding: Confronting the Gulf War Rift

In testimony before the Senate Armed Services Committee in late November 1990, former secretary of state Henry Kissinger suggested that America's leadership in the Middle East might be coming to an end. "We are in a transitional period," he explained. "I would think that over a period of 10 years, many of the security responsibilities that the United States is now shouldering in the Gulf ought to be carried by the Europeans who receive a larger share of the oil from the region."[1]

However, Saddam Hussein's invasion of Kuwait came while the United States was still the hegemonic power in the region. Kissinger explained that "we still have the post-war, global role and the military force capable of exercising it,"[2] while the Europeans lacked a security structure that would have enabled them to contain Iraq and play a role commensurate with their expanding political and economic power and their interests in the region.

"In the interim, the United States remains the key stabilizing factor in the region," emphasized Kissinger, giving his blessing to the American military attack on Saddam. But Washington would not carry the Middle Eastern torch forever, he concluded.

Did the Empire Strike Back?

The gulf war pointed out, as Kissinger suggested, one of the major dilemmas that the international system faces during transitional periods: finding ways for a declining hegemonic power to transfer some of its global and regional responsibilities to new and rising players. For various reasons, including force of habit, a hegemonic power resists giving up its leadership position. New powers, accustomed to being free riders, are not in a hurry to accept those responsibilities.[3]

From Washington's point of view, the Europeans were free riders during the gulf war. They expected that the hegemon, the United States, would as usual be there in the clutch and provide them with cost-free defense. After all, as one member of Congress put it, they could dial the 1-800-USA international emergency phone number.[4] President Bush, like any member of the World War II generation, would instinctively respond by sending the American policeman to establish order in this or that part of the world.

To many Americans, moreover, Europe's behavior during the war proved America's superiority. "There is still one superpower in the world and it is the United States," suggested one commentator.[5] It was Washington, not Bonn or Paris, that drew the line in the sand. While the United States made the hard decisions that served their interests, the Germans engaged in anti-American peace demonstrations and the French launched irritating diplomatic initiatives. What they should have done was to contribute to, or at least pay for, their own defense.

However, as the Europeans saw it, a crisis such as the one in the gulf could be used by the weakening global policeman to put down the new players who were beginning to question its hegemonic role. Seen from Paris and Bonn, the gulf war enabled a hegemon, the United States, to reassert its dominance and send its European challengers, who lacked the wherewithal to police the region, back to the corner.

The Europeans saw Bush as a sheriff in search of his *High Noon* role in the Arabian desert. His aim was "to drive a wedge between the Arab and European world, further slow down the creation of a grand European economic alliance, and set up a New World Order dominated by Washington."[6] French president François Mitterrand, responding to that European attitude, tried, on the eve of the gulf war, to lead an independent European diplomatic effort based on a linkage between an Iraqi pull-out from Kuwait and an Israeli withdrawal from the West Bank. Sounding a familiar Gaullist battle cry, he stated, "I do not feel I am in a position of a second-class soldier who must obey his commanding general."[7]

But the French-led European rebellion against America's leadership role was short-lived. Two months later, Mitterrand took his place as a junior partner in the new world order when he met with Bush on a sugar plantation in Martinique. "Our positions are closer than ever," announced a French spokesman after the Caribbean summit.[8] French foreign minister Roland Dumas stated that Paris might abandon its independent policy toward the Arab world, which France had pursued since the late 1960s when President Charles de Gaulle distanced his country from Israel.[9] An official of the European Community suggested that Europe would end up as a marginal player in the Middle East "completing, complementing and adding nuances" to U.S. ideas.[10]

The lesson of the war for Europe, as it proceeds toward economic and political integration, wrote the Washington correspondent for a conservative British daily, was that "Bush believes what he says: America is back, and the rest of the world should take note."[11] A Paris columnist for a left-leaning American weekly decried "Europe's submission" to Washington and its refusal "to become the new challenger to American domination."[12]

The Israeli Likud leaders applauded the marginalization of Europe in the Middle East; Prime Minister Yitzhak Shamir indicated that "we might allow" the Europeans to attend a regional peace conference but only as "observers."[13] At the same time, Palestinian nationalist and liberal reformers in North Africa, who looked to Paris for an alternative Middle Eastern agenda, felt betrayed by Europe's collaboration with the United States. "Adieu de Gaulle," wrote a pro-Palestinian publication in Paris, adding that the Arabs have learned their lesson from the gulf war: "why deal with the French valet when one can deal with the American boss?"[14]

Does the military victory of the American-led coalition in the Middle East mean, as neoconservative pundits have been suggesting recently, that "we have entered a period of Pax Americana," with an interventionist United States atop a unipolar world in which Europe will play at most a secondary role?[15] From that perspective, the war merely helped to formalize the new American-dominated international system that had resulted from the collapse of the Soviet empire. It reflected the new "division of labor" in the Western alliance in which Europe "delivers plenty of political support backed by hardware and a lot of money" while "leaving the driving to President Bush."[16] Should Americans and Europeans therefore abandon, as former British prime minister Margaret Thatcher argued, the "romantic" and "dangerous" notions of a united, diplomatically and militarily independent Europe that would be able to

109

share international security responsibilities in regions such as the Middle East?[17]

In the long run, however, a costly crisis, such as the gulf war, points to the weaknesses of a hegemonic power. It highlights the gap between the hegemonic power's continued pretension to leadership and the diminution of both its resources and the domestic support needed to advance its global role. After the hegemonic power becomes aware of that gap, as the French and the British did during the 1956 Suez campaign, it ceases to answer the international emergency phone. New powers are then induced to fill the vacuum and play an international role that is more commensurate with their economic resources, as did the United States in the Middle East after 1956.[18]

The dramatic military victory in the gulf may highlight the human, economic, and political costs of extending America's power in the kaleidoscopic system of the Middle East and of overextending its global commitments in general. Or it may eventually lead, as Kissinger predicted, to the shift of more diplomatic and security responsibilities from the United States to the European Community.

In many ways, the conduct of Europe and the United States in the Middle East in the post–gulf war era may determine the future relationship between the American hegemon and its Cold War allies, as well as the political map of the region.

The Middle East and the Rival Western Allies

The close cooperation and fierce rivalry that have marked the American-European relationship in the Middle East since 1945 and were brought to the surface during the gulf war reflect both the Cold War glue that tied the interests of the two Western players and their competition for preeminence in the region.[19] After World War II Britain and France, because of their military and economic weakness, passed the Middle Eastern torch to the United States.

Washington hoped that its oil companies would capture the British-dominated Middle Eastern oil market and that its anti-imperialist image would help it to replace the former colonial powers as the major player in the region. The Truman Doctrine, intended to thwart Soviet moves in the eastern Mediterranean that had threatened Western access to oil, was an assertion of American power in the region.

The 1956 Suez campaign and its diplomatic aftermath, including the use of U.S. political and economic power to pressure France and England to withdraw from Egypt, pointed to America's intention to undermine the status of those European nations. The 1957 Eisenhower Doctrine formalized America's preeminent position in the region. The British withdrawal from the gulf and France's recognition of Algerian independence marked the end of the domination of the Middle East by the European colonial powers. That domination was replaced by the American-Soviet competition.

However, the transformation of America's global military and economic position in the late 1960s and early 1970s—especially the U.S. involvement in Vietnam, the weakening of the dollar, and the U.S. alliance with Israel—enabled the Europeans, who were moving closer to economic and political unity, to once again start competing with the Americans in the Middle East. The tensions between Europe and the United States reached their painful climax in the 1973 Yom Kippur War and the ensuing Arab oil embargo. The Europeans pressured Washington to make concessions to the Arabs and, when it refused to do so, exploited the situation by making separate deals with the Middle Eastern states.

"Whereas the U.S. sees the problem of access to the Gulf in strategic terms, West Europeans see it primarily in political terms," said a former State Department official in an attempt to explain the fracturing of the Western alliance during the 1970s over Middle Eastern policies. The Europeans, "seeking to respond to the political and trade concerns of the nations of the Gulf region" and motivated by their own economic interest in increasing trade, including arms sales to the states in the area, wanted to forge an unbreakable political linkage between the Palestinian-Israeli conflict and the security of the Persian Gulf. The Europeans argued that U.S. refusal to accept such a linkage reflected the power of the Israeli lobby, and Americans interpreted Europe's commitment to that linkage as surrendering to Arab oil blackmail.[20]

The American-led Egyptian-Israeli peace process seemed to enhance U.S. power in the region. However, the Camp David accords failed to solve the Palestinian problem. The European Community, hoping to take advantage of that omission, came up in 1980 with the Venice Declaration, which demanded that the Palestine Liberation Organization (PLO) be included in a Middle Eastern conference that would lead to Palestinian independence. Although presented as an effort to complement American peace efforts in the region, the Venice Declaration was designed to win points with the members of the Arab bloc who were opposed to the Camp David accords and to tarnish the initial American diplomatic victory.

Israeli and American opposition helped to sink the European initiative. The oil shocks that followed the 1979 Iranian revolution, the Iran-Iraq war, and the economic and political crises that dominated European politics in the 1970s weakened Europe's ability to develop meaningful coordinated military and diplomatic efforts in the Middle East. The European weakness was further exposed after the Soviet invasion of Afghanistan, the promulgation in 1980 of the Carter Doctrine that made the Persian Gulf region an American protectorate, and the election of pro-Israeli Ronald Reagan as president of the United States.

The increasingly militant American-Israeli posture in the Middle East, evidenced by the 1982 Lebanon war and the 1986 American attack on Libya, paralyzed European initiatives in the region. Europe followed the American lead (in Lebanon and in the Iran-Iraq war), occasionally distanced itself from Washington (after the attack on Libya), and suffered the direct consequence of American-Israeli policies—increased Arab terrorism.

However, the American-Israeli alliance failed in its efforts to place the Palestinian problem on the back burner. The *intifada* confirmed the European thesis that the region would know no stability until the Palestinian question was settled. Reagan's decision to open a dialogue with the PLO and the growing tensions in early 1990 between the Bush administration and Israel suggested that the gap between Washington and the European Community on Middle Eastern policy was beginning to narrow.[21]

The Decline and Rise of America's Middle Eastern Paradigm

The end of the Cold War and the rise of Europe as a new global power raised questions about America's Middle Eastern paradigm in the early 1990s. First, Moscow ceased to be a threat to Western interests in the region, including the routes to the oil fields in the gulf. Hence, the need for an American military presence and diplomatic activity in the region to contain nonexistent Soviet expansionism was diminished.[22]

Second, although it may have been reasonable for the United States, as the hegemonic power in the region, to defend Europe's access to Middle Eastern oil during the Cold War, the new and stronger Europe, which was more dependent than the United States on the region's oil, seemed to be ready to take back the Middle Eastern torch.[23]

Third, although American aid had previously created incentives for Israeli intransigence, as Israel's role as America's anti-Soviet strategic asset became increasingly obsolete, Jerusalem's ability to divert attention from the Palestinian issue decreased.[24]

The decline of the Cold War Middle Eastern paradigm reflected the growing problems that were posed for the American leadership of the Western alliance by the diminishing Soviet threat and Europe's movement toward political and economic unity in 1992. A bilevel international system was emerging in which economic power would replace military power as the medium of international competition and in which Europe, probably under German-Franco leadership, would assume a status equal to that of the United States.[25]

In the United States the notion that without the Cold War Europe and Japan would be less willing to accept American leadership ignited a debate between those who advocated shifting economic resources from the military to the civilian sector so America could compete more effectively with Europe and Japan in the international market and those who supported a continued U.S. global military role. The latter group, dominated by members of the defense establishment who were worried about cuts in the military budget, argued that containing radical Third World bullies such as Saddam would enable Washington to reassert its global leadership role vis-à-vis Europe and Japan and suggested that the Middle East might be the ideal setting for new low- and mid-intensity conflicts.[26]

Enter the Middle Eastern bogeyman Saddam. Seen from Europe, the Iraqi invasion of Kuwait played directly into the hands of those who were concerned about American global declinism and the reassertion of European power. For the U.S. national security establishment, which sensed the irrelevance of its power in the new international system, the war provided an opportunity to prove that it was still indispensable.[27]

For the British leadership, who were interested in preventing America from decoupling from Europe, the war presented an opportunity to strengthen the special relationship between Washington and London. Not surprisingly, Bush's decision to send American troops to the gulf was made after a meeting with Thatcher in which she persuaded the president to take an unyielding stand against Saddam. (Britain's interest in the war also stemmed from the fact that Kuwaiti money helps to prop up the pound and strengthens its position in the world's financial system, as well as from historical ties to Kuwait.)[28]

For Israel and the Arab gulf states, worried over possible American disengagement from the Middle East, which would leave them alone to face radical regional threats, the gulf crisis provided a chance to attract U.S. military power to the region and to prove their relevance to U.S. strategic interests there.[29]

The American attempt to reactivate the Middle Eastern paradigm was therefore perceived in Europe as an exercise in reversing post–Cold War trends and in reestablishing American leadership of the Western alliance. The losers of the Cold War became the winners of the gulf war. The gulf war would bolster Britain's position in Europe and secure the interests of Israel and the Arab oil states. Hence, the speculation that the "Washington–London–Tel Aviv Axis" was attempting to keep Europe as an American protectorate.[30]

American Resentment, European Frustration

During the gulf war, a weakening hegemonic power, the United States, tried to tame its European allies. But the war revealed the gap between Washington's pretension to leadership and its diminishing economic resources. That point was underscored by the need for European military and economic support for the American action in the gulf and by Washington's resentment when that assistance was slow to arrive. Although the Europeans were trying to reassert their independence and to demonstrate that they did not automatically follow Washington's leadership, they found out that they still lacked the institutions and the alternative diplomatic agenda that they would have needed in order to challenge Washington. That realization made them angry with the big brother in Washington.

The initial reluctance of the European Community, with the exception of Great Britain, to commit large numbers of troops to fight in the gulf and to provide significant financial support for the

American intervention did not go unnoticed in Washington. "Is it going to be American taxpayers that are going to foot the bill so that when it's all over we end up with their economies enhanced?" asked Sen. David L. Boren (D-Okla.).[31] A growing number of voices in Washington suggested that the European approach reflected the free-rider problem: Europe, which is heavily dependent on Middle Eastern oil, wanted to have the benefits of a stable world order, including containment of the Iraqi dictator and security of the oil resources of the region, without bearing the costs.

When talks under the General Agreement on Tariffs and Trade collapsed in December 1990 as a result of the European nations' refusal to reduce subsidies to their politically powerful farmers, some in Washington detected an element of the theater of the absurd in the situation. The Europeans seemed to be preparing themselves for the coming economic-strategic battles between the major trading blocs by reasserting their protectionist policies against the United States while Washington was defending their economic interests in the gulf as part of a costly operation to which they were contributing little.[32]

The last-minute European-Soviet maneuvers in the UN Security Council, a visit to Baghdad by a Mitterrand adviser to plead with Saddam to withdraw from Kuwait, the anti-war demonstrations in Germany, and the refusal of Bonn's conservative leadership to contribute forces to the American military efforts all raised the specter of anti-Americanism and defeatism, if not that of a Munich-style appeasement, in Europe, according to American critics.[33] The realization that Paris had supplied Saddam with much of his sophisticated weaponry and that German scientists had helped him to develop his chemical weapons, to perhaps be used against the Jewish state, reawakened memories of Germany's Nazi past and of French collaboration with the German occupiers. Those facts suggested that Europe's action might be motivated by its pro-Arab, anti-Israeli policies as well as by traditional European anti-Semitism.[34]

On the Continent things looked very different. The gulf crisis brought back to the surface European intellectuals' and politicians' disdain for "unsophisticated" American diplomacy and globalist preaching. The consensus was that the Europeans, with their long experience in and knowledge of the Middle East, would have been

115

able to handle the problems with Saddam more effectively than did the United States "whose demonstrated ignorance of the Middle East is scary."[35]

European chauvinism, which had lain dormant during the Cold War alliance with Washington, was expressed by Robert Steuckers, who accused Washington in Florence's *Diorama Letterario* of "globalizing" local conflicts. "To limit deliberately one's action to his continental sphere of influence (that of Europe to Europeans, that of America to Americans) could automatically localize war and prevent it from spreading to the entire world."[36]

Iraq's annexation of Kuwait had very little impact on the Europeans. On the other hand, there was a feeling that a prolonged and bloody war with Iraq could produce chaos in the Middle East and harm that region's close economic and political ties with Europe. Although Europeans certainly had very little sympathy for the exiled leaders of Kuwait, many Europeans supported a solution to the Palestinian problem.[37]

The southern European nations, France, Italy, and Spain in particular, have large Moslem populations and a close relationship with North Africa. A war with Iraq, warned Spanish foreign minister Francisco Fernández Ordóñez, could lead to "a collision course between Islam and the West."[38] It could feed growing anti-European attitudes among Moslems in Europe and produce a wave of terrorism that would be felt immediately by the Europeans but never reach America's shores. Moreover, growing North African support for Saddam, manifested in several large pro-Iraqi demonstrations, might threaten the relatively moderate regimes in North Africa and lead to new waves of immigrants to France with all their explosive political dimensions.[39]

Germany drew major criticism from the United States for not contributing more directly to the war effort. Some Americans criticized the stand of the Germans, who seemed to be taking for granted the benefits of the international order secured by the United States while they sat in moral judgment of the Western countries that were taking steps to protect that order. Most elements on the German left reacted with knee-jerk anti-American pacifism; they adopted the slogan "no blood for oil." The pro-Israeli peacenik, singer, and poet Wolf Biermann accused some of his colleagues and compatriots of lack of sympathy for the Jewish state and of anti-American feelings that masked a reawakening of old German chauvinism.[40]

However, the political consensus expressed by Foreign Minister Hans-Dietrich Genscher, criticized by some as the "peace, cake, and happiness" mentality, reflected the belief that Germany should restrict its use of military force and play a "peaceful" international role befitting a "trading state." That belief, adopted by most Germans after World War II, was embodied in a constitution that, as German officials noted, was drafted under U.S. supervision in 1949 and limited the use of German forces to defending NATO territory.[41] The Germans also cited their national preoccupation with reunification as a principal reason for Bonn's reluctance to send troops to the gulf. Many Germans expressed concern that the war with Iraq might divert international attention and resources from the political and economic reconstruction of Eastern Europe and the Soviet Union, which they considered more important to Germany and Europe.

The war made it clear that Germany was not a superpower. Many Europeans saw Germany's discomfiture as part of an American grand design to weaken Europe's ability to project power in the post–Cold War era and to end the drive toward a possible German-Soviet-French connection by creating incentives for Moscow to establish instead a global American-Soviet condominium that would control everything from the UN Security Council to the Middle East.

An Italian senator, Umberto Bossi, pointed out that the war in the gulf and the suppression of Lithuanian independence were parallel developments. "The War in the Gulf and the repression of the autonomous tendencies in Lithuania serve the same objective: to reimpose the division of the world into two blocs as in the time of Yalta," he suggested. "On the one hand, there is Bush flexing his muscles in the Gulf. On the other hand, there is Gorbachev repressing the struggle for independence."[42]

Former French defense minister Jean-Pierre Chevènement, an early opponent of Paris's backing the American goals in the gulf, called the war "America's war" and suggested that by sending troops to the gulf "France has accepted to help the U.S. restore a world domination that its economic situation no longer assures."[43]

117

According to him, the war was an effort by Bush to remedy America's economic problems and to avert a recession by going to war to position the United States permanently in the Middle East to control its oil sources. For Chevènement, a founding member of the France-Iraq Friendship Association who entered French politics in colonial Algeria when it was torn by its war for independence, France is first and foremost a Mediterranean country whose primary interest is in a strong Mediterranean region, and thus in an independent Middle Eastern policy. The fact that Washington set out to destroy Iraq, France's main and most powerful ally in the gulf and a counterweight to the more pro-American Saudi Arabia, was seen as part of an effort to erode Paris's interests in the region and weaken its Middle Eastern project. Chevènement eventually resigned in protest against Mitterrand's pro-American stance.

The views of the Socialist Chevènement were shared by major figures on the extreme left, including members of the weakening Communist party, and on the extreme right, including the racist Jean-Marie le Pen, who visited Saddam as part of a last-minute "peace mission." They were joined by more mainstream figures such as Phillipe de Gaulle, son of Charles de Gaulle, who voted against France's participation in the gulf war on the ground that it violated France's Arab interests, as well as by several of France's "wise men," including former foreign ministers Maurice Couve de Murville, Michel Jobert, and Claude Cheysson.[44]

On the French left, which had been united until the gulf crisis in a struggle against racism, a division developed that mirrored the one on the German left. It pitted anti-war figures such as former Marxist Regis Debray, who called for the "return of Europe to the Europeans," and Harlem Désir, leader of the anti-racist group SOS Racisme, against pro-Israeli socialist intellectuals such as author and painter Marek Halter and Bernard Henry Levy, a former Maoist and a "New Philosopher." The latter supported France's entry into the war as a way of defending Israel and were accused by their colleagues of replacing their old Moscow-Havana itinerary with a speedy trip to Washington via Tel Aviv.[45]

No Taxation without Representation

On the French right former prime minister Jacques Chirac accused Bush of masterminding a major scheme. President Bush,

Chirac argued, had foreseen that Europe (and Japan) would be economic great powers 20 years hence. Since both lack independent sources of oil, Bush set out to make control of oil America's equalizer.[46] The prevailing attitude among European leaders was that Washington was trying to force them to implement its policies in the gulf and to bear the costs of a war, such as terrorism and oil shortages, without asking them to participate in the decisionmaking. "Behind the public facade in London as well as in Bonn and Paris there is impatience and not a little exasperation with the U.S. Administration," reported the *Guardian* of London in December 1990. It quoted an EC official who complained, "It is the classic case of taxation without representation." That American revolutionary battle cry had been used earlier by then EC president, Italian foreign minister Gianni de Michelis. "How can the Americans expect the Europeans to provide a pro rata contribution to the multi-national force, when they have no say in overall strategy?" asked the European diplomat.[47]

Those Europeans were arguing that if Washington wanted them to cease being free riders, it should allow them to sit in the driver's seat of Middle Eastern policymaking. After all, if Europe had been able to seriously influence Middle Eastern policies in the last decade, it might have been able to avoid disasters such as the 1982 Lebanon war or push more effectively for an Israeli-Palestinian peace, which could have strengthened the moderate Arab bloc and thereby made the region less hospitable to Saddam's aggression. The message behind the European reservations about America's moves in the gulf was that Bush could not have his cake and eat it too: he could not continue to call the shots and expect Europe to pay the costs of unilateral U.S. action.

The European perception was a mirror image of the view from Washington, which implied that the United States was forced to come to the aid of Kuwait for the sake of its European allies who were unwilling to pay the costs. "We cannot expect the United States to go on bearing major military and defense burdens worldwide, acting in effect as the world's policeman," argued Thatcher, echoing that American perception. She turned the European criticism on its head, suggesting that unless Europe marched to the American tune and sent a "positive and swift response" to Washington, there was a serious danger that the allies would be left without their American protector.[48]

7. The Coming American-European Struggle over the Middle East

European resentment of American hegemony—which had been expressed during the gulf war in statements that indicated that the Europeans did not want to serve simply as check-writing machines to finance American military operations and would like to be consulted on policy issues—gave way after the war to critical self-examination. It gradually became clear to many European officials that one of the major reasons for their inability to meet the American challenge during the war had been the lack of European institutions for developing independent political and security policies. That lack was especially apparent when it came to out-of-area conflicts and Europe's continuing reliance for defense on an American-led NATO.

As a result, as one newspaper put it, during the war Europe appeared "hesitant and haggling."[1] Another announced that "war brings out the mouse in Europe's prosperous giant."[2] One American observer suggested that the gulf war showed that "the 12 European Community nations are still incapable of defining their common foreign policy interests clearly and concisely enough to act together to protect and promote those interests."[3] "To be brutally honest, public opinion sensed that Europe was rather ineffective," explained President Jacques Delors of the EC Commission. "We will have to face up to the lessons to be learned in due course."[4]

Washington's criticism of Europe's free riding during the war was supplemented in its aftermath by growing recognition that by providing American security as a free good, Washington discouraged Europe from sharing in the burden of its own defense. That recognition led to new efforts to assign the European nations a greater role in any Western defense structure so that the they would respond better the next time there was a call to arms in the Middle East or elsewhere. However, Washington also has had to confront what might be called the "European unity paradox." The United

States has long supported the idea of a united Europe; during the Cold War, Washington had hoped that a united Europe would provide a bulwark against Soviet expansionism. Washington had also taken for granted that a Europe that spoke with one voice would be a simpler and more straightforward entity to deal with as part of a general Western approach to various global problems, such as the crisis in the gulf. A strong and united Europe was perceived in that context as an American asset.

But Washington seems to have failed to take into consideration the possibility that a common European voice would not necessarily be a sympathetic one.[5] "Certainly the evidence suggests that had Europe had a common foreign policy and common defense structures at the time of the Iraq seizure of Kuwait, Britain would have been restrained from giving the support it did," suggested one European analyst.[6] In particular, it seems unlikely that a British leader would have urged America to go to war, as Prime Minister Margaret Thatcher did in the summer of 1990. Hence, there was a growing sense in Washington, after the gulf war, that progress toward a unified and strong Europe might actually harm American interests.[7]

Europe and the United States: Partners or Rivals?

The gulf war sent European and American strategists and politicians back to their drawing boards to wrestle with the basic questions of their security relations in the post–gulf war era. Everyone seemed to agree that military power still counted and that world peace could not be secured through economic power alone. As Delors told the European Parliament, the European Community was expected to become a "major power, and not just an economic one."[8] The gulf crisis highlighted the dilemmas involved in securing peace in a world in which rigid certainties have been replaced by a more fluid system, symbolized by the dangerous structure of Third World regions, including the Middle East. The underlying question is whether Europe will become a rival or a partner of Washington in the world in general and in the Middle East in particular.[9]

Two alternative scenarios for the American-European security arrangement have been constructed since the war. The first envisions the continuing existence of NATO under American leadership to deal with broadly defined security threats to the members of the

Western alliance. The second envisions European control of the Continent and a more independent policy toward other regions.

New Atlanticism

Under the first scenario, American military forces would remain, albeit in reduced numbers, in Europe, and Washington would continue to provide the European nations with a nuclear umbrella. NATO's mission would be redefined to include responding to out-of-area threats, such as the one in the Middle East. That scenario envisions the rise of a stronger "European pillar" of a new transatlantic security structure. A more diffuse NATO would remain in place; the nine-nation West European Union (WEU), whose goal is to strengthen European political and military coordination, would serve as a bridge between the United States and the European Community; and the commandership of NATO would alternate between the United States and Europe.[10]

Under that structure, Europe would be more independent but not insular, a more mature partner to Washington but not a rival. It would enjoy more say in decisionmaking and bear a greater share of the defense burden, especially on the Continent. However, it would still rely, especially in non-European regions, on American security leadership. Secretary General Manfred Wörner of NATO was referring to that scenario when he told the Brussels-based Center for European Policy Studies that "the task is to give the alliance a stronger European character."[11]

Since the gulf war, the Bush administration has been advancing that scenario, which it calls the new Atlanticism. It talks about the need to establish within NATO a large, multinational rapid reaction force that will respond immediately to crises (e.g., the gulf crisis) outside Europe. In that context, NATO commanders agreed in April 1991 to expand the alliance's European-staffed rapid reaction force, by perhaps as many as 100,000 troops, to deal with such eventualities.[12]

The gulf war clearly pointed to the need to redefine NATO's out-of-area role, over which the United States and Europe have often clashed. During the 1973 Yom Kippur War, Bonn strongly objected to the movement of U.S. tanks from bases in West Germany to Israel because that movement went beyond NATO's defined mission. In 1987, when the United States provided a naval escort to protect

Kuwaiti tankers from Iranian gunboats, the British and French participated in the mission but carefully refrained from identifying it as a NATO operation.[13] Some analysts argue that political differences over out-of-area issues, especially those involving the Middle East, are going to continue to divide Europe and America. If those analysts are right, the short-lived consensus that developed during the gulf war was an exception to the rule that cannot be expected to hold across the board.

The war accentuated a number of political problems. NATO gave Ankara assurances that it would assist Turkey if it were attacked by Iraq. The NATO Air Mobile Force, which included 18 German aircraft, was sent to Turkey. But Bonn rejected Ankara's goal of extending NATO's responsibility to the Middle East by emphasizing that those forces were to be used only in defense of Turkish territory, not for attacks on Iraq.[14] American planners, however, argue that the gulf war proved that no individual country or combination of European states would be able to produce the military forces necessary to contain the large armies, the competent air forces, and the weapons of mass destruction that might be controlled by future extremist regimes in the Middle East. Growing security threats from that region make it inevitable that America and Europe will coordinate their military policies for the region.

France and England might be able to tame an Arab dictator for a short period by bombing raids or gunboat diplomacy. However, only huge land powers and large naval forces, of the kind that Washington mobilized during the war and that it could bring to bear in future conflicts in the Middle East, could contain serious threats to Europe from its southern flank. The sine que non of Europe's security policy in the Middle East would continue to be America's large navy, marine, and airborne divisions, which the new Atlanticism would provide.[15]

Under the new Atlanticism scenario, Germany would be anchored to the Western alliance but, guided by America and without provoking London or Paris, would be able to gradually expand its security responsibilities outside Europe. The decision by Bonn to send several hundred soldiers to aid relief efforts for the Kurds, the first major deployment of German ground forces outside the NATO theater since World War II, fits with that general American scheme.[16] Washington wants to convince Germany that its position as a powerful trading state can be preserved only if it helps to protect militarily the world trading system; the exclusive pursuit of check-book diplomacy will not suffice.

Immediately after the gulf war there were some indications that Europe would be receptive to those America ideas. Some European observers were suggesting that perhaps Europe's new line on NATO should be, "Yankee don't go home!" (The 220,000 American troops now assigned to Europe, down from 325,000 in August 1990, are widely expected to be reduced by half and perhaps even to 60,000.) With the apparent rise of hard-liners in the Soviet Union, the disarray in Europe, and the perception of possible new dangers emanating from the Middle East, such as ballistic missiles in the hands of new Saddam Husseins, there appeared to be a certain eagerness to keep America in Europe. The United States "is the only real superpower and it is badly needed to balance the force of the Soviet Union," stated Joachim Thies, editor of the *German Journal of Foreign Affairs*.[17]

Some analysts even argued that France's decision to send troops to the gulf stemmed from its interest in keeping U.S. troops in Europe to offset Germany's pacifist tendencies and economic clout. "To argue for an American presence in Europe, there had to be a French presence in the Gulf," explained Dominique Moisi, deputy director of the French Institute for International Relations.[18] His country's performance suggested that French president François Mitterrand wanted to prove to Washington that France is a reliable ally, especially "if we want to sit down at conference tables and have a say in world affairs," as Defense Minister Pierre Joxe put it.[19] The possibility that France might be willing to follow the U.S. lead in the postwar era was strengthened when Paris joined in a NATO strategic review and allowed some use of French facilities by U.S. forces.[20]

New Atlanticism sounds like a marvelous idea that would make everyone happy. Institutional changes would be made to give the European allies more power in NATO and to equip the organization to deal with out-of-area problems. Europe would not only be taxed but would also take part in security and political decisionmaking. It would cease to be a free rider and a blind follower as it moved to the front seat. New burden-sharing arrangements would relieve the United States of some of the economic costs of the alliance, but the U.S. share of those costs would not be reduced so dramatically as to call into question America's commitment to Europe or the U.S. right to lead.

The problem is that the Europeans still might not feel that they were in the driver's seat, a position they believe is commensurate with their rising economic power. Reforms in NATO might disguise U.S. hegemony, but they would not eliminate it. And Americans might resent continuing to shoulder the heavy burden of leadership and providing security to their allies across the Atlantic while Europe beat them in the international marketplace and eroded their economic security. That resentment, which is symptomatic of the current fluid international system and was magnified by the gulf war, is bound to be exacerbated by new political differences on Middle Eastern issues. A new management structure for NATO will not, in and of itself, erase that American resentment.

Europe for the Europeans

The second scenario, "Europe for Europeans," reflects more pessimistic expectations about the European-American relationship. According to that scenario, an independent European bloc would make its own decisions about defense and then present them as faits accomplis to Washington. That vision is now supported by France and Germany, and it enjoys growing backing in Britain. The gulf war has been viewed as a reason to redouble efforts to more closely integrate the political and security policies of the European nations. "From patronizing the United States as the country of can't-shoot-straight bumbledom, European elites have once more turned to envying and admiring it as the competent organizer of a dazzlingly smooth high-tech victory," commented one observer.[21] At the same time, concern that Washington's victory would lead to a triumphal attitude and an attempt to reassert U.S. hegemony enhanced support for the idea of a new European political and security order. Making Europe into a superpower whose military status would be comparable to that of the United States, an idea for which there is now growing enthusiasm, would have been seen as "costly folly before the thrilling video games of the Gulf War."[22]

Hints of a more assertive Europe troubled the Bush administration. The president sent a top State Department official to warn German, French, and British leaders not to adopt a more radical posture. Washington was worried that trends in Europe might lead to an "internal bloc within NATO" and eventually to the disintegration of the organization. The American response, however, seemed only to have heightened European concerns about Washington's drive for hegemony.[23]

Although there is no clear consensus in Europe on the institutions that would supersede NATO, in recent months there have been several moves toward serious exploration of a distinct security role for the European Community. In February 1991 German chancellor Helmut Kohl and Mitterrand met to discuss a general plan for developing greater coordination of EC foreign and security policies. In March 1991 the EC nations agreed to study a possible "organic relationship" that would include a defense dimension for the WEU as part of an attempt to build political unity in the European Community, not as part of a European pillar of NATO.[24]

A draft treaty presented by the EC presidency to the Intergovernmental Conference on European Union proposes that as a first step the WEU be upgraded from a debating society to an organization that might become a European caucus, within NATO, that would accept guidelines from the community. Eventually, the WEU would be merged with the European Community.

Complementing those moves have been efforts by European states to strengthen bilateral security arrangements within the alliance. Paris has vigorously pursued the establishment of a Franco-German security arrangement. That pursuit has brought the two nations' key military planners into a close working relationship. In 1990 French and British leaders began to explore closer coordination of their conventional and nuclear forces. (For years London had spurned French efforts to discuss coordination of the two nations' nuclear forces.)[25]

Bonn's refusal to commit military troops to the gulf war and the economic and social problems Germany is facing as a result of reunification—slowing economic growth, rising unemployment, and the slide of the German mark—are allaying French and British fears of a resurgent German power at the center of Europe. The earlier concern that Germany would try to establish independent security arrangements with the Soviet Union, which could have broken the tradition of close German cooperation with France and the West, do not seem very realistic now. Hence, there is diminishing interest in maintaining American troops in Europe to neutralize the German threat.[26]

To many Americans it appears that Kohl is following the French "down the primrose path of gutting NATO so the EC can assume European defense responsibilities."[27] The question now is not whether Germany will be anchored to the West and eventually agree to share responsibility for security outside Europe but whether European, including German, security will be the responsibility of a reformed American-led NATO, in which Europe has slightly more influence, or of an independent European security structure, which France is advocating.

Concern in Washington that Germany and even Great Britain and the Netherlands are leaning toward the French position led, in the summer of 1991, to the decision to postpone the NATO summit, which the Americans had hoped would bless the new Atlanticism approach. Bush and his advisers were worried that instead of embracing new Atlanticism, the summit would bring to the surface the resentment and anger, which were beginning to replace the initial postwar, pro-American euphoria, occasioned by continued American hegemony.[28]

In a move that angered the Bush administration, and highlighted growing American-European tensions over the future of NATO, in May 1991 the French government proposed the creation of a rapid deployment force under EC auspices. According to the plan, which Washington perceived as an attempt to compete with its own proposal for a similar NATO force, multinational military forces would have been assigned to defend European interests within and outside Western Europe. Those forces would have been under European control and taken part in everything from peacekeeping and humanitarian assistance to direct military action against Middle Eastern bullies. Spain, Italy, Greece, Belgium, and Luxembourg expressed support for the proposal. U.S. officials, on the other hand, saw it as a way of accelerating the demise of NATO and creating the basis for independent European political and security policies.[29] Only with the application of enormous political pressure was Washington able to get the European nations to adopt its position and create such a force under NATO's auspices.

Resisting the Neoconservative Paradigm

Europe's skeptical nod to the new Atlanticism should not have come as a surprise. The American plan is regarded in Europe as an attempt to further what is perceived to be the real agenda behind the intervention in the gulf: maintaining U.S. control of American-European relations in the post–Cold War era. For that purpose, Washington chose to flex its muscle in the Middle East, an adjunct region of the Western alliance that is a major out-of-area bone of contention.

Indeed, the new Atlanticism reflects the neoconservative paradigm that envisions an American hegemony, a U.S.-dominated new world order, and a reformed American-led NATO. Europe would have just a little more say in the new NATO, which would remain the guarantor of the security of the Western alliance and be expanded to cover out-of-area regions, in particular the Middle East. Neoconservatives contend that America overcame the Vietnam syndrome and is ready once again to play the role of global policeman, with Israel as its Middle Eastern deputy. According to that view, U.S. military power would continue to function, as it did in the gulf war, as the ultimate arbiter of international conflicts. Europe (and Japan) would share the financial burden of such arbitration, and the Middle Eastern countries (and the Third World), out of fear or friendly persuasion, would be content to conform to the interests and views of the only remaining superpower.[30]

The Pax Americana world view calls for continued American-European unity based on the common political and cultural history of what the *Economist* characterized as "Euro-America" and the need to contain threats posed by an angry and frustrated Russian bear; resurgent German militarism; and radical political and military forces in the Arab and Moslem worlds, which the *Economist* termed "Islamistan."[31] According to that world view, cultural and political-military tensions between Euro-America and Islamistan will grow, and new Saddams will emerge in the 19 Moslem states that lie between Morocco and Iran. Those states, with their young and poor populations, are vulnerable to radical, anti-Western nationalistic and religious ideologies. That militancy will be exported to Euro-America through immigration, terrorism, and new gulf wars.

With its control over oil and large military forces, Islamistan directly threatens the core interests of Euro-America. According to the neoconservative paradigm, the gulf war proved that only a unified American-European structure, aided by Middle Eastern powers such as Saudi Arabia, Israel, and Turkey, will be able to contain future threats from Islamistan and maintain the status quo in the Middle East. Indeed, the main goals of Euro-America in the Middle East will be to maintain stability and to refrain from engaging in any major crusade for democracy or self-determination for Kurds, Palestinians, or other minorities. Hence, Euro-America should be content to see the rise of a user-friendly Saddam in Iraq instead of taking steps that might lead to Kurdish independence, which could threaten Turkey or Syria. It should learn to treat with benign neglect Israel's annexation of the West Bank and its continuing resistance to Palestinian independence.

Europe does not seem to be interested in adopting the American-made new Atlanticism paradigm. The tragic fate of the Kurdish people in Iraq and the apparent failure of Washington to resolve the Israeli-Palestinian problem are leading many Europeans to think that the gulf war was not an attempt to establish a new world order but an exercise in advancing Washington's interests behind the mask of grand moral principles. Europe challenged Bush's policy of neglect toward the suffering Kurds and adopted a more activist approach. It will probably also reject any new American attempt to place the Palestinian issue on the back burner.

Notwithstanding the French-American agreement on the future of the Middle East and current European support for Washington's diplomacy in the region, France and the United States still differ seriously about the appropriate solution to the Middle Eastern conflict. France's views on creating an independent Palestinian state are much closer to those of Spain, Italy, and even Britain than they are to Washington's. After his meeting with Bush, Mitterrand was especially insistent that the Palestine Liberation Organization (PLO) was still the legitimate representative of the Palestinians, and he stressed the need to do away with double standards in the Middle East. The UN resolutions that created Israel called for the establishment of an independent Palestine, he pointed out, adding that "it's dangerous to refuse a people any form of identity."[32] French foreign minister Roland Dumas was returning to the Gaullist tradition when, despite criticism from the Bush administration, he met in early April 1991 with PLO leader Yasir Arafat.

Will Europe Rise to the Challenge?

Europe's ability to emerge as an independent political and military force in the world in general, and in the Middle East in particular, will depend to a large extent on the willingness of Britain to depart from the Thatcherist axiom that there is no alternative to Europe's continued submission to America's political-military leadership. Any movement toward an independent European security role and a corresponding weakening of NATO will correlate with the diminishing perception, especially in France, of a rising German colossus. A Berlin-Paris-London axis could then develop as a counterweight to the Washington–London–Tel Aviv axis.

A powerful Europe, with more than 10 million Moslems living within its borders, might wish to develop special economic and political ties with its Middle Eastern periphery. Europe might then emerge as an alternative to the Cold War American-led alliance, whose goal during the gulf war was, according to a *Le Monde* columnist, to divide and marginalize the Moslem and Arab worlds.[33]

An expanded European role in the post–gulf war Middle East will not be a function of emerging independent European political-military institutions alone. Europe will gain new prestige and power in the Middle East not by imitating the American model with its use of military power in pursuit of new imperialist adventures but by trying to offer an alternative paradigm. Europe's role will depend on its success in winning the hearts and minds of the region's people, as opposed to submitting them to external political control through naked military power and trying to return them to a "pre-industrial age."[34]

Mitterrand's emphasis on the need to support self-determination for the Palestinians and the Kurds and France's overall agenda for political and economic reform in the Middle East—based on attempting to tackle the deep-rooted political, social, and economic problems of the region and on trying to offer its people an equal say in a new arrangement with Europe—might provide an alternative to America's obsession with stability and its support of the status quo in the region. European moves in support of the Kurdish refugees in southern Iraq, which ran contrary to American desires, may reflect the shape of things to come.[35]

As a catalyst for peace and change in the region, Europe will be able to win allies among the political and intellectual elites in North

Africa, Jordan, and Yemen, societies that have begun moving toward democracy and have been quite critical of the American-led gulf operation. Geographic proximity, demographic ties, economic interdependence, and cultural links, together with a more forward-looking and idealistic agenda, could help Europe to play a larger role in the region. However, if all Europe does is scrap with America over the spoils of victory, signing a few billion-dollar contracts as part of the reconstruction of Kuwait or a new arms deal with the Saudis, it will probably win some economic crumbs but lose the larger battle for influence in the region.[36] It will continue to be a follower, not a leader, and will leave Washington to pursue a destructive Middle Eastern policy.

Southern Europe and the Mediterranean

France and Italy, along with Spain and Portugal, have been the European states most actively advancing an independent European approach to the Middle Eastern problem. They have proposed a Conference on Security and Cooperation in the Mediterranean (CSCM).[37] If that proposal is adopted by the European Community, the CSCM could serve as the basis for a new policy that would either complement or challenge American diplomacy in the Middle East, especially if and when U.S. peace efforts reach a dead end. Those southern European states' geographic proximity to and strong demographic ties with the Middle East, especially with North Africa, tend to make them sensitive and sympathetic to Arab interests and concerns. In contrast, the northern European states, particularly Great Britain, have a more pro-American and pro-Israeli point of view. In the post–gulf war era, southern Europe can be expected to lead any independent European effort in the Middle East.[38]

The CSCM idea was first launched by the Italian government in December 1989 at the Euro-Arab Conference in Paris. It was put forward again at Palma de Mallorca by Italy and Spain in the midst of the gulf crisis and was adopted in Lisbon at the beginning of 1991 by France, Italy, Portugal, and Spain after those four countries had discussed the idea with, and received general support a month earlier from, several Arab countries.[39]

The CSCM plan is modeled after the Conference on Security and Cooperation in Europe (CSCE), known informally as the Helsinki process, which has served since 1975 as an umbrella for talks between East and West on issues ranging from arms control to cultural exchanges and human rights. The Helsinki process laid the foundation for the peaceful reunification of a divided Europe by codifying a common standard of human rights, recognizing established borders, and promoting trade relations among ideologically antagonistic states.[40]

The CSCM idea originally stemmed from the southern European states' concerns about possible social and economic instability in Arab North Africa. The Maghreb is for Paris and Rome what Mexico is for Washington. Growing economic and demographic disparity between the northern and southern shores of the Mediterranean tends to give rise to radical forces in countries such as Algeria and Morocco, and radical activity, in turn, produces new waves of immigration to southern Europe. The CSCM is supposed to serve as a forum for helping the North African countries to deal with their acute social and economic problems.[41]

The growing electoral power of Islamic fundamentalist groups in Algeria, which became apparent in that country's first open election, pointed to the potential for dangerous political explosions in the Maghreb. As revolutionary socialist institutions, including Algeria's ruling party, went politically bankrupt and Tunisia's pro-Western political elite declined, Islamic fundamentalism emerged as a powerful alternative.[42] The huge anti-American and pro-Iraqi demonstrations that took place in Rabat, Algiers, and Tunis during the gulf crisis were reflected in the neutral if not pro-Saddam positions adopted by the incumbent governments. Those positions increased European concern about the potential popularity in the Maghreb of "Saddamism," a mix of anti-Western Arab radicalism and Islamic fundamentalism that could outlive its medium, Saddam. Those worries spurred the Mediterranean European group to increase its efforts to push forward the CSCM plan, as a way of dealing with the political and economic problems of the region, and to expand it to other geographic areas and issues, such as the gulf and the Arab-Israeli conflict.[43]

One of the interesting aspects of the CSCM is its attempt to expand the very definition of "security." As Delors explained in a recent speech before the International Institute for Strategic Studies, security includes not only maintaining militarily defensible borders but also providing a livable environment, economic prosperity, and stable and legitimate political institutions.[44] Whereas the American approach to the Iraqi-Kuwaiti and the Arab-Israeli conflicts is to view them through political-military lenses, focusing on issues such as the regional balance of power or the provision of military guarantees, the CSCM perspective adds other dimensions. It suggests that a real and lasting peace will depend on solving nonmilitary problems, such as the social and economic gap between the have and the have-not states, diminishing water resources, human rights, self-determination, and educational and environmental issues.

The CSCM could follow the pattern set by the CSCE and address three distinct types of issues: security, economic cooperation, and human rights. It could take a comprehensive regional approach to traditional security problems such as disarmament, including denuclearization of the region, the recognition of the inviolability of frontiers, and the implementation of military confidence-building and arms limitation measures. The CSCM's regional security system would not be imposed from the outside by foreign military forces, according to Italian foreign minister Gianni de Michelis. It would instead depend on local players and be supported by international guarantees. It would create the basis for regional economic cooperation strengthened by outside backing, especially from the European Community, for development projects. And it would be a forum for solving regional disputes, such as those in Lebanon and Cyprus and the Palestinian-Israeli conflict.[45]

Instead of the rigid structure of a Middle Eastern peace conference sponsored by Moscow and Washington or by the UN Security Council, the CSCM would provide Israelis and Arabs with an informal forum for preliminary discussion of the problems that divide them. It could also allow them to focus on such regional problems as water scarcity and to develop confidence-building measures before addressing the more complex political and security problems. An important goal of the CSCM would be "to codify a set of rules and principles that would apply equally to all participants," explains de Michelis. "No regional system can be imposed from outside. The primary responsibility lies with those who will belong to that system whether sovereign states or entities recognized by the United Nations."[46] The CSCM is expected to include the EC members and the Middle Eastern states (including the PLO), as well as other interested powers, such as the United States. In the long run, it could serve as a nucleus around which to establish a unified European–Middle Eastern structure.

The CSCM proposal was received with enthusiasm by Algeria, Morocco, Tunisia, Libya, and Mauritania. Those countries, which have formed a North African common market, and the southern European states had already established a permanent forum for political consultation and economic cooperation, the Four Plus Five Forum for Regional Cooperation in the Mediterranean. During the war, southern European public opinion was agitated by news of anti-Western protests in North Africa. The daily *El Pais* headlined an article on the Maghreb "The Threat of the Southern Front," and added that "the advance of Islamic fundamentalism brings the gulf war close to the Spanish frontier."[47] After the war, Spain took the lead in trying to mobilize the European Community to increase aid to North Africa.

The southern European nations were relieved that the Maghreb had not been swept by a major anti-Western tide of Saddamism. However, the potential for social and economic problems remains, and there could well be a delayed backlash against Saddam's defeat. "The situation in the Maghreb is not explosive, but neither is it reassuring," argues Miguel Angel Moratinos, who is in charge of North African affairs in the Spanish Foreign Ministry. "The Gulf crisis has accelerated the process of sociopolitical change there."[48] The possible rise of an Islamic fundamentalist government in Algeria is creating anxiety in Paris and Rome and among the secular elites in North Africa. The Westernized and progressive intellectuals and politicians in the Maghreb hope that by maintaining Western influence in the region, through a system like the CSCM, it will be possible, especially by using economic incentives, to tame the radical Moslem elements. Continued Western influence alone can prevent new tides of educated professionals from emigrating from countries such as Algeria and Morocco to Europe.

Turkey embraced the CSCM plan and expressed a special interest in leading a regional effort to share water resources. For Ankara, the CSCM would be a way of getting into the European Community through the back door and furthering Turkey's traditional interest in acting as a bridge between Europe and the Middle East.[49] The

CSCM proposal was also supported by Palestinian intellectuals and activists and by Syria.[50] A modified version was adopted by the Jordanian government, which presented the plan as its own during discussions with American and European officials. Israel, while not adopting the CSCM by name, announced its interest in a Helsinki process for the Middle East. The Likud government formed a committee to study a proposal of that sort as an alternative to an international peace conference.[51]

As noted, the end of the Cold War and the gulf crisis, which have raised major questions about Israel's ability to continue as America's strategic asset, have produced a lively debate in Jerusalem about the need to complement or even replace its dependence on Washington with new international orientations. In that context, some Labor leaders are looking to Mitterrand, not to Bush, as a potential catalyst for a peace process. Labor leader Shimon Peres, who was the architect of the special relationship with France in the 1950s, enjoys a close relationship with Mitterrand, who in 1982 was the first French head of state to make an official visit to Israel.[52]

Moroccan-born Likud member David Levy is the first Israeli not fluent in English to serve as foreign minister. Like other members of the large, politically influential, and mostly pro-Likud North African community in Israel, he feels more comfortable in Paris than in New York. Levy, who has maintained a personal friendship with members of the French right, in particular with Jacques Chirac, has been critical of Prime Minister Yitzhak Shamir's efforts to exclude the Europeans from the peace process. He believes that the cold shoulder Israel is giving the European Community will harm Israel's chances of joining that community.[53]

Europe's Economic Role in the Peace Process

Indeed, even without complete implementation of the CSCM, Europe could become a major economic partner of Israel and the Arab states. Europe's economic role in the Middle East was emphasized in 1987 as part of a peace initiative launched in Brussels. The European Community stressed the need to establish a linkage between peace and economic development and give that linkage a definite form. In particular, unconditional support was promised for the economic development of the West Bank and the Gaza Strip.[54]

"Without prejudging future political solutions, the Twelve wish to see an improvement in the living conditions of the inhabitants of the occupied territories, particularly regarding their economic, social, cultural and administrative affairs," said the Brussels statement.[55] The European Community decided to grant aid to the Palestinian population of the occupied territories and to allow certain products from those territories preferential access to the community's markets. Since the early 1980s Britain, France, Italy, and West Germany have been committed to assisting various development projects in the West Bank and Gaza. In 1986, for example, the European Community helped to launch the first venture capital fund for Palestinian industry. After 1988 the community pressured Jerusalem to allow Palestinian farmers from the West Bank and Gaza to market their fruits and vegetables independent of Israel's state-owned marketing agencies, thus encouraging Palestinian farmers to crack Europe's produce markets.[56]

The political implications of those economic efforts were reflected in the welcome Palestinian leaders, such as former Gaza mayor Rashad Al-Shawwa, gave the idea of treating the West Bank and Gaza as a distinct entity, separate from both Israel and Jordan. The close economic ties between Israel and the European Community have also been used to pressure Jerusalem to change its policies toward the Palestinians.[57] Israel, whose primary exports to Europe are agricultural products and diamonds, wants to penetrate the EC high-tech industry. It hopes that its strong technological and educational base will enable it to join the community in the future. Brussels has made it clear to Jerusalem that any agreement on permanent association of Israel with the European Community would have to be part of a general political solution to the Israeli-Palestinian problem. One idea, raised several times by EC members, is to hold "parallel" peace conferences: a political forum concerned with a diplomatic settlement and an economic forum, led by the European Community, to work on ways to improve the economic lot of the Palestinians and others in the Middle East.

Economic conditions in the Middle East since the gulf war provide an opportunity for such European action. Jordan's economy is in ruins; the economic system in the West Bank and Gaza has been devastated by the *intifada* as well as by the repercussions of the war. Israel is facing major economic challenges as a result of the gigantic wave of Soviet Jewish immigrants.[58] In their March meeting, after the cease-fire in the gulf, the EC foreign ministers clearly signaled a more activist policy by approving a package of $330 million for Israel and for the West Bank and Gaza. Israel will receive about $214 million in loans and an additional $37 million in interest subsidies; the Palestinians will receive a grant of $80 million.[59]

The wisdom of such government-to-government economic aid is doubtful, but the European Community can encourage economic change in other ways. The community could provide Israel and the Arab entities with economic incentives to reach a diplomatic solution. It could, for example, offer Israel, Jordan, and a Palestinian state associate membership as part of a political agreement. Unimpeded access to the European market would provide new opportunities for economic development in those three Middle Eastern political entities—a crucial consideration given the need to absorb the Soviet Jewish immigrants into Israel and to resettle Palestinian refugees, including a few hundred thousand who are leaving Kuwait.[60]

Associate EC membership would make the three states more attractive to foreign investment capital. Such investments could be directed, for example, toward the reconstruction and revitalization of the Gaza Strip and its refugee camps. The Gaza Strip is today a center of Palestinian misery, a kind of Middle Eastern Calcutta. It could be turned into a Middle Eastern Hong Kong, whose industrious population would turn its port, Gaza, into a commercial center linking Europe and the Middle East.

Israel could do business with European companies and take advantage of its highly educated and professional Soviet immigrants if it created high-tech industrial parks in the Israeli Negev and Galilee. Other economic projects that could evolve from a European-Arab-Israeli structure include Israeli-Jordanian cooperation in attracting European winter tourism, Jordanian-Palestinian efforts to form centers for Arab publishing and media, and Israeli-Palestinian development of European-financed agricultural laboratories that would address the problems of Third World (especially African) countries.

The Israeli-Palestinian-Jordanian association could become the nucleus of an economic renaissance that would reawaken the old "spirit of the Levant," which once made the region the center of

Mediterranean trade and commerce and a political, economic, and cultural link between Europe and the Islamic orient. The Israelis and the Palestinians, and later the Lebanese and the Syrians, who have similar views of education and business, could become the leaders of that renaissance. Similar economic entities, such as the Maghreb group, a Nile confederation of Egypt and Sudan, and a gulf grouping that could link Iraq and Kuwait, might also establish their own agreements for association with the European Community.

Just as Germany could gradually emerge as Europe's leader in the reconstruction of the East European nations, and eventually associate them with the European Community, France and southern Europe could emerge as leaders in the Mediterranean and the Middle Eastern periphery. The CSCE and the Helsinki process contributed to the fall of the Berlin Wall, to the return of freedom to Poland and Hungary, and to the reunification of Germany and its reemergence as a major European power. The CSCM and a "Mediterranean process" could contribute to the fall of the walls between Israelis and Arabs, to a shift of political and economic power from northern to southern Europe, and to the emergence of France as a major Mediterranean power.

A Pax Americana in the Middle East?

On the surface, however, the gulf war seemed to have shattered any possibility of a European challenge to American foreign policy in the Middle East. With American prestige enhanced by the triumph over Saddam, the EC members have seen no alternative but to play silent partner to Washington in its Middle Eastern diplomacy. They have quit insisting on the need to convene an international conference on the Middle East and have expressed support for the U.S. double-track approach: pursuing peace negotiations between Israel and the Arab states and between Israel and the Palestinians.

At a mid-April 1991 meeting in Luxembourg, the EC members pleaded with U.S. secretary of state James A. Baker III, who was en route to the Middle East to discuss convening a regional conference chaired by Washington and Moscow, for a role in the new U.S. drive for peace. After a March 1991 tour of the Middle East undertaken by an EC ministerial team, the "troika" headed by Luxembourg's foreign minister, Jacques Poos, and his Italian and Dutch counter-parts, the Europeans asked for a "significant role" in resolving the Arab-Israeli conflict.[61] However, the Europeans received a skeptical response from Baker. He promised only that he would try to make sure that the peace conference would be "inclusive rather than exclusive" and suggested that the European Community would have observer status and be expected to confine itself to dealing with economic development issues.[62] During an emergency meeting of the community on April 8, 1991, several leaders expressed "fears that the EC may be sidelined in the Middle East by Washington."[63] Indeed, during the 1991 Madrid peace conference, representatives of the European Community were relegated to observer status.

The CSCM plan received an equally cold shoulder from the Bush administration during a recent visit to Washington by the Italian foreign minister. "The American response to our plan has been lukewarm if not pretty negative," admitted an Italian official, adding that, without independent political-military muscle, Europe "finds it difficult to challenge Washington in the Middle East."[64] Indeed, Washington seems to be intent on imposing its agenda on the Middle East and on excluding the Europeans from any meaningful role there. However, in the long run, Washington's stance will only increase the costs to the United States. Washington's insistence on U.S. hegemony could produce a rerun of Britain's experience after World War I. Britain tried to exclude France and other European powers from decisions about the division of the Ottoman Empire, but eventually growing economic problems at home and increasing difficulties in solving the problems and conflicts of the Middle East forced Britain to plead with Paris and Washington to share the costs of maintaining order in the region.

"It is not right that the burden of taking action should fall on the British Empire alone," wrote a British leader in 1922. In words that could apply to the American global role today he warned: "We cannot alone act as the policeman of the world. The financial and social conditions of this country make that impossible." He added that unless the United States came to Britain's aid in the Middle East, London might "retire into an exclusive concern with her own national interests."[65]

Washington is already becoming aware of the costs of implementing the goals Bush set for the postwar Middle East, such as establishing a regional security arrangement and pursuing an Arab-Israeli peace. The longer-than-expected American military presence in the gulf and the bloody turmoil in Iraq are already shattering the myth that the war was a cheap high-tech military adventure, and some Americans are wondering if the putative victory was worth the cost. A new American-induced arms race in the region and the slow progress of the peace process have highlighted the gap between the stated moral grounds of the gulf crusade and its true realpolitik basis. That gap has been dramatized by television images of dying Kurds, the emir of Kuwait's new palace, and the new Jewish settlements in the West Bank.[66]

Those developments are beginning to weaken the unique international coalition and the domestic grouping of liberal internationalists, pro-Israel neoconservatives, and a Rockefeller Republican administration that led the United States into a war in support of the Arab oil-producing regimes. Neoconservative and liberal columnists have blasted Bush for hesitating to come to the aid of the Kurds. The pro-Saudi inclinations of the administration may force it to confront Israeli intransigence, which could lead to growing tensions between Washington and Jerusalem as well as among the administration, neoconservative intellectuals, and the Democratic-controlled Congress. If Washington does not attempt to soften Israeli intransigence, the United States could face criticism from Brussels and encounter growing resentment in the Arab world. Such criticism and resentment might, in turn, threaten the power of the Arab regimes Washington rushed to defend in the war.[67]

Since the fall of the Ottoman Empire, no external power has been able to impose its policies on the local actors of the Middle East, in which numerous national, regional, and extraregional political players combine and divide in ever-shifting patterns of alliances and rivalries.[68] Washington is going to learn that its ability to dominate the diplomacy of the region, characterized by a mishmash of local and global issues, is limited. The more the United States tries to impose a Pax Americana, the more it will become involved in issues that have nothing to do with its original interests. It may well become hostage to local powers, ranging from Kurdish rebels in Iraq to the militant government in Jerusalem. Because U.S. Middle Eastern policies are so "domesticated," involving powerful political players such as the American Jewish community and the oil companies, failures in the Middle East can represent major political costs for a president.

The continuing mess in the Middle East, coupled with a growing economic recession at home, may coincide with increasing trade competition from Europe, whose access to Middle Eastern oil was secured by the gulf war. If the Europeans continue to erect protectionist measures against U.S. products, American economic nationalists' calls for cutting the defense budget and disengaging from costly commitments, such as the one to the Middle East, are likely to win support in Washington.[69]

Hence, instead of cementing the Western alliance, the gulf war seems to have signaled the beginning of political and economic divisions in Euro-America. There is a distinct possibility that the European and North American pillars of NATO will evolve into independent political-military structures, each setting different priorities and pursuing different interests vis-à-vis Eastern Europe, various Third World regions, and Islamistan.

Instead of reassuring us that America is "walking tall again," the conclusion drawn by neoconservative analysts, the military adventure in the Middle East and its repercussions may bring official Washington closer to the view of large segments of the European political spectrum as well as to that of Americans who favor reduced American military intervention abroad. According to that view, the "financial weakness of the U.S. is likely to rule out the idea of establishing a Pax Americana in the Middle East."[70] In the gulf war, it took 75 percent of America's tactical aircraft and 40 percent of its tanks to defeat a country with the gross national product of Portugal. Washington could not have afforded such an effort without the pledges of aid, which amounted to $53.9 billion, from its allies. That kind of aid is unlikely to be forthcoming again, and the United States is unlikely to continue maintaining forces that would permit action on such a scale.

In the post–Cold War era, as the gulf war indicated, "America may feel a disproportionate responsibility to lead, but even its allies will not always and everywhere feel inclined to follow."[71] But maintaining and restoring "order" throughout an anarchic international system will be beyond any single player. Moreover, we are moving from a territorial-military-political age into an economic-financial-technological age.[72] Massive U.S. military power will not necessarily translate into greater influence. Economically powerful entities, including the European Community, will be increasingly able to resist Washington's pressures and to pursue their own policy agendas. The gulf war, as Henry Kissinger pointed out, was "an almost accidental combination of circumstances unlikely to be repeated."[73] It has not altered the inexorable erosion of U.S. global dominance.

It is possible that in the short run Washington will be able to maintain the status quo in the Middle East and preserve the dividends of its dramatic victory in the gulf. After all, the military machine of Iraq was destroyed, and the economies of two other regional bullies—Iran and Syria—are in ruins. The Arab monarchies of the gulf can therefore breathe more easily and can rest assured that, for a while at least, their regimes will not be threatened by any serious regional challenger. Israel, which regained its military supremacy in the region, can continue to consolidate its rule in the West Bank, confident that the American president is not going to stand in its way, at least until after the 1992 presidential election.

However, experience has shown that we must not construe the region's current apparent quiet to mean that the anti-American tide in the Middle East has crested. "As in the Suez crisis, the gravest consequences usually lag behind events."[74] The gulf war opened a Pandora's box of ethnic rivalries, devastated an Arab country, inflicted more than 200,000 casualties, and created an environmental nightmare.

The population explosion in the Middle East, the growing economic and social problems of Egypt and other North African countries, and the persistent questioning of the legitimacy of most of the regimes in the region—coupled with the unsolved Palestinian problem—sooner or later will undoubtedly produce an increase in anti-American sentiments. Those feelings could take the form of radical political activism and terrorism and lead to the collapse of the pro-American coalition at a time when Washington was facing the growing costs of its military overextension.[75] Hence, the legacy of the gulf war may be different from what some of its supporters suggest today. In the future America may be compared with Great Britain, which after World War I, along with its Zionist and Arab

143

allies, carved up the Ottoman Empire, turned its remnants into a European protectorate, and made it "a breeding place for a future war."[76]

The British victory over the Ottoman Empire, which was applauded at the time as a sign of new imperial dynamism, was later seen as a prelude to global decline. Similarly, the gulf war may turn out to have been not the first chapter in the new American-dominated world order but the last hurrah of a waning global power whose diminishing economic resources constrained its ability to expand its diplomatic and security role.

8. Israel and Palestine: Toward a Federal Solution

Zionism and Pan-Arabism have been two of the 20th century's most powerful national-ideological movements. The confrontation between Jewish nationalism, with its goal of gathering all of world Jewry in the biblical homeland of the Hebrew people, and Arab nationalism, with its grand design of reestablishing an Arab empire stretching from Morocco to the borders of Iran, is almost a century old. That dramatic conflict has been taking place in one of the most strategically important regions of the world, the Middle East, which controls the globe's largest oil reserves. The controversy focuses on a territory, the Holy Land, and its capital, Jerusalem, to which the three major religions, Christianity, Islam, and Judaism, have strong cultural and historical ties. And it involves two peoples, Jews and Arabs, who have had a major influence on world civilization and whose history has been intricately intertwined with that of the West.

U.S. involvement in the conflict as a result of America's moral commitment to the Jewish state, on the one hand, and its oil and strategic objectives in the Middle East, on the other hand, has occupied a top position on the U.S. foreign policy agenda. It was a major part of U.S. Cold War strategy, and it also has had some major domestic political repercussions.

The Arab-Israeli conflict, as it came to be known after the establishment of the Jewish state in 1948, has produced several major regional wars and almost led to a nuclear confrontation between the two superpowers in 1973. The rivalry is still bloody both on the communal level—between Israeli Jews and Palestinian Arabs—and on the international level—between Israel and most of the Arab states, with the exception of Egypt, which signed a peace agreement with Israel in 1979. Even after the end of the Cold War, the conflict continues to draw the attention and the intervention of outside powers, including the United States.

Israel and the Arab states are not just nation-states striving for security. The conflict between them is also the product of the explosive engagement between the ideologies of Zionism and Pan-Arabism. Until those two movements reach an accommodation, recognizing the legitimate national rights of both populations in the land they share, the chances of solving the technical aspects of the conflict, such as demarcation of the borders of the states of Israel and Palestine and issues related to arms control, remain slim.

Unless some solution to the Israeli-Palestinian conflict is found soon, there is a danger that the antagonism between the two movements will go beyond a relatively simple territorial dispute between states and political movements and become a messianic war between Moslem and Jewish fundamentalists. Messianic wars cannot be ended by rational compromise.

The Roots of the Conflict

Zionism and Pan-Arabism share common historical roots. They both emerged at the end of the 19th century, as a delayed reaction to European nationalism, among people living on the margins of Europe—the East European Jews concentrated in the Russian Empire and the dispersed Arabic-speaking Moslems in the Ottoman Empire. Both movements were led by secular intellectuals—assimilated Jews and Christian Arabs—who had been educated in the cultural centers of Western Europe and influenced by the dominant ideological currents of the era.[1]

The Zionist and the Arab nationalist intellectuals attempted to respond to the same dilemma: how could the religious basis of their Jewish and Moslem communities be reconciled with the secular nature of modern nationalism? The solution was to square the circle. Both Judaism and Islam were given a new interpretation based on secular-nationalist grounds that were not much different from those of Italian, Polish, and Pan-Slavic nationalism, for example.

While the religious element remained in the background, the definitions of Jewish and Arab nationalism were broadened by the addition of other elements—language, culture, history—with which assimilated Jews, such as Theodore Herzl, and Christian Arabs, such as George Antonius, felt more at home. More significant, both movements provided formulas according to which their

146

peoples could enter the modern era and the nation-state system without losing their historical identities. Hence, the founders of the two movements proposed that modern Jewish and Arab national-ism could become more inclusive and serve as bases of identity, especially for Jews and Arabs who had rejected their religion as a common group denominator.

The most important added element was the political one. The Zionists and the Arab nationalists set out to free their communities from the political control of the Russian Empire and the Ottoman Empire, respectively, and to acquire national self-determination and political independence. Where the independent Jewish and Arab territories would lie and who would be liberated remained unclear.

While many Zionists regarded the biblical territories of Eretz Israel (the land of Israel), known since the late Roman era as Pales-tine, as the historical homeland in which the Jewish people should regain their independence, many of them, including Herzl, were willing to accept other territories, such as Uganda, as a homeland. Even those who focused on Palestine as the ideal geographic locale had only a very fuzzy idea about where the borders of the new homeland would lie.

The early Zionists regarded the Jews of Eastern Europe as the initial target for self-determination. Central and West European Jews were expected to join the movement at some later point, and Arab Jews, who are today the majority of Israel's Jewish population, were marginal to the Zionist project. American Jews were regarded only as a source of financial and political support. Herzl and the other early Zionists assumed that after the establishment of the Jewish commonwealth most Jews would immigrate to the new state, while those who remained in the Diaspora would eventually assimilate and cease to exist as a viable Jewish community. Most East European Jews, however, rejected the Zionist prescription. The majority tried to assimilate in one way or another, to establish an independent Jewish existence in the Diaspora, or to emigrate to North America.

Arab nationalists focused on Greater Syria (which included mod-ern-day Syria, Lebanon, Israel, and Jordan) and the Arabian Penin-sula as the locus of their political aspirations. The "Arab West," which consists of North Africa and Egypt, did not initially figure very clearly in the Arab nationalist vision. Egypt, which after 1945 became the leader of the Arab world, was not regarded by many Arab nationalists, and certainly not by the Egyptians themselves (whose intelligentsia for many years propagated the notion of a separate Egyptian nationalism tied to a pre-Arab cultural-historical identity), as part of the future political Arab homeland. Like the Zionists, the Arab nationalists were members of a vanguard intellectual group with very weak links to the mainly peasant, Arabic-speaking communities of the Middle East whose main group identity remained religious and tribal.

World War I and the disintegration of the Russian and Ottoman empires provided the two national movements with major diplomatic dividends. They both had bet on the winning horse, the British Empire, to mobilize international support for their political aspirations. London, motivated by complex strategic and political considerations, established political and military alliances with both Zionists and Arab nationalists as a way of getting international and regional support for its long-term imperial goals in the Middle East. It is doubtful that the two movements—which lacked serious support among, respectively, the masses of the Arabic-speaking communities in the Ottoman Empire and the Jewish communities in Eastern Europe—would have been able to achieve their initial political goals without British support.[2]

Interestingly enough, the British policymakers did not see any reason "why either British or Jewish aspirations should not be in harmony with Arab aspirations."[3] As one of them noted, "Most of us younger men who shared this hope were . . . pro-Arab as well as pro-Zionist, and saw no essential incompatibility between the two ideals."[4]

Neither the Arab military forces, fighting on the side of Great Britain, nor international Jewish diplomacy played a major role in the British victory over the Turks. However, the role played in post–World War I Middle Eastern intrigues by the tribal leaders of the oil-producing territories of the Arabian Peninsula and by Western Jewish leaders pointed to the crucial role they would later play in Middle Eastern diplomacy. Great Britain, however, found itself committed after the war to sometimes conflicting promises to the Zionists and the Arab nationalists.

Certainly, Britain's promises to establish a Jewish homeland in Palestine and to create an Arab Syrian state (which was expected to include the territory of Palestine) seemed incompatible. Initial efforts to reach an agreement on cooperation between Zionists and Pan-Arabists—most notably British efforts to bring the Zionist leader Chaim Weizmann and the Arab prince Feisal, son of Hussein ibn Ali-Sherif and emir of Mecca who later became king of Iraq, to a compromise on Jewish settlement in Palestine—led nowhere because of Palestinian Arab opposition to Jewish colonization.[5] A great confrontation between the two nationalist movements seemed inevitable.

The leaders of the first wave of Jewish immigrants to Palestine, who arrived at the end of the 19th century and established Jewish colonies, tended, as did the small older Sephardic community in Palestine, to pursue a limited political agenda based on the need to cooperate with the Arabic-speaking majority that inhabited the country and to achieve some kind of political-cultural autonomy for the Jewish population. They tended to be affiliated with the more moderate wing of the Zionist movement, whose vision of a homeland was of an autonomous Jewish colony in Palestine under some kind of international regime.[6]

A crucial development took place after the Russian Revolution with the arrival of the second wave of Jewish immigrants who espoused a Zionist-socialist agenda. The younger new leadership that gradually took political control of the Zionist movement, as well as of the Jewish community in Palestine, combined communist and socialist ideologies with Eastern and Central European notions of organic nationalism and espoused a more militant agenda. Their goal was to establish in Palestine a political and economic structure based on exclusive Jewish authority.

Early signs of the new leadership's greater militancy included successful efforts to force Jewish farmers in Palestine to refrain from hiring Arab labor and confine their workforce to Hebrew labor. That action, coupled with the purchase of land from Arab owners and the establishment of independent political, economic, and later military institutions, created the basis for the future Jewish state.

Zionism like Pan-Arabism began to face the major dilemmas that have since bedeviled both movements. The Zionists, who wanted to bring a "people without a country to a country without a people," were confronted with a cruel reality. Palestine was already inhabited by a "people"—a non-Jewish Arabic-speaking population that did not fit into the long-term Zionist scheme. Some suggested that the Arabs be converted to Judaism; others advocated their transfer to the Arab parts of the region as part of an agreement with the governments there. Also, the majority of East European Jews did not follow in the footsteps of the Zionist leaders. Instead, they remained in Europe or continued to emigrate to the United States, until restrictive immigration quotas were imposed in 1921.

Moreover, the initially politically dormant Arab population began to oppose the flow of Jewish immigrants and was increasingly influenced by Arab nationalists who resented Britain's failure to fulfill its commitments. Anti-British Palestinian uprisings, the first signs of an independent Palestinian nationalism, and the surrounding "independent" Arab states put pressure on London, which began to limit the number of Jewish immigrants to Palestine and to downplay its commitments to Jewish political independence. Those actions, of course, created enormous resentment among the Zionist leadership.

Arab nationalism with its ambitious goals also faced problems, especially the failure of Arabism to become a unifying force in a region dominated by competing separatist national, ethnic, and religious groups. In addition to non-Arab entities such as Persia and Turkey on the periphery and non-Moslem religious-ethnic groups such as the Maronites in Lebanon, the Assyrians in Iraq, and the Copts in Egypt, the Arab world included non-Arab national groups such as the Kurds in Iraq and Syria and the Jews in Palestine. Those groups refused to be assimilated in a large Arab nation. The divide-and-rule tactics of the French and British imperialists tended to accentuate those conflicts.[7]

The Arab-Israeli Conflict and the Cold War

Whereas the results of World War I enabled Zionists and Pan-Arabists, who took advantage of the fall of the Russian and Ottoman empires and the interests of the British Empire in the Middle East, to jump on the last bandwagon of 19th-century European nationalism, the outcome of World War II created the requisite conditions for the two movements to lead the first wave of late 20th-century anti-colonial Third World nationalism.

Britain's desire to maintain its strategic interests in the region during and after World War II played into the hands of Pan-Arabists and resulted in the establishment of the Arab League, the gradual erosion in the British commitment to Zionism, and the granting of political independence to Arab states. At the same time, World War II and the Holocaust, as well as the need to resettle the European Jewish refugees, led to growing sympathy for Zionist ambitions in the Western nations, including Great Britain and the United States.

Washington, which began to replace London as the major Western power in the region after 1945, therefore came under the same conflicting pressures that England had felt in the preceding years. Sympathy for the plight of European Jews, which was used effectively by a growing and politically vibrant American Jewish community, led to support for the establishment of the Jewish state. Zionism enjoyed the support of the more idealistic and anti-imperialist elements of American public opinion. At the same time, the perceived need to preserve its strategic and oil objectives in the region put pressure on the United States to consider Arab interests. A coalition that included the oil companies and members of the defense establishment gradually became the backbone of American support for Arab interests.[8]

Zionist leaders took advantage of both American sympathy and Soviet interests in ejecting the British from the region to win support for their goals in the late 1940s. There resulted a unique diplomatic constellation in which the two superpowers were united in their support for the partition plan in 1947 and their recognition of the new Jewish state in 1948. The Arab states were ruled at the time by reactionary oligarchies that were backed by the weakening forces of British imperialism and the new American Cold War establishment.[9]

The modus vivendi that was reached between Israel and the Arab states after the 1948 war was based in part on an informal agreement between the Israeli government and the pro-British Hashemite Kingdom of Jordan to prevent the establishment of an independent Palestinian state by annexing the West Bank to Jordan (Gaza remained under Egyptian control).[10] At the same time, the massive flow of Arab refugees from what became the state of Israel and the arrival of Jewish immigrants from Europe and the Arab countries allowed Israel to treat the small minority of Palestinians who became Israeli citizens as a manageable problem. The Arabs became second-class citizens in a state that was based on an exclusive Jewish nationalist concept (which stipulates that any Jew who moves to Israel automatically becomes an Israeli citizen but denies that right to Arab refugees who left the country in 1948).

The Palestinian-Israeli conflict remained on the back burner until 1967, and the conflict between Zionism and Arab nationalism was framed as a confrontation between Israel and the Arab states. That quarrel, in turn, became intertwined with the Cold War as the elites on both sides began to draw military and economic benefits from the Western and Soviet blocs. The perpetuation of the Arab-Israeli conflict enabled Israeli and Arab leaders to maintain powerful national security states and public antagonism toward the external enemy.

More radical Arab nationalism surfaced in the Middle East after the rise of Gamal Abdel Nasser, who was quite hostile to the West, to power in Egypt in 1954 and the Israeli leaders' decision to ally themselves with the West at about the same time. Those changes led to a new superpower realignment in the region. Moscow emerged as the main backer of militant Arab nationalism, and Washington was increasingly identified with Israeli interests, especially after the 1967 Six-Day War.

The Cold War alignment meant that the Zionist and the Arab agendas would both remain unfulfilled. The division of the Arab world into pro-Western and anti-Western camps made a mockery of any idea of Arab unity—an idea that would have been impossible to realize in any case because of rivalries among and within the Arab states. The Palestinian people became the main victims of the new constellation of power and were used cynically by various Arab states as a weapon against Israel and their Arab rivals.

Israel's siding with the West in the Cold War left the large East European and Soviet Jewish communities, who were regarded by Israeli leaders as a natural pool of immigrants to the Jewish state, behind the Iron Curtain, unable to make choices about their individual rights and national self-determination. Instead of moving to Israel, as classical Zionism prescribed, American Jews became a powerful force for mobilizing American support for Israel against what was beginning to emerge as a Soviet-backed Arab bloc.[11]

The Six-Day War began to gradually return the Arab-Israeli conflict to its pre-1948 conditions, to the original intercommunal struggle between Israelis and Palestinians. The Arab states still maintained their confrontational stance against Israel, but the 1973 Yom

Kippur War and the Egyptian-Israeli peace process symbolized an attempt by the leading Arab state, Egypt, to begin to decouple itself, with American support, from the Arab-Israeli conflict. The 1982 Lebanon War, the Iran-Iraq war, and later the gulf war continued to weaken the anti-Israeli Arab coalition.

However, the 1967 Six-Day War also intensified the communal conflict between the Israeli Jews and the Palestinians over the land they share. The Palestinian Arabs, whose social structures and political institutions had been shattered during the turbulence of 1947–49, ceased to be a major political factor in the Arab-Israeli conflict at least until the creation of the Palestine Liberation Organization (PLO) in 1964. Israel's 1967 invasion of the West Bank and Gaza was an important catalyst for Palestinian nationalism and for mobilizing international and Arab support for that cause.[12]

On the Israeli side, the war radicalized Jewish Israeli nationalism and helped to activate the political power of the Sephardic Jews. Their support brought to power in 1977 the Likud government, which has been committed to Israel's political control over the West Bank and Gaza. Since then, both sides have escalated their claims to an exclusive national right to Israel/Palestine.

The Palestinian-Israeli Conflict and the End of the Cold War

The *intifada* that began in 1987 brought to a new peak the Palestinian-Israeli war. That uprising began at a time when the superpower rivalry was coming to an end. The diminished rivalry led to two parallel developments.

The Soviet Union, which had broken off diplomatic relations with Jerusalem after the Six-Day War and had viewed Israel as an exclusive bastion of American interests in the Middle East, began to open diplomatic channels to the Jewish state and signaled its willingness to allow Soviet Jews to emigrate to Israel. The United States, which had refused to recognize the PLO, referring to it as part of a Soviet-sponsored terrorism network, opened a diplomatic dialogue with the Palestinian group. The dialogue produced a willingness to accept the idea of Palestinian self-determination.[13]

The PLO's recognition of Israel in December 1988 and Prime Minister Yitzhak Shamir's 1989 plan for elections in the occupied territories were attempts to respond to the new international environment. However, the PLO's refusal to condemn a planned terrorist attack on Israel by a member group and Shamir's rejection of

American efforts to implement his own peace plan stalemated efforts to begin Israeli-Palestinian talks.

The end of the Cold War and the gulf war represents a turning point for both the Palestinians and the Israelis. The end of those wars has brought changes in both the regional and the international environment. A Palestinian-Israeli agreement could lay the groundwork for a political and economic federation in Israel/Palestine. That federation could, in turn, serve as the basis for a new political and economic alignment in the region—an alignment that could turn the Middle East into a new player in the international system.

Conversely, the continuing Israeli occupation of the West Bank and Gaza and the perpetuation of the Palestinian-Israeli conflict will strengthen the forces that are preparing to turn the Zionist-Arab conflict into messianic battles that could eventually lead to a wider war between the West and Islam. Such a war could bring an end to the third Jewish commonwealth and make the plight of the Palestinian Arabs less important in the international scene. The nightmare of a Middle Eastern Armageddon could become reality and involve the region and outside players in a destructive war that would almost certainly include the use of chemical, biological, and nuclear weapons. The gulf war may be either the last chapter of a regional power struggle or a warning about the shape of things to come.

Indeed, the end of the Cold War and its related political and economic developments have presented Israelis and Palestinians, and the region as a whole, with some stark choices.[14] They can either reform their political and economic systems and establish new regional systems based on economic cooperation and free trade, which would allow them to gradually become part of the new international economic system, or they can perpetuate their bankrupt economies and maintain old ethnic and religious rivalries, which would almost guarantee that they would become marginal to the rising economic and political powers of Europe, East Asia, and North America.

The Future of the International System

The fall of the Berlin Wall signaled the defeat of collectivist programs, both fascist and communist, by the liberal democratic ideals of individual political, economic, and cultural freedom. That apparent democratic victory has led some to believe that we are indeed witnessing the "end of history."

The emergence of a unified Europe raises the possibility of moving beyond nationalism and state-controlled systems toward more unifying confederal and federal structures. The rise of Japan and of the economic tigers of East Asia as powerful trading states reflects the superiority of the capitalist system and suggests that economic power may be replacing military power as the cornerstone of a new international system.[15]

At the same time, the collapse of the Soviet empire unleashed new reactionary nationalist, ethnic, and religious forces. Similar developments seem to be taking place in other parts of the world as well—for example, the disintegration of Yugoslavia and the civil war between Serbians and Croatians and the separatist movement that is gaining political power in Quebec. The growing "balkanization" of American society and politics into different ethnic and racial groups with exclusionary agendas points to similar, albeit milder, problems.

The disintegration of the bipolar Cold War international system, therefore, also threatens to produce a more chaotic and dangerous system. Moreover, the gulf war suggested that military power will probably still play an important role in determining the outcome of conflicts over economic resources and strategic interests. There are also signs that the transformation of the post–World War II international trade system may lead to new trade wars between the major economic powers that are controlled by central bureaucratic authorities bent on pursuing protectionist policies. Finally, parts of the world, such as sub-Saharan Africa, are being marginalized and are turning into political and economic basket cases.

The new post–Cold War international system will be characterized by elements of both the euphoric end-of-history vision and the more pessimistic international chaos scenario.[16] There will be a core of politically stable and economically prosperous democratic and capitalist states, in particular the United States, the European Community, and Japan. Those states, it can be argued, had been engaged in a century-long "civil war" between the forces of liberalism and authoritarian ideologies (communism, fascism). That struggle ended with the victory of liberalism and the agreement of the major players to deemphasize the use of military force to solve their problems.[17]

The governments of the core states will try to manage more effectively and peacefully the relationship between the principal political and economic centers (Washington, Brussels, and Tokyo) and the decentralizing and libertarian forces pressuring for more political, economic, and cultural freedoms so that those struggles do not degenerate into zero-sum conflicts. Although the rivalries among the new trading blocs may be fierce and antagonistic, the core states will attempt to deal with the diplomatic and economic competition among them without resorting to the use of military force.

On the periphery of the international system will be the "losers," mainly Third World states and societies—in sub-Saharan Africa, parts of Asia, and portions of Latin America—that, because of their failure to advance to the more democratic and capitalist stages of political and economic development, will stagnate. They will be controlled by corrupt military dictatorships and plagued by bloody civil wars and economic underdevelopment.

At best, those countries will be marginalized by the international system, treated with indifference by the core states, and occasionally receive financial aid from multinational organizations such as the World Bank. (Unfortunately, such aid tends to perpetuate the more destructive features of authoritarian political and economic systems.) At worst, they will become the focus of regional military conflicts over the control of economic and political resources.

In the middle, between the core states and the peripheral states, will be a third group of states and regions, such as East Asia, Eastern Europe, the former Soviet Union, and parts of Latin America. Those areas will be the battleground for the struggle between the forces of reaction, authoritarianism, collectivism, and chauvinism, which promote militant nationalism, religious intolerance, and centralized economies, and the forces of economic progress and liberty, which support economic liberalism, political decentralization, and structures that accommodate different national and religious entities. The struggle between those forces, which today takes various forms in the former Soviet Union, Poland, Yugoslavia, South Korea, Mexico, and Brazil, will determine whether the middle states and regions will join the core or the periphery of the international system.

The success of the rapidly industrializing nations of East Asia, such as Korea, Singapore, and Taiwan, suggests that those nations, whose gross national products surpass those of Portugal and Greece, may become core nations, especially if their economic transformation is complemented by political liberalization. Eventually, they could serve as a model for similar changes in China. Hence, the Pacific Rim, probably led by Japan, could become one of the most prosperous and successful parts of the industrialized liberal core.

Victory for the coalition of the old guard Communists and chauvinistic and anti-Semitic groups in Russia would condemn that country to economic chaos and civil war that could lead to the rise of a new authoritarian regime. A similar outcome may be expected in Yugoslavia if the communist nationalist movement stays in power in Serbia. The most likely outcome would be the disintegration of the country into a backward, chauvinistic, and protectionist Serbia and the more Western-oriented, market-based systems of Croatia and Slovenia. A worse outcome would be the perpetuation of an authoritarian Serbian-dominated government for the entire Yugoslavian federation.

If the liberal coalitions in Poland and Hungary successfully implement their programs, those countries could be drawn into the European core. Devolution of the central power in the former Soviet Union and creation of a confederal system coupled with continuation of glasnost and perestroika might allow the Commonwealth of Independent States to join the European core as well.

Similarly, greater economic and political liberalization in Mexico could lead to establishment of a free-trade area between that country and the United States. Such an area would increase the odds that Mexico would become part of the North American core area. It is possible that the same thing might happen with other reforming systems in Central and Latin America, such as Brazil, Argentina, and Peru, where free-market and democratic ideas, advanced by such thinkers as Hernando de Soto, seem to be prevailing over both the decaying political and economic orientations backed by the old military oligarchies and those supported by Marxist revolutionary groups.[18]

The Future of the Middle East
The Middle Eastern nation-states produced by Zionism and Arab nationalism will have the opportunity to determine where they will

fit in the new international system. Israel and its Arab neighbors might join, or at least become adjuncts to, a successful core region or be exiled to the periphery.

The Westernized intellectual and political elites that led the Zionist and the Arab nationalist movements were instrumental in bringing their respective communities into the modern age by freeing them from foreign political control and establishing independent nation-states. However, those new states have not been able to solve their deep-rooted structural problems.

Israel, although it has freed itself from foreign domination, established a modern political and economic system, and provided a homeland for survivors of the Holocaust and refugees from Arab countries, has failed in its efforts to entice the 12 or so million Jews around the world to immigrate to the new state. It has actually created dilemmas of dual loyalty for Jewish citizens of other countries.

Jewish nationalism has not even succeeded in establishing a secular identity for the Jewish citizens of Israel. Israel is today a theocracy in which state and religion are intertwined, and the more Orthodox religious view of Judaism is gaining public support and political influence. The absorption into Israel of hundreds of thousands of Jews from Islamic countries, whose own sources of Jewish life and culture were traditional and religious, weakened the power of the more secular Western European elite that established the state. Their vision of a liberal and open Jewish commonwealth in the east has been gradually replaced by a vision of a new Jewish ghetto on the Mediterranean.

More important, the concept of an exclusively Jewish state has made it impossible for Israel to absorb politically and economically the Palestinian Arabs living inside its borders and in the territories it occupied in 1967. The more militant Zionists who came to power in 1977 refused to recognize the rights of those Palestinian Arabs to self-determination and maintained Israel's political and ideological commitment to the control and eventual annexation of the West Bank and Gaza. The Orthodox and anti-Western groups that are leading the Jewish settlement movement in the West Bank represent an extreme wing of Zionism that is gaining power.[19]

Lack of a solution to the Palestinian-Israeli conflict makes it difficult for Israel to solve its problems with the surrounding Arab states and to integrate itself into the region. The political elites that have dominated Israel since its establishment were able to take advantage of the Cold War to advance Israel's security interests and to perpetuate the country's decrepit socialist economy. Serving the interests of British and French imperialism during the 1950s and after 1967 those of the Cold Warrior elements of the American foreign policy community saved the Israeli political elite from having to face the economic and diplomatic music.

In exchange for its services as a strategic asset helping to defend American interests in the region and in other areas of the Third World as part of the Cold War strategy, Israel received the support it needed to maintain and expand its national security and welfare state and continue to suppress an alienated Arab population and deny its political rights. Ironically, American and European Jews who were supposed to move to Israel, as well as other supporters of the Jewish state in the West, became a source of political and economic survival for Israel and helped to construct the Cold War ideology, an important component of which was Moscow's hostility toward Israel and its refusal to allow Jews to leave the Soviet Union. American neoconservatism became the crucial intellectual link between militant Israel and American Cold Warriors.

Israel, as are the former Soviet Union, Poland, and Yugoslavia, is home to both progressive and reactionary elements. The progressive elements are concentrated in Tel Aviv and other coastal cities where Israel's academic institutions, high-tech industries, and artistic and literary life are located. Those cities are dynamic commercial centers dominated by a secular and culturally permissive population oriented toward a materialistic, even somewhat hedonist lifestyle. The intellectual currents, popular music, and women's fashions of the coastal centers imitate those of London, Paris, and New York. That part of Israel is politically liberal, has a Western outlook, and hopes to reach an accommodation with the Palestinian population, to integrate the state into the region, and to make it part of the forward-looking global economy. It is an Israel that wants to reform the country's economy, to separate state and religion, and to adopt a constitution and a bill of rights.

Jerusalem and the Jewish settlements in the West Bank are reactionary. The majority of the population looks to the past and thinks in terms of "us," the Jews, against "them," the goyim: the murderous Palestinians and the hostile Arabs, the unreliable and ineffectual United States, and the decadent, anti-Semitic West. Theirs is a ghettoized Israel, a theocracy whose identity is religious, mystical, and messianic. They hope to "Judaize" Judea and Samaria, annex those territories, and eventually force the Palestinian Arabs to leave the country or to remain under an apartheid-like system. They see Israel engaged in a never-ending, all-out war with the Arab world and with Islam, a war that can end only when one side wins decisively.

The nearly half million Israeli Jews who have immigrated to the West, in particular to North America, since 1948 have reduced the pressure for political and economic reform in Israel. In a way, that emigration saved Israel's *nomenklatura* from a potential revolutionary force. Instead of storming Israel's decaying political institutions, many young Israeli professionals chose to build their future on Wall Street or in Silicon Valley.

However, there are still many Israelis who continue to demand the transformation of their society, seek economic reform, and hope to weaken the political power of the Orthodox parties. Growing unemployment and worsening economic problems may be catalysts for such changes. Moreover, the hundreds of thousands of mainly secular and professional Jews who are moving to Israel from the former Soviet Union could strengthen the opposition to the present nationalist-socialist clerical government.

"These secular Russian immigrants have a clear interest—both personal and collective—in a secular Israel in which they will not have to conform to religious laws they don't believe in,"[20] explained one analyst. In addition, they are appalled by Israel's socialist bureaucratic state. One Russian immigrant summed up the aspiration of the new Israelis: "Here in Israel no communism. Here capitalism, here freedom."[21]

The Arab World: Sources of Stagnation and Reform

Arab nationalism succeeded in freeing the Arabic-speaking people from Ottoman rule and later from French and British imperialism. It achieved political independence in the form of new nation-states that were expected eventually to unite and produce one Arab nation. However, Arab nationalism has failed to act as a unifying force; indeed, moves toward Pan-Arab unity have exposed and accentuated the structural problems that complicate attainment of that goal. Those problems include balance-of-power struggles among geopolitical entities in the Arab world (Iraq versus Egypt); separatist nationalist tendencies that are based on pre-Arab identities that have been preserved (in Egypt, Lebanon, and Iraq); and major ideological and political conflicts between traditional monarchies, such as that of Saudi Arabia, and secular regimes, such as those in Iraq and Syria.

Arab nationalism has also failed to deal with national minorities such as the Kurds in Iraq and the black Christians in Sudan. The Arab regimes in Baghdad and Khartoum attempted to suppress and even destroy those groups. Arab Christians, who had been in the vanguard of Arab nationalism, found themselves discriminated against as Pan-Arabism became increasingly identified with Islam, which is the official religion of all the Arab states except Lebanon. Its unwillingness to accept the existence of Israel, a non-Arab state, in the midst of the Arab world and the destruction of Lebanon as a relatively open and free Arab society have been the most dramatic examples of Arab nationalism's inability to deal with its own contradictions. Lacking any political legitimacy in the eyes of their populations and unable to deliver economic and social progress to their citizens, most Arab regimes resorted to authoritarian methods of rule. "Revolutionary" military dictatorships that espoused a militant form of Arab nationalism replaced decaying monarchies in Egypt, Iraq, and Libya. Arab oil, especially after 1973, helped to enhance the financial and political power of regimes in Iraq and Saudi Arabia and expand their huge military machines. But it also highlighted the gap between the oil-rich and the oil-poor Arab countries.[22]

The Cold War helped to enhance the power of the Arab regimes. The traditional monarchies relied on the West for military and financial support and in return provided access to oil and a strategic foothold. The more radical dictatorships tried to play one superpower against the other as part of a "neutralist" Third World strategy. Israel and the problem of the Soviet Jews became the centerpiece of the Cold War neoconservative ideology; the Palestinian problem and Arab unity became a major focus of the Soviet-supported anti-American Third World strategy.

The dismal economic performance and the political brutality of the Arab regimes; the growing social and economic gaps in the Arab countries; the demographic explosion (especially of young, unemployed, and radicalized populations in Egypt and Algeria); the rise of new social forces in Arab societies, such as the Shi'ite minority in Lebanon; and the continuing rivalries and conflicts within and among the Arab states have all raised major questions about the ability of secular Arab nationalism in all its variations to serve as a unifying ideology.

The end of the Cold War accentuated and magnified many of the problems facing the Arab world. As tyranny ended in Eastern Europe, many Arabs were reminded of their own Ceausescus who were still riding high. While the European Community took giant steps toward integration, Arabs were becoming increasingly aware that their own efforts to achieve economic coordination through the Arab League and other organizations such as the Gulf Cooperation Council, the Arab Maghreb Union, and the Arab Co-operation Council had met with general failure. In addition, as the Soviet Union initiated closer relations with the West, the Arab world received less and less military and economic support from the Communist bloc. The end of the Cold War has led to an improvement in relations between Israel and Poland, Hungary, and Czechoslovakia as well as to the flood of Jewish immigrants to Israel.

The Arab world faces a major population explosion. Its 200 million and more people will double their numbers in the coming two decades, and most of the increase will occur in countries that cannot provide jobs for their present citizens. Many basic services are already fully exploited, which is causing growing social discontent, even among the professional, urban middle class. "Squeezed between soaring populations and drooping economies, unable or unwilling to meet their people's rising clamor for democracy, Arab regimes find it convenient to revive the Zionist bogeyman," suggested one analyst.[23]

Saddam Hussein's regime and his invasion of Kuwait typify the condition in which the Arab world finds itself today—ruled by brutal strongmen and divided into various hostile camps. Even the Palestinian problem can no longer serve as a unifying force. The only vibrant opposition to either the secular military dictators or the traditional Moslem monarchies, whose survival depends on their ability to continue to squeeze outside players for financial and military aid, is found in groups that subscribe to various brands of mystical and messianic Islamic fundamentalism. However, those groups lack serious political or economic agendas. If they come to power, they are unlikely to be able to reform and manage the political and economic systems they inherit.

Nevertheless, some isolated portions of the Arab world still maintain remnants of the old "spirit of the Levant" that dominated the region during the heyday of the Ottoman Empire. Under the empire, the region was a mosaic of ethnic and religious groups that maintained their individual political and cultural autonomy yet together created trade and business centers that provided links with the outside world and served as a commercial and cultural bridge between Europe and the Middle East.

Will it be possible to reproduce that spirit? With the destruction of Lebanon, which was the last bastion of the old Levantine attitude, and with the rise of radical Islam, that is probably more a hope than a realistic scenario. There are, however, some elements pushing in that direction.

The forces that support the notion of regional and geographic separatism; the growing educated and Western-oriented middle class in Syria, Iraq, North Africa, and among the Palestinians; the existence of national and ethnic minorities, such as the Kurds and the Shi'ites in Iraq and the Maronites, the Druze, and the Shi'ites in Lebanon; and restive young populations should not inevitably produce destructive currents in the Arab states. Instead, those forces could weaken the existing central authorities and establish new regional configurations.

Indeed, the experiments with democratic institutions and parliamentary elections in countries such as Jordan, Algeria, and Tunisia and the failure of revolutionary Iran to become an ideological magnet for the Arab Moslem world are signs of hope for the Middle East. They suggest that there are forces in the region that might encourage political and economic freedom. A recent survey of the Arab world found that "ordinary Arabs have little trouble understanding what the West, and now increasingly the East, mean by democracy. . . . Arabs are as keen as Indians, Americans, Poles and Romanians to see their rulers' autocratic power constrained by checks and balances" and "would like the chance to remove

163

unpopular leaders through the ballot box instead of uprisings or coups."[24] A growing number of Arabs are willing to admit that the main problems facing the Arab world are self-inflicted and that solving them should begin with political reform at home.

The Arab states face a dilemma similar to that faced by the Commonwealth of Independent States, Yugoslavia, Czechoslovakia, or for that matter Canada: finding a way to evolve into decentralized and diffused confederal or cantonized systems based on the rule of law and individual political and economic freedoms. Those systems will need to allow the different national, ethnic, and religious groups greater political autonomy yet secure the political and economic rights of all citizens. There is also a need to construct new regional arrangements, based on economic cooperation and free trade, that will link the different states in broader economic markets, not force upon them some mythical pan-national identity.

Lebanon could be divided into Maronite, Druze, Arab Shi'ite, and Arab Sunni cantons each of which would enjoy its own political, economic, and religious-cultural autonomy while a central government in Beirut took care of defense and foreign policy problems. Iraq could be reconstructed as an Arab-Kurdish federation that would give the Shi'ite and Sunni Arabs additional religious autonomy. In Syria the Druze and the Alawites could be granted autonomous cantons. Similar confederal or canton-based arrangements could be developed to solve the conflicts between Arabs in the north and blacks in the south in Sudan, between Arabs and Berbers in Algeria, and between the Persian majority and the Arab and Kurdish minorities in Iran.

There is no one model that can be applied to all the states of the region. A canton system might suit Lebanon with its fairly well integrated ethnic and religious groups that are nearly equal in size. The significant differences between Arabs and Kurds might necessitate a more devolved federal system in Iraq. Sudan might adopt an in-between arrangement, and minorities in Syria and Iran might need little more than local autonomy.

Two major dangers attend political decentralization. First, on the domestic level, the division of the current states into cantons or autonomous regions, which would free citizens of different national, ethnic, and religious groups from central authoritarian regimes that have been trying to impose a unifying identity (Arab, Persian) on them, might place them under the heel of provincial dictators or even local warlords. Those new rulers might impose their own authoritarian regimes and unifying local identities on the citizenry, including the minorities of the new subunits. For example, Iraqi Kurds might celebrate the removal of the central authoritarian power of the Sunni-based regime in Baghdad only to find themselves ruled by a Kurdish dictator who wished to suppress non-Kurdish minorities, such as the Turkemans.

That danger cannot be eliminated, but a limited central constitutional government that secured the right of all citizens to live wherever they chose in the state and a free-market system that was conducive to trade among the various subunits would minimize the danger. In the long run, the Pan-Arabist and Pan-Islamic regional unity movements would be replaced by national identities. For example, Iraqi Arabs and Kurds, who maintained their local autonomy as well as their cultural ties to other Arabs and Kurds in the region, would be united under a new national identity.

The second danger is found at the regional level. Although there is nothing sacred about the existing borders of the states in the region, disintegration of the current system could lead to new regional conflicts if not total chaos. For example, Kurdish autonomy in Iraq might trigger calls for Kurdish separatism and even secession in Turkey, which could lead to intervention by Turkey in Iraq, which in turn could produce new conflicts among Ankara, Tehran, and Damascus.

Power should, therefore, be devolved in a way that maintains the inviolability of the existing borders yet opens the way to agreed-upon border changes and territorial exchanges in the future. Regional markets would allow members of the various ethnic groups, who are separated by the existing borders, to move freely among all the states of the region. Such freedom of movement and commerce would prevent new pressures for ethnic-territorial secession from developing. Examples of such regional markets might include a North African economic community composed of Morocco, Algeria, and Tunisia and a Nile-based economic grouping of Egypt, Sudan, and Ethiopia. The free movement of products and people would greatly enhance the prospects for peace and stability.

Toward an Israeli-Palestinian Federation and an Economic Confederation of the Levant

Notwithstanding their current political problems, the Israelis and the Palestinians may be able to create a nucleus for political and economic change in the Middle East. After all, very few observers would have imagined that the German and the Japanese people, who were committed during World War II to the expansion of their military power, would turn into nations of traders and businessmen after 1945. A similar change is theoretically possible in the Middle East.

It is conceivable that the Palestinian terrorist and the Israeli general of today may become the trader and the chief executive officer of tomorrow. The decline of Zionism and Pan-Arabism might produce a new secular and territorial identity, based on a decentralized political arrangement and a free-market economic system, that would allow the Israelis and the Palestinians—the two most educated and business-oriented groups in the region—to coexist politically and cooperate economically instead of shifting their allegiances to religious fundamentalism and messianic nationalism.

Middle East analysts have tended to ignore the economic aspects of the Israeli-Palestinian conflict and the way the distorted Israeli economic system has polarized the relationship between Jews and Arabs. Although Israeli rule may have raised the standard of living of the Palestinians in the territories, Israel treats them—even more than its own citizens—with infuriating discrimination, arbitrariness, and favoritism. The system has given rise to bitterness among Palestinians, "especially among those with little means of protection against the routine abuses of our senseless bureaucracy," according to Daniel Doron, director of a free enterprise–oriented Israeli think tank.[25]

When Israeli citizens permit their government to distort the economy, they pay for it with stagnation, which they rationalize as a necessary sacrifice for "national security" and "social development." The Palestinians are less likely to passively accept the hardships to which the Israelis have become inured. Most of the Palestinians in the territories are unorganized laborers and small-scale entrepreneurs who lack the defenses, such as trade unions and interest groups, that most Israelis have. For that reason, among others, the Palestinians are demanding changes in the political structure and mobilizing behind political leaders they hope will obtain for them the same wealth, jobs, patronage, and status the Jews enjoy.

Doron argues that young, educated Palestinians who had nowhere to go in Israel's statist economy were a rootless proletariat that made the explosion in the territories inevitable. His perceptive analysis was confirmed by two distinguished Israeli journalists, Ze'ev Schiff and Ehud Ya'ari, in *The Intifada*. According to a secret Israeli intelligence report, they reveal, many Palestinians who have been jailed since the beginning of the uprising listed economic factors such as unemployment and a harassing bureaucracy, rather than the demand for a Palestinian state, as their major reason for participating in the *intifada*.[26]

Economic reform must go hand in hand with a political solution. Any peace agreement will last only as long as the Palestinian economy prospers and economic development has a chance to cement the fragile strands of political stability. To put it another way, the solution to the Palestinian-Israeli conflict should reflect libertarian principles with their emphasis on both economic and political freedoms. It should include a plan for both political devolution and economic deregulation.

American and Israeli leftists propose the establishment of an independent Palestinian state as a solution to the conflict between the two peoples. However, unless increased economic freedom for both sides and new mechanisms for political and economic integration of the two states are put in place, an independent Palestinian state could simply serve as a base of operations for a destructive Palestinian political elite. That would guarantee the continuation of the conflict between Palestinians and Israelis in a new form— between two states instead of two communities.

When peace comes, it will be the free flow of people and products that will bind Palestinians and Israelis together. "Commercial activity is the only sphere where Jews and Arabs have learned to interact—not in the artificial and rarefied atmosphere of conferences and seminars but in daily life and in a framework that . . . is mutually beneficial."[27]

The libertarian solution advocated here would include the establishment of a federation of Israel and Palestine that would consist of Israel within its pre-1967 borders and a Palestinian state based in the West Bank and Gaza. (All territorial exchanges and border changes would have to be acceptable to both sides.) A united Jerusalem, divided into Palestinian and Israeli counties, would serve as the political capital of the new federation.[28]

Citizenship would be dual. Each individual would be a citizen of either Israel or Palestine and of the federation. Each state would

167

have its own parliament and local governments and would organize its administration in its own way. The political autonomy and responsibilities of each state, which would have to be agreed upon in advance, could be fairly great. For example, the two states might wish to restrict citizenship and establish different relationships with outside states. Palestine might become a member of the Arab League, and Israel might join the World Jewish Congress. Israel and Palestine would probably, at least in the initial stages of the federation's development, encourage Jewish and Arab immigration to their respective territories.

Constitutionally guaranteed freedom of movement of both people and wealth between the two states would create pressures for cooperation. Free trade and a thriving market would bind Israelis and Palestinians with ties of mutual self-interest. What Frances Kendall and Leon Louw, in their plan for a confederation in South Africa, called the "demonstration effect,"[29]—competition between the two constituent states, which would arise in a system with severe restrictions on the central government—could help to produce peace and prosperity. "My dream," Faisal el Husseini, a young Palestinian leader in the West Bank, told Schiff and Ya'ari, "is that 10 years from now the conflict between us will involve the fact that we lowered the prices of the computers we produce so as to squeeze you out of the market."[30]

The new federation would have a central government based in Jerusalem that would be viewed less as a governing body than as an agency for the protection of the two states and the basic rights of their citizens. The government would consist of two houses of equal status, one elected directly by all the citizens of the federation on the basis of proportional representation and the other made up of equal numbers of delegates from the two states, regardless of the size of their populations.

A cabinet would be elected by both houses sitting in joint session. It would promote cooperation between the local Israeli and Palestinian governments and handle foreign policy and defense issues. A national government limited by a constitution and a bill of rights would be based on the principles of maximum devolution and strict limitation of central government power, with a clear separation of judicial, administrative, and legislative functions.

In the long run, after Israel and Palestine have settled the Jews and Arabs who want to immigrate, the existence of the federation will create pressures for the "de-Zionization" of Israel and the "de-Arabization" of Palestine. Israelis might gradually develop an independent identity based on language, culture, and territory without loosening their cultural ties to the rest of the Jewish world. Israel might even absorb non-Jews. A Hebrew-speaking Christian might be accepted as an Israeli citizen in the same way an Italian-speaking Jew is accepted as an Italian citizen.[31]

A similar process would take place on the Palestinian side. While they maintained cultural ties with the Arab world, the Palestinians, like the Israelis, would develop their own independent identity based on geography and their own history and culture. Eventually, the federation would make possible a new Israeli-Palestinian identity that would be a mixture of the products of Jewish and Moslem civilizations and Western and Eastern cultures.

By itself, the federation could become a major center of finance, trade, and technology. Israelis and Palestinians, with their high levels of education, strong middle classes, and extensive external ties to the West and the Arab world, could turn the federation into a commercial bridge between Europe and the Middle East. The federation could seek to establish a free-trade area with the United States and to link itself to the European Community as an associate member, which would provide interesting opportunities for international investors and traders. Israel's large Russian-speaking population could make the federation a laboratory for business ties between the United States and the Commonwealth of Independent States, and the Palestinians could make it a major publishing and media center for the Arab world.

The federation could also become the nucleus of a new regional political and economic arrangement. It could become part of a larger economic market that would include Jordan, Lebanon, and Syria. Those three states and the new federation are one geographic-historical unit, Greater Syria, that has always served as a bridge between the Middle East and Europe and has had stronger links to Mediterranean Europe than to the sheiks of the gulf. The strong demographic ties among the federation, Jordan, Syria, and Lebanon and their large educated and Westernized middle classes and professional and business communities could gradually turn those states into a single economic market, which would allow its people to make maximum use of their human potential as well as their dwindling economic resources, in particular water.

Choices

Israelis and Palestinians, Jews and Arabs, like other players in the emerging international system, will face clear choices. They can continue to fight over the graves of Jewish prophets and Arab sheiks in the West Bank and be marginalized in the international system, or they can compete in the international stock markets and in regional trade shows and join the core nations.

Arab leaders and intellectuals can create either conditions that will lead to the revival of the spirit of the Levant or those that will allow the corrupt Arab sheiks and military dictators to be replaced by the rising forces of religious fundamentalism and messianic nationalism. Israelis face similar choices. Either the secular and commercial Tel Aviv will come to symbolize Israel, or the fanatic religious Orthodox Jerusalem will.

In the long run, the Middle East can either destroy itself in a bloody apocalyptic struggle between the dark forces of Judaism and Islam, which are going to inherit the remnants of modern Zionism and Arab nationalism, or it can use its mosaic of ethnic and religious groups to turn the region into a productive center of peace, free trade, and prosperity. The Middle East, in short, can become a prosperous and successful core region or be pushed to the periphery of the international system.

In the short run at least, the pessimists are going to win the day. It is not inconceivable that the "tribes with flags" that dominate the Middle East will make that region more chaotic than ever. Contrary to many expectations, the gulf war did not improve prospects for peace and stability in the region, and it is very doubtful that Washington's actions are going to make a lot of difference.

Washington, as one of the primary core players in the world, is in a position to produce incentives for both Israelis and Arabs to make peace and reform their political and economic systems. Instead, the United States has been pursuing policies that run counter to that goal. The gulf war has highlighted the bankruptcy of American policy in the region. The war helped to make the Middle East safe for the interests of the feudal monarchies and the military dictatorships in the Arab world and for the continued Israeli occupation of Arab territories. It tied America's position in the region to the pro–status quo powers whose policies almost guarantee that the Middle East will remain on the periphery of the international system.

More important for America's long-term interest, by continuing to pursue its present policies in the region, Washington is almost guaranteeing that the forces of change that will emerge in the future will direct their frustration and anger against the United States.

9. Conclusion: Is There a Way Out of the Middle Eastern Morass?

The successful military outcome of Operation Desert Storm created unrealistic expectations that were fanned by President Bush's rhetoric. In a Wilsonian address before Congress on March 6, 1991, the president promised "to create new opportunities for peace and stability in the Middle East" and proposed a "new regional structure" for the gulf based on local military forces (characterized by some as a Middle Eastern NATO) that would allow him to bring U.S. troops home.

"Our commitment to peace in the Middle East does not end with the liberation of Kuwait," Bush told the cheering audience. He stated that he would lead the way to a "comprehensive peace" based on the principle of land for peace and on guaranteed security for Israel and "legitimate Palestinian political rights." Bush and his advisers, as well as other analysts and pundits, also proposed a grand plan for arms control in the region, including the elimination of weapons of mass destruction; put forward ideas about closing the economic and social gaps between the have and the have-not states in the region; and discussed the possibility of establishing a constitutional monarchy in Kuwait.[1]

Indeed, there was in the United States, in the days immediately after the military victory in the Persian Gulf, a sense of omnipotence similar to the euphoria that dominated Israel after the Six-Day War in 1967—a feeling that everything was possible in arranging the political cards in the Middle East; that after Saddam Hussein, an Iraqi Thomas Jefferson would come to power in Baghdad, and a window of opportunity would be opened for democracy, stability, and peace in the region.[2]

However, ever since the Madrid peace conference, there has been a growing sense in Washington that the window has turned into a peephole that might close entirely. Moreover, the television images

of the suffering Iraqi civilians, the tragedy of the Kurds, the harass-
ment of Palestinians in Kuwait, and the expanding Jewish settlements in the West bank are graphic testimony to the discrepancy
between Bush's declared idealistic agenda and his actual policies.

Like a natural storm, Operation Desert Storm wreaked havoc on
the region: hundreds of thousands of casualties, physical destruction, an environmental catastrophe, and close to 5 million refugees.
A UN report stated that allied bombing has relegated Iraq to a "Pre-
Industrial Age."[3] New alliances were formed during the war as
different players—Saudis, Egyptians, Israelis, and Syrians—all
took advantage of the storm and its temporary effects to advance
their interests.

The Egyptians were able to return to the center of Arab politics,
to destroy the power of their Iraqi competitor, and to secure the
continuing flow of American money to support their shaky economy. Syrian dictator Hafez al-Assad settled his scores with his
Ba'ath rival in Baghdad and took the opportunity to formalize and
legitimize his control of Lebanon (with tacit approval from Washington). The Egyptians and the Syrians along with the Arabian
desert sheiks (who had learned that bribing an enemy does not
always secure power and safety) allowed the American ally to cut
the threatening Iraqi tribe down to size. Now, they can all return
to managing their hostile relationships by combinations of military
threats, financial payoffs, and the exploitation of external players,
such as the United States. They can continue to participate, that is,
in the never-ending game of alliance building and untying, which
is sometimes characterized as "stability."

Desert Storm left misery and destruction, but it also left each of
the regional players, with the exception of the Palestinians and
the Kurds, with some booty. Even Saddam is back in business in
Baghdad, consolidating his power with the blessing of his recent
antagonists. The Persian Shi'ite mullahs, the enemies of yesteryear
and now the silent winners of the war, are welcome guests in the
tents of the Arab Sunni sheiks. And the members of the Israeli and
Palestinian tribes are again sharpening their knives and axes and
returning to their very private and bloody shepherds' war.

After a storm, be it political or meteorological, passes over the
Middle East, the region returns to its eternal stillness, as though
nothing has happened. The people come out of hiding, remove the

174

sand from their faces, shake the dust from their clothes, and return to the desert's routine: the daily struggle over water wells and grazing spaces. The desert's tribes go back to the ritual of signing and breaking alliances, and their leaders meet at night before the fire to contemplate the next raid against their hostile neighbors.

It is in front of the burning fire that the American guest is treated to another ritual of Middle Eastern hospitality. The tribe's elders listen to his advice and nod with polite approval as the foreigner, the child of some faraway green pasture land, suggests that the time has come to replace primal desert hatred with eternal peace. As the American guest outlines his vision of the new world order, a product of the Western mind with its contemporary images of board room directors raising a glass of scotch after the signing of a successful business deal, the elders, sipping their orange juice, recall the other foreigners who have passed through the region: the Greeks, the Romans, the crusaders, the British, the French. Those foreigners and others all hoped to recreate the region in their own image only to retreat from it humiliated and exhausted, abandoning their regional allies and leaving nothing more than their imprint on some precious archaeological item.

The More Things Change . . .

As the dust settled in the Middle East, Washington found to its chagrin that few things had changed. The war left the region in more or less the same political and economic condition in which it had found it. We are reminded once again of Carl Brown's kaleidoscope. The kaleidoscope has been turned, and a new configuration has emerged. But as always the configuration includes the same players and the same problems that will drive the region into yet another time of chaos out of which will emerge a new, equally temporary configuration.

Indeed, the new science of chaos has some interesting relevance to the Middle Eastern system. Chaos theory offers a way of seeing order and pattern where formerly only the random, the erratic, the unpredictable—in short, the chaotic—were observed.[4] Despite its chaotic tendencies—social upheavals, political revolutions, regional wars, and global entanglements—there are, as the preceding chapters suggest, a certain order, stability, and continuity that have characterized the system since the fall of the Ottoman Empire.[5]

The main feature of the region is ruling political, social, ethnic, and religious elites who fight for their survival by creating and dissolving shifting alliances with domestic, regional, and external players. Each move by a regional or an external player, like the famous Butterfly Effect, tends to produce new alliances and configurations, and a certain stability ensues as long as the various ruling elites sense that their interests are being maintained, at least for a while.[6]

The imposition after World War I of a nation-state system on the Middle East, and the institutionalization of that system after World War II by the grant of political independence to new states, did not bring lasting order. Instead, the nation-state system provided a new arena in which the ruling elites, especially the proponents of Zionism and Pan-Arabism, attempted to advance their interests.

The Middle East's unwillingness to adopt a more stable structure is explained by the fact that "in the Middle East there is no sense of legitimacy—no agreement on rules of the game—and no belief, universally shared in the region, that within whatever boundaries, the entities that call themselves countries and the men who claim to be rulers are entitled to recognition as such."[7]

Most of the region's states are superficial entities that were produced by British and French imperialism. Those states, in addition to lacking political legitimacy, have had neither economic viability nor experience with liberal or democratic traditions. In those societies, various ethnic and religious groups are engaged in a fierce competition for power. That competition is typically won by whichever military clique controls the national television system and usually spills over into other states in the region in the form of secessionist or irredentist movements.

External players who have tried to impose their will on the region have failed. They may occasionally gain important short-term dividends from their intervention, such as access to oil. However, as this book suggests, in the long run the costs of intervention and alliances with the region's ruling elites have usually increased in direct proportion to the external power's attempts to increase the power of one regional player at the expense of other players or to dominate the region by excluding competing external players.

Moreover, it is difficult to determine whether the intervention of external powers in the Middle East leads to "better" outcomes. Like the Butterfly Effect, it produces new, different, and unpredictable outcomes. Those new outcomes are pregnant with opportunities, but whether they are seized to advance a productive or a destructive end depends, in the final analysis, on the regional players themselves.

Until they solve the problem of legitimacy and accept some rules for their game, the regional ruling elites, as well as competing elites, will be engaged in a continuous, bloody struggle for power. Foreign intervention has a tendency to aggravate the situation by creating inducements in the form of military and economic aid and diplomatic support. Such aid and support encourage the regional elites to hold on to their power and to refrain from reforming their systems and from reaching agreement with their rivals. As a result, they establish neither political legitimacy nor a regional order under a set of accepted rules.

Not only does the intervention of an external power aggravate the problems of the region; such intervention also harms the long-term interests of the external power. The problem is that the more an external player, such as the United States, invests in the Middle Eastern game, the more it expands its regional commitments and encourages the development of new domestic constituencies who have a vested interest and emotional involvement in the production of a public good—America's Middle Eastern policy.

Predictably, the gulf war resulted in new commitments to defend the Arab gulf states against potential threats from Iran, new arms sales to those states as well as to Israel, new promises to bring peace between Israelis and Palestinians, and new pressures to "do something" about the Kurdish tragedy or the continuing rule of Saddam.

For a while after each Middle Eastern upheaval, such as Desert Storm, there is an illusion of stability and order as the system and its players adapt to the new configuration. Then a new explosion— a terrorist attack, a threat to an existing regime, a new regional war—occurs and causes the overcommitted external power, in this case the United States, under pressure from its regional allies and domestic constituencies, to take military action or diplomatic initiatives.

Any effort by the external player to minimize the risks of its involvement in the Middle East usually results in a no-win situation that has major costs. The decision not to invade Baghdad produced political and moral costs (Saddam remains in power, and the Kurds and the Shi'ites are suppressed) that have led to domestic criticism and public outcry and to various pressures from regional players. However, a decision to invade Baghdad would have led to a new and even more bloody quagmire for Washington. It could have destroyed the power base of the ruling Sunni elite and might have led to the disintegration ("Lebanonization") of Iraq, including the possible formation of independent Kurdish and Shi'ite entities. Such fragmentation of the country might have resulted in the overt or covert intervention of Turkey and Iran in Iraq and in years of general anarchy that would have further destabilized the region.

Hence, the Bush administration's foreign policymakers, after urging Iraqis to rise up and remove Saddam from power, now find that his ouster could cause the breakup of Iraq and the rise of religious fundamentalism linked to Iran. If the choice is between the latter scenario and the continued survival of Saddam's regime, Washington would no doubt prefer to see the devil it knows remain in power in Baghdad—although clearly the administration would prefer to see a more "user-friendly" Iraqi government drawn from the Sunni elite.

The outcome of the gulf war illustrates the policy dilemmas Washington faces in the Middle East. U.S. policy has created conditions that will be less conducive to political reforms and to solving the area's interstate conflicts. Moreover, the goals that were enunciated in Bush's war rhetoric—establishing democracy in the Middle East, forming regional security arrangements, moving toward arms control agreements, and bringing peace between Arabs and Israelis—have only created unfulfilled expectations that are bound to lead to new American commitments and entanglements.

Mission Impossible: Making the Middle East Safe for Democracy

Notwithstanding official American rhetoric encouraging democracy in the gulf region, Washington, bearing in mind the alternatives, continues to tolerate the autocratic rule of the sheiks. Under pressure from Saudi Arabia, it even gave up on the modest effort to push for some democratic opening of the system in Kuwait, where women are still denied even the most basic civil rights, residents who are not members of the ruling family are offered only crumbs of political power, and Palestinians and Shi'ites are harassed and frequently persecuted.[8]

The gulf war pointed to the long-term problem facing traditional Middle Eastern monarchies: to survive politically, they must continue to rely on direct and indirect American aid and military support. But that dependence exposes their populations to Western political and economic models and creates politically explosive expectations. The discrepancy between the traditional ruling elites' pretensions of resisting the influence of outside "infidels" and the elites' alliances with those very infidels is revealed. Opposition from both modernizing and fundamentalist forces is quite likely at some point.

Those developments underscore a major fallacy of U.S. Middle Eastern policy. Neoconservative intellectuals in the United States insist that the global spread of democracy will also produce an increase in pro-American sentiment.[9] That is not the case in the Middle East. Anti-Americanism pervades the Arab and Moslem worlds and stems, as noted, from resentment of both the tacit U.S.-Israeli alliance and the direct American intervention in the region. Indeed, such states as Jordan, Algeria, and Yemen, which have experimented in recent years with quasi-free elections, have seen fundamentalist and anti-Western groups gain strength. In those countries during the gulf war, strong anti-American elements put pressure on the incumbent regimes, especially that of Jordan's pro-American King Hussein, to adopt a more sympathetic policy toward Saddam.[10]

The chances of making the Middle East safe for democracy, along with Washington's power to move the region's states in that direction, are extremely limited. American efforts can create a backlash and produce major political costs for perceived American interests in the area since such efforts are bound to unleash anti-Western, authoritarian forces. At the same time, an alliance with the status quo regimes in the Arab world, such as those in Saudi Arabia and Kuwait, will inevitably turn Washington into a symbol of repression in the eyes of democratic and revolutionary factions.

The United States faces a no-win situation in its relationship with the existing political regimes. Attempting to democratize them would produce political and social instability and create a vacuum that would entice militant domestic and outside forces to act. Trying to secure the power of the existing regimes would create conditions that could lead to the rise of anti-American successor governments.

In the short run, the region's people will face three political alternatives: decaying traditional monarchies, such as those of Saudi Arabia and Kuwait; religious fundamentalism, symbolized by Iran and its supporters in the region; and military dictatorships that espouse a relatively benign secular nationalism (Egypt and Algeria) or a ruthless secular nationalism (Iraq).

In all probability, Washington will continue to ally itself with benign dictators and traditional monarchs. For every regional friend it wins, Washington is bound to gain 10 enemies for whom America represents not the winds of desirable change but the status quo of reactionary forces. When radical factions come to power, Washington will suffer the consequences of its policies, as it did in Iran.

Americans will then express surprise and astonishment at the anti-American rhetoric and violence that will dominate the policies of the new regimes. Most Americans will be unwilling to accept the proposition that past U.S. policies had something to do with those adverse developments—that an Iraqi child who lost his parents under the rubble of a Baghdad apartment building destroyed by American bombers might one day hijack an American airliner.

The Middle East is unlikely to be swept by the forces of democracy and economic freedom in the foreseeable future. As was suggested in Chapter 7, there are islands of reform in the Middle East. They include Kuwaitis who have studied in the United States; Egyptians who have business ties with America; Jordanians who watch American television programs and films; and the more secular Israelis, Palestinians, and Lebanese. Indeed, business, educational, and cultural ties are the best way to increase the likelihood that the American model will take root in those societies at some point in the future.

Military intervention and alliances with reactionary regimes or attempts to launch democratic crusades will only tend to neutralize the positive effects of the American model of liberty on the region's people and create hostile attitudes toward the United States. Americans who thought it was difficult to bring democracy and free markets to the Soviet Union, which had strong historical ties to the West, will discover that trying to implant those concepts in Middle

Eastern systems, which are just emerging from the Middle Ages, is a long and almost impossible mission.

Perpetuating the Region's Balance-of-Power Games?

Competing with the goal of promoting democracy in the Middle East after the war was the idea of creating, through regional balance-of-power arrangements and American military commitments, a regional zone of stability and security. Some suggested that an extensive U.S. military role could be avoided by creating a security arrangement that would combine the military forces of the Arab gulf states and Egyptian mercenary forces (in exchange for Saudi financial aid for Egypt's ailing economy).[11]

However, such a security arrangement would be as stable as the shifting sands of Arabia and could actually create more long-term problems. The principal effect would be to foster the illusion in the United States and throughout the Arab world that Washington can ensure the security of the region without a large-scale military presence merely by deploying some naval forces and keeping some military equipment there.

There are several problems with such an updated application of the Nixon Doctrine. Not only are there questions about Egypt's political will and military capacity to maintain the balance of power against the military forces of Syria, Iran, and Iraq, but Saudi Arabia has never welcomed a high-profile Egyptian role. Moreover, the gulf states, especially Saudi Arabia and Kuwait, are experiencing major financial problems as a result of the gulf war; their own economies need postwar reconstruction. They are, therefore, in no mood to help restructure the economies of have-not states such as Egypt.[12]

If Washington insists on maintaining a balance in the gulf that is favorable to the United States, it will have to maintain armed forces there to deal with contingencies and protect the Arab gulf states. (No regional security arrangement will be able to do that.) That mission would lead inevitably to more Pentagon spending and plans to improve U.S. "long-reach" military capabilities in the region. Such steps would certainly entail maintaining a rapid deployment capability and perhaps even the peacetime presence of ground troops.[13]

Such a development would go beyond the over-the-horizon U.S. presence originally envisioned. It would entail political costs for

U.S. politicians, and it might actually undermine the already precarious legitimacy of the traditional regimes in the gulf. The gulf war, therefore, would not result in the rise of a viable regional security organization but in an increasing U.S. commitment to the direct defense of the Arab oil states and the growing dependence of those states on Washington.

American officials expressed the hope that after the gulf war Washington's Arab allies would establish an effective balance-of-power structure. But with the eclipse of the Arab League as a forum for managing intra-Arab conflicts, the region's states lost another incentive for managing their own interests through a regional mechanism. They also lack both the military power and the political will to form an independent regional security structure. As a result of the war, the United States will become a more active player, an external balancer, that will continue to be drawn into the kaleidoscopic balance-of-power games of the region at growing military and diplomatic costs.

Indeed, the Middle East will continue to be inhospitable to collective security schemes as long as Washington provides military assistance to and projects its power into the region. Such U.S. actions are disincentives for the various regional players to create their own security arrangements. For example, by sending a message to the rulers of Kuwait that Washington will always be ready to come to the emirate's defense, Washington has apparently taken it upon itself to secure a post–gulf war balance of power in the region, a mission that is both unrealistic and dangerous.

Washington is currently trying to maintain a very fragile balance by micromanaging security in the gulf. The United States is planning to station the forward element of its Central Command (now based in Tampa, Florida) in one of the gulf states (probably either Oman or the United Arab Emirates) and has asked some of the countries in the region to make storage places available for heavy American and perhaps European materiel. Washington has also committed itself to a program intended to more than double the Saudi armed forces (to about 200,000) over the next five to seven years and to strengthen the defenses of the six Gulf Cooperation Council countries.

However, those ideas and the efforts to implement them are already facing obstacles. There is congressional opposition to selling new military equipment to the gulf states, and Saudi and other leaders in the region are reluctant to increase cooperation with the United States. Notwithstanding the postwar talk about Saudi Arabia's willingness to reassert its military and political power and strengthen its ties with Washington, the kingdom's rulers are concerned about opposition both from domestic fundamentalist groups and from Iran.[14]

Unfortunately, American policymakers have learned the wrong lesson from the war. The lesson of the gulf war is not that the United States needs to more effectively restore the regional balance or to more efficiently micromanage U.S. ties with the regional players, as some are suggesting. The real lesson is different: being part of the Middle Eastern kaleidoscope entails heavy costs, which cannot be calculated in advance. Those costs are borne by all the players and especially by the United States, which has invested the most in the game.

It is impossible, after all, to keep the kaleidoscope's configuration in place for long after a move, such as the U.S. victory. Any player finds that after a while a positive outcome in one configuration (Iraq containing Iran) becomes negative in another configuration (a strengthened Iraq invading Kuwait) and necessitates a new move (the gulf war). The Middle Eastern game is never ending, and the United States is bound to encounter new entanglements and higher costs. As it cuts one head off the hydra of instability, Washington will see several new ones spring forth.

It is not inconceivable that new commitments resulting from the gulf war—combined with pressures from the Arab oil and Israeli lobbies to contain new villains and magnified by the notion that the gulf war "proved" that Washington can play (with few costs) the role of international policeman—might lead the United States to a new intervention in the area. After all, some would argue, after paying the costs of destroying one bad guy, do we really want to see another bad guy—perhaps President Assad of Syria—take advantage of our victory? Let's get rid of him so we can finally create a lasting regional balance. A new American intervention could range from indirect nonmilitary aid, channeled through the Saudis, to support for various guerrilla groups "fighting for democracy" in Iraq to direct U.S. military involvement in future regional conflicts.

As should any real drive for political and economic freedom, a serious move toward a balance-of-power system in the Middle East, including the development of security arrangements, should come from within and reflect the interests of the regional players. It should not be imposed from without by Washington or other external powers.

However, as has been noted, Israel and the Arab states are not just nation-states striving for security. They represent powerful ideologies, such as Pan-Arabism, Islamic fundamentalism, and Zionism, that are used by the ruling elites to mobilize domestic and external support. As long as those ideologies continue to play a prominent role in the politics of the region and the core problems they thrive on, such as the Palestinian-Israeli conflict, are not solved, the possibility of moving toward a viable nation-state system that can be open to balance-of-power arrangements will be slim.

Potential American disengagement, not possible new U.S. military commitments, might force the ruling elites to finally deal with the problems of the region and to set the stage for political accommodations between Zionism and Pan-Arabism. Such accommodations might, in turn, lead to creation of normal international relationships. Without a solution to the Arab-Israeli conflict, the chances for an effective nation-state system disappear. The danger will then be that the most extreme fundamentalist groups on both sides will gain power and lead the region, and the United States, into a zero-sum messianic conflict.

Arms Control: Early Expectations, Early Disappointments

In early June 1991, the president unveiled his long-delayed plan for arms control in the Middle East, including the possible end to the production of material for use in nuclear weapons. The plan, however, secures Israel's nuclear monopoly and focuses very little on ways to curb the spread of conventional weapons.[15]

Two days after Bush presented his plan, Secretary of Defense Richard Cheney announced during a visit to Israel that the United States was planning to stockpile American military equipment there for use in new regional conflicts. Cheney added that Washington would also give Israel 10 used F-15s and continue to supply three-quarters of the funds for an American-Israeli anti-ballistic missile project, the Arrow.[16]

"There is nothing inconsistent" about pursuing arms control in the region on the one hand and providing for the "legitimate security requirements" of Israel on the other, explained Cheney. Israeli officials rejected even the hint in Bush's proposal that Israel at some point would have to open its nuclear program to international inspection. In what seemed to be a scene from *Alice in Wonderland*, one Israeli official suggested, after Cheney's announcement of the stockpiling of American weapons in Israel, that the Bush plan should focus on controlling conventional weapons in the region.[17]

There is little doubt that encouraging an arms control agreement, especially on weapons of mass destruction, has even less chance of success than does trying to structure regional defense pacts. Comprehensive approaches to regional arms control would have to involve a large number of states, from Morocco to India, with varying capabilities and motives—a most difficult prospect. Moreover, although arms control agreements both reflect and contribute to changes in the political environment, they cannot substitute for those changes. If the Middle East continues to spawn unpredictable political rivalries, it is probable that, to secure their fragile margins of security, the region's states will continue to build their military machines, especially at a time when sources of arms are not exactly drying up. The gulf war has opened a new cycle of regional military build-ups, led by the champion of Middle Eastern arms control, the United States.[18]

In addition to deciding to stockpile weapons in Israel and making other arms agreements with that country, the administration asked Congress to approve the sale of 46 F-16 fighter jets to Egypt at a total price of $1.6 billion and has indicated that it is considering $18 million in arms sales to some of the Arab gulf states, a move that will stimulate requests by Israel for similar deals.[19]

The lesson that Israel and America's gulf allies have drawn from the gulf war is that their security rests on acquiring more, not fewer, high-tech weapons. If one takes into consideration the strong regional demand for conventional and unconventional weapons and the existence of old and new sources of supply (such as the American and West European arms industries that are searching for new markets; the expanding arms businesses of North Korea, Brazil, Czechoslovakia, Poland, and the former Soviet Union; and Israel's independent, advanced defense industry), one does not have to be an expert in the international arms market to predict a new and more destructive regional arms race.

It is impossible, even with the best of intentions, to curtail arms sales to the region. The complex and secretive arms trade environment and the availability of billions of petrodollars on the demand side virtually guarantee continued activity. Israel, Turkey, and the moderate Arab states will probably continue to request more weapons to defend themselves against "new Saddams," and Washington, pressured by the Israeli and Arab lobbies and encouraged by the now-rejuvenated military-industrial complex, will find it difficult not to provide those weapons.

The gulf war made it possible for Israel to regain its regional nuclear monopoly. No Israeli leader, even a moderate Labor leader, will give up what most Israelis consider their nation's weapon of last resort or open Israel's nuclear program to international inspection. The only incentive for Israel to begin reducing its nuclear arsenal would be another regional power's acquisition of nuclear weapons or progress on a political settlement of the Arab-Israeli conflict. Ironically, by destroying Iraq's capability to produce nonconventional weapons, Washington has probably slowed progress toward a nuclear balance of terror between Israel and Iraq. Such a balance might have given Jerusalem an incentive to consider (as part of regional political negotiations) nonconventional arms control agreements.

Neither the United States nor Israel can in the long run prevent other Arab or Moslem countries from gaining access to technology that will enable them to develop nuclear or other weapons of mass destruction. Other factors in addition to the Arab-Israeli conflict, such as the problems between India and Pakistan, make the development of an "Islamic bomb" almost inevitable. An Islamic bomb, however, could actually lend stability to the relationships among the Middle Eastern states in the same way the nuclear threat is apparently helping to prevent a military confrontation in the Indian-Pakistani conflict over Kashmir.[20]

Eventually, only the political settlement of Middle Eastern conflicts and the creation of greater regional stability will give rise to an environment conducive to discussions on ending the arms race. Such discussions will be the political horse that must pull the cart of arms control.

Benign Neglect of the Palestinian-Israeli Dispute?

Despite Washington's success in reviving the Arab-Israeli peace process, U.S. diplomatic efforts have failed to produce any major progress in settling the core Palestinian-Israeli problems. The Likud government seems to be more committed than ever to the principle of Greater Israel and has made it clear that it will not willingly grant the Palestinians in the West Bank and Gaza any form of political independence. Indeed, Shamir and his colleagues are intensifying their efforts to settle the territories and expand Israeli control over them.[21]

The stalemate in the Arab-Israeli negotiations, coupled with the changes taking place in the former Soviet Union and growing economic problems in the United States, is causing Washington and the American people to lose interest in the Middle East.[22] That state of affairs gives American policymakers a new opportunity to reassess their hyperactive diplomatic approach to Arab-Israeli peace. The activist approach has been based on a perverse assumption: Washington should pay the financial and diplomatic costs of helping Arabs and Israelis to stop killing each other, since an end to the slaughter would do more for Washington than for the combatants.

That assumption was derived from Washington's Middle Eastern policy paradigm, which assumed that unless America helped to make peace between Israel and its Arab neighbors, there would be several unpleasant results. First, Washington, as a result of Arab resentment, would find it difficult to safeguard Western oil and strategic interests in the gulf. Second, the United States would endanger its moral commitment to Israel, since that state's security can be guaranteed in the long run only by recognition and acceptance by its neighbors. Finally, U.S. failure to secure peace would produce regional instability that would invite Soviet meddling and expansionism.

The end of the Cold War and the collapse of the Soviet empire have largely eliminated the third factor from the overall American calculation, although Washington will have to recognize Moscow's legitimate interest in its Middle Eastern geopolitical back yard and should not exclude the Russians from any regional diplomatic effort.

The gulf war at least weakened, if not removed, the first factor: the linkage between the Arab-Israeli issue and American interests in the gulf. Washington was able to form a pro-American Arab coalition, which included an Arab state, Egypt, that has signed a peace agreement with Israel, and to defend its interests in the gulf without solving the Palestinian problem. With the linkage between the Palestinian problem and American interests in the gulf so weakened, more Americans may wonder why the United States should invest diplomatic time and energy to resolve a conflict between two adversaries who do not seem to be interested in taking advantage of such American efforts.

Continued Israeli occupation of the West Bank and Gaza has raised major questions about the second element of America's Middle Eastern paradigm: Washington's moral commitment to the Jewish state. American support and aid, as the preceding chapters suggest, help to maintain a repressive militant government in Jerusalem and a bankrupt socialist economy. If Israel wants continued American public support, which is based on the argument that Israel is a democratic nation that is different from the surrounding Arab authoritarian and dictatorial regimes, it will eventually have no choice (in its own interest) but to decouple itself from the occupied Arab territories, reach some modus vivendi with its Arab neighbors, and reform its political and economic systems.

By clinging to its Middle Eastern paradigm, Washington is actually removing incentives for diplomatic and economic change on both the Israeli and the Arab sides. Washington's high-profile involvement in trying to make peace between Arabs and Israelis creates the impression that the diplomatic stakes are higher for Washington than for the regional adversaries—that it owes them diplomatic support or financial compensation in return for concessions. The United States also becomes a party to domestic political battles in the Middle East as Israelis and Arabs opposed to U.S. moves begin to direct their frustration against Washington. Moreover, by creating the expectation that it can deliver a solution, the United States is bound to produce an eventual backlash when its commitments to each side are not fulfilled.

The time has come for Washington to consider replacing its activist approach to the Israeli-Palestinian conflict with benign neglect— the kind of attitude it has adopted toward other regional conflicts such as that between India and Pakistan. That approach might persuade more Israelis and Palestinians that, unless they seriously attempt to solve their conflict, they, not the United States, will be the ones to bear the costs of their intransigence.

If the conflict remains unresolved, the Palestinians will remain under Israeli control for the foreseeable future. Despite the solidarity rhetoric from their Arab brothers, the Palestinians and their problem could be marginalized both regionally and internationally. The costs to Israel of perpetuating the conflict are also obvious. It will retain the burden of occupation in the midst of bloody communal conflict; gradually lose the Western support it regained during the gulf war; and be unable to meet its rising economic and social challenges, particularly the absorption of Jewish immigrants from the former Soviet Union.

One important reason that American mediation between Egypt and Israel was successful in the late 1970s was that both Cairo and Jerusalem were willing from the outset, even without American intervention, to accept the land-for-peace formula as the basis for solving their conflict. Similarly, in the present situation, Washington should be ready to help the Israelis and the Palestinians only when they are ready to help themselves, and then it should offer its services only as a mediator and an honest broker. However, in contrast to its conduct during the Egyptian-Israeli peace negotiations, the United States should avoid creating undue expectations about its ability to deliver a solution and making a commitment to pay the two sides for agreeing to settle their differences.

Recommended: Constructive Disengagement from the Middle East

The growing difficulties the administration is encountering in trying to revive the Arab-Israeli peace process might encourage Washington to adopt a more low-key approach. The pragmatic Bush might be tempted to continue to maintain the facade of diplomatic momentum in the region but not push for substantive progress. That tactic would allow him to hold together his war coalition without exerting too much political energy, which might entail major costs for him before the 1992 election.[23]

In the short run, however, it seems unlikely that Washington will treat the Arab-Israeli conflict with the kind of benign neglect recommended here or that it will move toward gradual disengagement from the Middle East. The gulf war weakened, for a short period, the position of those in the foreign policy establishment who were interested in seeing the United States divert resources from the military and restructure its economy for more effective competition in international trade. The "splendid little war" played into the hands of members of the military-industrial complex who wanted to see Washington play the role of global police officer and extend its military commitments in various parts of the globe, especially in the Middle East.[24]

Moreover, the continued existence of the powerful Middle Eastern iron triangle and issue network makes it very difficult for Washington to adopt a lower profile in the region. The result will be new chapters in America's no-win strategy there. For example, pressures from pro-Israeli members of Congress will make it impossible for the administration to cut economic or military aid to Jerusalem. Sources close to Bush and Baker suggest that the administration may refuse to guarantee billions of dollars in loans to be used to absorb Jewish immigrants unless Israel terminates its settlement policies in the West Bank and adopts a more flexible approach to the peace process. But as the 1992 election campaign gets closer, it will become more and more difficult for the White House to challenge a Congress in which Democrats and Republicans will probably be vying to approve the larger aid package for Israel.[25]

However, Washington's continued support for the Likud government, especially if the *intifada* flares up again, will put growing pressure on the Arab members of the U.S.-led Middle Eastern coalition to demand that Bush do something to end the Israeli occupation of the West Bank and Gaza. The pressure brought to bear by the Arabs and the Europeans will create a diplomatic momentum, facilitated by extensive media coverage of the Middle East, that Bush or any other president will find difficult to check.

Massive arms sales to Saudi Arabia and other Arab allies will create the usual tensions between the president and Congress when the latter demands an increase in military support for Israel. The Jewish state's supporters in Washington have already begun a public relations campaign against Syria, demanding that the United States attempt to isolate Damascus diplomatically. Even if the administration resists that pressure, the anti-Syrian public campaign, like the anti-Iraqi one that took place before the Iraqi invasion of Kuwait, could lead to increased conflict between the United

States and Syria, against the possible backdrop of growing military tensions between Jerusalem and Damascus.

Moreover, Washington will ultimately begin to feel the regional political repercussions of the gulf war. Middle Eastern societies have always exhibited delayed reactions to domestic and regional crises. For example, it was several years after Israel's establishment in 1948 that dramatic political changes in the Arab world, including the rise of Gamal Abdel Nasser in Egypt, took place. Similarly, the Arab defeat in 1967 did not produce immediate repercussions. They emerged only in the early 1970s in the form of PLO terrorism, the 1973 Yom Kippur War, and the oil embargo.

The continuing socioeconomic problems of the Arab world, coupled with growing hostility toward Washington because of its support for Israel and its war against Iraq, could contribute to a similar delayed reaction to the gulf war. We might even see a resurgence of Saddamism, a combination of Arab radicalism and Islamic fundamentalism that might well outlive Saddam himself. The United States and the conservative Arab regimes that supported it during the war would then face a regional anti-American *intifada* that would threaten American citizens and interests as well as pro-American governments in the Middle East.

American neoconservatives, reflecting the pro-Likud line of the day, will argue that an anti-American Middle Eastern *intifada* proves that the question of the West Bank is a side show and that the United States and the West as a whole face a political, cultural, and military conflict with a new global threat: the forces of Arab radicalism and Islamic fundamentalism. Neoconservatives and other supporters of Israel will identify Palestinian nationalism with the new Arab Moslem bogeyman in the same way they tied it to the Soviet-sponsored terrorism network in the 1980s. They will then suggest that Israel can again serve as a strategic asset against radicalism in the region. And Israel will once again be the Middle Eastern neighborhood cop assisting the United States, the global policemen.

Members of the Arab oil lobby will see the new *intifada* in a different light and will echo the arguments made by the leaders of the moderate Arab regimes. Their thesis will be that the regional anti-American *intifada* is the result of continued Israeli occupation of the West Bank and Gaza. If only Washington could pressure

Israel to withdraw from the occupied territories and agree to establish an independent Palestinian state, the Middle East would know peace and stability. Unless Washington takes that step, they will argue, its oil and strategic interests in the gulf will again be threatened and new Saddams, who thrive on the festering Palestinian problem, will come to power.

The American administration will again find itself in a no-win situation. Following the neoconservatives' pro-Israeli advice will only strengthen anti-American attitudes in the Arab and Moslem worlds and may draw Washington into a diplomatic and military confrontation with radical forces in the region. Such a confrontation will increase the power of the militant Likud government with its annexationist agenda. Israel and its supporters will then be able to obtain increased funding for the American entitlement program for the Jewish state, and no incentives for diplomatic flexibility and economic reform will be created.

Following the pro-Arab line will lead to a growing conflict with Israel, with the usual destructive domestic consequences, without any guarantee that exerting pressure on the Jewish state will lead to the establishment of a Palestinian state or secure American interests in the region. Unable to "deliver Israel," Washington will risk growing antagonism from both sides.

The best-case scenario for the rival policy twins, the Israeli and the Arab oil lobbies, would be one in which American interests in the Middle East converged in opposition to a threat to both Israel and the moderate Arab regimes, as was the case with Saddam Hussein. But the chances for a rerun of that scenario seem to be slim.

Short of such a rerun, Washington will find itself trying to juggle its policies in response to conflicting pressures from Jerusalem and the pro-American Arab capitals. Those pressures will lead Washington to make new diplomatic and financial commitments in an attempt to deal with the Arab-Israeli conflict as well as with other sources of domestic and regional instability. Those commitments, coming at a time of increasing economic problems at home and rising trade tension with Europe and Japan, could finally lead to public realization of the costs involved in the Middle Eastern engagement. That realization might at last neutralize the power of the Middle Eastern iron triangle and issue network and eventually result in America's bidding farewell to the region.

The United States could avoid being forced by domestic and Middle Eastern pressures, as Great Britain was after World War II, to exit humiliated from the Middle East. Washington could devise a policy that would allow it to gradually and honorably disengage from the Middle East and begin shifting some of its security and diplomatic responsibilities to other global and regional players. A policy of disengagement would create incentives for the regional players to seek a diplomatic solution to their conflicts and to begin to reform their political and economic systems.

A U.S. policy of disengagement should include gradual elimination of American military commitments to the Arab military dictatorships and traditional monarchies. Loss of U.S. protection and aid might finally force those governments to make badly needed political changes. The possibility of shifts toward greater radicalism in those societies should certainly be of concern to Washington, and the United States should be prepared to deal in a rational way with anti-American violence. However, such developments should not deter the United States from taking steps that are in its own long-term interest.

After all, the transformation of those tradition-based societies is inevitable and will occur sooner or later as the new educated elites and popular frustration produce change. It is better that such revolutionary change take place at a time when Washington has ceased to be identified as a source of economic and military support for the declining elites and serves instead as a model of liberty and progress. Indeed, the United States should be willing to help all the Middle Eastern states adopt free-market systems and establish free-trade areas. The American private sector can help Middle Eastern businesses help themselves by encouraging Western investment, improving marketing techniques, and providing training programs to facilitate entrepreneurial activity.

Although democratic values may be alien to the political cultures of the Middle East, respect for the traditional market, the bazaar, is not. The expansion of islands of free enterprise in countries such as Egypt, Tunisia, and Jordan can strengthen their existing business communities and increase the power of the young professional middle class. Those segments of society, which tend to be Westernized and pragmatic in their political orientation, could eventually serve as a counterweight to both the decaying military regimes and the rising fundamentalist groups.

American expectations must be realistic. U.S. efforts should be low key and modest. In the next few years, political groups that espouse radical nationalism and Islamic fundamentalism are more likely to come to power in the Middle East than are groups that support democracy and free markets. Washington should avoid falling into the trap of castigating the new radical regimes as enemies of the West and automatically assuming that they will pose a serious political and military threat to the United States—which they will then do.

As the case of Iran suggests, after a bloody revolutionary period, even a radical fundamentalist regime like that in Tehran is in need of investment from and trade with the West, especially the United States. Such a regime, notwithstanding its revolutionary rhetoric, then opens to the West. Such openings inevitably play into the hands of the more Westernized professional classes. A United States that was neither hostile nor threatening could be a very important catalyst for change.[26]

Washington should also end economic aid to Israel and gradually reduce its military commitment to the Jewish state. Those changes would remove impediments to economic reform in Israel and encourage it to adopt a more moderate diplomatic posture. An Israel that rid itself of the burden of occupying a territory in which close to 2 million angry Arabs live and that moved to adopt an economic system based on free-market principles could become a prosperous and secure trading state. That Israel would cease to be dependent on the United States and could maintain and even strengthen its friendship with the American people.

Washington should welcome the possibility that France, the other Mediterranean European states, and the rest of the European Community will return to play a more active diplomatic and military role in the Middle East. The European Community might establish political and economic arrangements with the Middle Eastern states in a number of ways. Forming a Conference on Security and Cooperation in the Mediterranean and linking Israel, a Palestinian entity, and Jordan to the European Community as associate members are two examples of the constructive role Europe could play in the region with which it is connected by geographic proximity, demographic ties, and economic interests.

Most important, the United States should refrain from entering a new cycle of military commitment and diplomatic hyperactivity, which could lead political elites in the region to look again to Washington to solve their domestic and political problems and contain regional threats. By renewing military and diplomatic commitments, the United States would remove the incentives for those regimes to reform their political and economic systems, to create stable balance-of-power systems and viable security arrangements, and to reach diplomatic solutions to their conflicts. Instead of becoming a symbol of political and economic freedom, the United States would be identified with repressive regimes and become a symbol of evil in the eyes of new rising elites. Washington would also risk becoming a party to regional conflicts and being drawn into one military intervention after another.

The recent American intervention in the Persian Gulf and the revival of the peace process point to the dilemmas inherent in American policy toward the Middle East. President Bush and his advisers are already discovering that getting into the gulf crisis was easier than getting out. Instead of letting itself be lured into new entanglements, the United States should seize the opportunity provided by the end of the Cold War and the completion of the gulf war to finally replace its decaying Middle Eastern paradigm with a more cautious and disengaged approach, one that is commensurate with American interests and values and helps to advance the long-run security and prosperity of all the peoples of the Middle East.

Notes

Chapter 1

1. Francis Fukuyama, "The End of History?" *National Interest* 16 (Summer 1989): 4–5. On the debate on American foreign policy in the post–Cold War era, see John J. Mearsheimer, "Why We Will Soon Miss the Cold War," *Atlantic*, August 1990, pp. 35–42; Richard J. Barnet, "The Age of Globalism," *New Yorker*, July 16, 1990, pp. 46–60; and Earl C. Ravenal, "The Case for Adjustment," *Foreign Policy* 81 (Winter 1990–91): 3–19.

2. On the changes in American-German relations, see Daniel Burstein, *Euroquake* (New York: Simon & Schuster, 1991).

3. Quoted in Jerry W. Sanders, "Retreat from World Order: The Perils of Triumphalism," *World Policy Journal* 8, no. 2 (Spring 1991): 236.

4. William W. Kaufmann, *Glasnost, Perestroika, and U.S. Defense Spending* (Washington: Brookings Institution, 1990); and Stephen Alexis Cain and Natalie J. Goldring, "Restructuring the U.S. Military: Defense Needs in the 21st Century," Report by the Defense Budget Task Force of the Committee for National Security and the Defense Budget Project, Washington, March 1990.

5. See Richard Rosecrance, *The Rise of the Trading State: Commerce and Conquest in the Modern World* (New York: Basic Books, 1986).

6. Michael T. Klare, "Policing the Gulf—And the World," *Nation*, October 16, 1990, pp. 401–5, analyzes that debate. I borrowed the terms "geo-strategic" and "geo-economic" from Klare to refer to the two main orientations in that debate. Also see Edward N. Luttwak, "From Geo-Politics to Geo-Economics," *National Interest* 20 (Summer 1990): 17–23.

7. See Theodore Sorensen, "Rethinking National Security," *Foreign Affairs* 69, no. 3 (Summer 1990): 1–18.

8. John McCain, "The Need for Strategy in the New Postwar Era," *Armed Forces Journal International* 127, no. 6 (January 1990): 43–47.

9. Klare, p. 408.

10. For the libertarian approach to the subject, see Ted Galen Carpenter and Rosemary Fiscarelli, "America's Peace Dividend: Income Tax Reductions from the New Strategic Realities," Cato Institute White Paper, August 7, 1990. For a discussion of the debate on foreign policy on the political right, see Paul A. Gigot, "Isolationism Returns to Life on the Right," *Wall Street Journal*, August 17, 1990; and Irving Kristol, "In Search of Our National Interest," *Wall Street Journal*, June 7, 1990.

11. See Ted Galen Carpenter and R. Channing Rouse, "Perilous Panacea: The Military in the Drug War," Cato Institute Policy Analysis no. 128, February 15, 1990.

12. Coral Bell, "Why Russia Should Join NATO," *National Interest* 22 (Winter 1990–91): 37–47.

13. Charles Krauthammer, "The Unipolar Moment," *Foreign Affairs* 70, no. 1 (America and the World 1990–91): 23–33.

14. See Robert Higgs, "U.S. Military Spending in the Cold War Era: Opportunity Costs, Foreign Crises, and Domestic Constraints," Cato Institute Policy Analysis no. 114, November 30, 1988.

Chapter 2

1. James Blackwell, *Conventional Combat Priorities: An Approach for the New Strategic Era* (Washington: Center for Strategic and International Studies, May 1990), p. xx.

2. Ibid.

3. "Will America Be Safe When the Third World Goes Ballistic?" Transcript of "American Interests," PBS telecast, June 30, 1990, p. 9.

4. See Senate Committee on Armed Services, *Crisis in the Persian Gulf Region: U.S. Policy Options and Implications,* 101st Cong., 2d sess. (Washington: Government Printing Office, 1990). The members of the foreign policy establishment who testified before the committee criticized the tactics employed by the Bush administration in the gulf. None, however, raised any major questions about the basis for the administration's policy in the gulf.

5. For an example of calls for democraticizing the Arab world, see David Ignatius, "In the Coming New Gulf Order, We Must Help the Arab World Join the Global Democratic Revolution," *Washington Post,* August 26, 1990.

6. Quoted in Michael T. Klare, "Policing the Gulf—and the World," *Nation,* October 15, 1990, p. 420.

7. For a discussion of changes in Soviet policy in the Middle East, see Avigdor Haselkorn, "Does Soviet 'New Thinking' Apply in the Mideast?" *World & I,* June 1989, pp. 122–29.

8. Eliyahu Kanovsky, quoted in Hobart Rowen, "Singing OPEC's Tune," *Washington Post,* August 2, 1990. See also David R. Henderson, "Do We Need to Go to War for Oil?" Cato Institute Foreign Policy Briefing no. 4, October 24, 1990.

9. The Likud party, formed in 1973, brought together several right-wing groups, including the Herut and the Liberals. The party, which was initially led by Herut's leader, Menachem Begin, and has been committed to Israel's political and military control of the West Bank and Gaza (Greater Israel) and to the Jewish settlement drive in those Arab territories, which Israel occupied in the 1967 Six-Day War. The Likud won the 1977 Knesset (parliamentary) elections and has since dominated all of Israel's coalition governments. The party is currently headed by Yitzhak Shamir.

10. Semadar Peri, "Abraham Tamir Reveals: I Met with Members of the Iraqi Leadership," *Yediot Aharonot* (Hebrew), February 15, 1991.

11. See Leon T. Hadar, "Looking for an Israeli Gorbachev, a Palestinian de Klerk," International Papers, International Youth Crusade for Freedom, Fairfax, Va., September 1990.

12. For an expression of those concerns, see Thomas Dibacco, "Mideast Getting Short Shrift," *Washington Times,* June 25, 1990.

13. Brian Duffy, Louise Lief, Peter Cary, et al., "Saddam Most Dangerous Man in World, *U.S. News & World Report,* June 4, 1990, pp. 38–51.

14. Hassan bin Talal, "Moderate Arabs, Israelis Must Talk," *New York Times,* May 26, 1990. See also Itamar Rabinovich, "To Combat the Growing Iraqi Threat, *New York Times,* May 10, 1990.

15. Barry Rubin, "Reshaping the Middle East," *Foreign Affairs* 69, no. 3 (Summer 1990): 142.

16. Michael Collins Dunn, "Cold War or Not, Middle East Remains Key U.S. Security Concern," *Washington Report on Middle East Affairs,* July/August 1990, p. 27.

17. See Robert S. Greenberger, "Saudis' View of Israel Softens, but Kingdom May Back Away," *Wall Street Journal,* March 4, 1991. For a discussion of the close

relationship between the Israeli and Arab oil lobbies, see John Judis, "On the Home Front: The Gulf War's Strangest Bedfellows," *Washington Post*, June 23, 1991, or the longer version of the article that appeared in the May/June 1991 issue of *Tikkun*.

8. See "Bandar, the Son of the Saudi Defense Minister . . ." *Israeli Foreign Affairs*, March 21, 1991, p. 8. The relationship between Bandar and Solarz and the ties between the pro-Israeli and the pro-Saudi elements in Washington are also discussed extensively in Michael Massing, "The Way to War," *New York Review of Books*, March 28, 1991, pp. 17–22.

19. For a discussion of the group and its goals, see Robert A. Clark, "Things You Ought to Know: Who Funds the Pro-War Organizations," *Washington Report on Middle East Affairs*, February 1991, p. 19. For a reponse, see Frank C. Carlucci, "Those Were Cheap Shots," Letter to the editor, *Washington Report on Middle East Affairs*, April 1991, p. 5.

20. Quoted in "American Jews Are Divided over Wisdom of the Gulf War," *Special Interest Report*, American Council for Judaism, Alexandria, Va., January/February 1991, p. 1. Also, for AIPAC's role in the debate on Capitol Hill, see Rowland Evans and Robert Novak, "Israel's Call for Action," *Washington Post*, September 9, 1990.

21. *Washington Jewish Week*, January 17, 1991.

22. "American Jews."

23. Cokie Roberts quoted in "American Jews," p. 1.

24. On Kuwait's public relations efforts in Washington, see Glenn Frankel, "Iraq, Kuwait Waging an Old-Fashioned War of Propaganda," *Washington Post*, September 10, 1991.

25. On Turkey's concerns at the end of the Cold War, see Sam Cohen, "U.S., EC Rebuffs Force Turkey to Look Elsewhere," *Middle East Times*, July 24–30, 1990, p. 6.

26. On the Soviet moves, see Bill Keller, "In Moscow, Gulf Crisis Ranks Second," *New York Times*, September 1, 1991; Bill Keller, "Junior Partner No More, Gorbachev Raises Role to Major Player in Crisis," *New York Times*, September 11, 1991; Thomas L. Friedman, "Big-2 Horse Trade," *New York Times*, January 31, 1991; and Michael Dobbs, "Kremlin Seeks Distance from U.S. on War," *Washington Post*, February 6, 1991.

27. For initial reactions on the left to the gulf crisis, see Robert L. Borosage, "Countering Bush's Gambit in the Gulf," *Nation*, September 24, 1990, pp. 293–8.

28. Jeane Kirkpatrick, Testimony before House Committee on Armed Services, December 4–20, 1990, in *Crisis in the Persian Gulf: Sanctions, Diplomacy and War* (Washington: Government Printing Office), p. 734.

29. See, for example, Paul Gigot, "Iraq: An American Screw-Up," *National Interest* 22 (Winter 1990): 3–10.

30. See Al Miskin, "Mediations," *Middle East Report*, January/February 1991, p. 33.

31. Laurie Mylroie, "The Baghdad Alternative," *Orbis* 32, no. 3 (Summer 1988): 339–54.

32. Judith Miller and Laurie Mylroie, *Saddam Hussein and the Crisis in the Gulf* (New York: Times Books/Random House, 1991).

33. Quoted in Peri.

34. For the Iran-Contra angle, see Samuel Segev, *The Iranian Triangle* (New York: Free Press, 1988).

35. On the developments leading to the war, see John Newhouse, "The Diplomatic Round: Misreadings," *New Yorker*, February 18, 1991, pp. 72–78; and Massing.

Chapter 3

1. The discussion between Welles and Elath is described in Eliahu Elath, *The Struggle for Statehood* (Hebrew) (Tel Aviv: Am Oved, 1983), vol. 1, pp. 144–45.

2. James M. Buchanan and Gordon Tullock, *The Calculus of Consent: Logical Foundation of Constitutional Democracy* (Ann Arbor: University of Michigan Press, 1965), p. 286.

3. Ibid.

4. Ibid., p. 287.

5. Ibid.

6. Hugh Heclo, "Issue Networks and the Executive Establishment," in *Public Administration: Concepts and Cases*, ed. Richard J. Stillman II (Boston: Houghton Mifflin, 1983), p. 417.

7. For a complete critical analysis of the Israeli lobby's efforts in the United States, see Richard H. Curtiss, *Stealth PACs: How Israel's American Lobby Took Control of U.S. Middle East Policy* (Washington: American Educational Trust, 1989). For a more recent discussion of the lobby, see Lloyd Grove, "On the March for Israel," *Washington Post*, June 13, 1991; and Lloyd Grove, "The Men with Muscle," *Washington Post*, June 14, 1991. For a discussion of the network of terrorism experts in Washington, see Edward Herman and Gerry O'Sullivan, *The Terrorism Industry: The Experts and Institutions That Shape Our View of Terror* (New York: Pantheon Books, 1989).

8. For a critical study of the Arab oil lobby, see Steven Emerson, *The American House of Saud: The Secret Petrodollar Connection* (New York: Franklin Watts, 1985).

9. For a revealing discussion of the way American diplomatic pressure on Kuwait and other Arab countries helped to undercut Arab efforts to reach a diplomatic solution to the Persian Gulf crisis, see Pierre Salinger and Eric Laurent, *Secret Dossier: The Hidden Agenda behind the Gulf War* (New York: Penguin Books, 1991). See also Christopher Layne, "Why the Gulf War Was Not in the National Interest," *Atlantic*, July 1991, pp. 55, 65–81.

10. Robert Higgs, "U.S. Military Spending in the Cold War Era: Opportunity Costs, Foreign Crises, and Domestic Constraints," Cato Institute Policy Analysis no. 114, November 30, 1988, p. 17.

11. Heclo, p. 418.

12. For an analysis of public and elite attitudes toward the Arab-Israeli conflict, see Cheryl A. Rubenberg, *Israel and the American National Interest* (Urbana and Chicago: University of Illinois Press, 1986), especially chap. 8.

13. Robert Higgs, *Crisis and Leviathan: Critical Episodes in the Growth of American Government* (New York and Oxford: Oxford University Press, 1987).

14. On changes in American media coverage of the Arab-Israeli conflict, see Ze'ev Chafetz, *Double Vision: How the Press Distorts America's View of the Middle East* (New York: William Morrow, 1985); and Edmund Ghareeb, *Split Vision: The Portrayal of Arabs in the American Media* (Washington: American-Arab Affairs Council, 1983).

15. See Arthur Hertzberg, *Being Jewish in America: The Modern Experience* (New York: Herzl, 1979), pp. 210–27.

16. For a discussion of those points, see William Quandt, *Decade of Decision* (Berkeley: University of California Press, 1977); and Joe Stork, "Israel as a Strategic Asset," *MERIP Report*, May 1982, pp. 3–13.

17. See David Fromkin, *A Peace to End All Peace: The Fall of the Ottoman Empire and the Creation of the Modern Middle East* (New York: Avon Books, 1989), especially part 3, "Britain Is Drawn into the Middle Eastern Quagmire."

18. For studies on the origins of the modern Middle East, see J. C. Hurewitz, *The Struggle for Palestine* (New York: Schocken, 1976); and Christopher Sykes, *Crossroads to Israel, 1917–1948* (Bloomington and London: Indiana University Press, 1973).

19. Quoted in Fromkin, p. 297.

20. Quoted in Wilbur Crane Eveland, *Ropes of Sand: America's Failure in the Middle East* (New York: W. W. Norton, 1980), p. 20.

21. Ibid., pp. 35–55.

22. See Elie Kedourie, *England and the Middle East: The Destruction of the Ottoman Empire, 1914–1921* (Hassocks, Sussex: Harvester, 1978).

23. See Leonard Stein, *The Balfour Declaration* (London: Valentine Mitchell, 1961).

24. Quoted in Fromkin, p. 257.

25. See Albert Hourani, *The Emergence of the Modern Middle East* (Berkeley: University of California Press, 1981).

26. See Daniel Yergin, *The Prize: The Epic Quest for Oil, Money and Power* (New York: Simon & Schuster, 1991), especially part 2, "The Global Struggle." See also Leonard P. Liggio, "Oil and American Foreign Policy," *Libertarian Review,* July/August 1979, pp. 62–69; and Sheldon L. Richman, "Where Angels Fear to Tread: The United States and the Persian Gulf Conflict," Cato Institute Policy Analysis no. 90, September 9, 1987.

27. Yergin, pp. 203–6.

28. Ibid., pp. 409–31. See also Theodore Draper, "American Hubris: From Truman to the Persian Gulf," *New York Review of Books,* July 16, 1987, pp. 40–48.

29. Richman, "Where Angels Fear to Tread," p. 22.

30. Liggio, p. 65.

31. Richman, "Where Angels Fear to Tread," p. 23.

32. Yergin, pp. 391–408.

33. See Peter Grose, *Israel in the Mind of America* (New York: Alfred A. Knopf, 1983).

34. Paul Johnson, *Modern Times: The World from the Twenties to the Eighties* (New York: Harper & Row, 1983), p. 480.

35. On Eisenhower's Middle Eastern policy, see Steven L. Spiegel, *The Other Arab-Israeli Conflict: Making America's Middle East Policy from Truman to Reagan* (Chicago: University of Chicago Press, 1985), pp. 50–93.

36. For an account of the complex ties among the Soviet Union, communism, and the Arab world, see Mohammad Heikal, *The Sphinx and the Commissar: The Rise and Fall of Soviet Influence in the Arab World* (London: Collins, 1978); and Patrick Seale, *Asad: The Struggle for the Middle East* (Los Angeles: University of California Press, 1988).

37. Quoted In Jonathan Steele, *Soviet Power* (New York: Simon & Schuster, 1983), p. 184.

38. Ibid., pp. 180–81.

39. See Galia Golan, *Yom Kippur and After: The Soviet Union and the Middle East Crisis* (Cambridge: Cambridge University Press, 1975).

40. L. Carl Brown, *International Politics and the Middle East: Old Rules, Dangerous Game* (Princeton, N.J.: Princeton University Press, 1984), p. 171.

41. For an account of the Egyptian-Israeli peace process, see William Quandt, *Camp David: Peacemaking and Politics* (Washington: Brookings Institution, 1986).

42. "Muslim Militia Leader Seeks to Block Talks," *New York Times,* October 19, 1991.

43. Brown, p. 16.

44. On the TWA hijacking and its repercussions, see David C. Martin, *Best Laid Plans* (New York: Simon & Schuster, 1988); and Jane Mayer and Doyle McManus, *Landslide: The Unmaking of the President 1984–1988* (Boston: Houghton Mifflin, 1988).

45. Sheldon L. Richman stresses the need to understand the interactions between the supposedly isolated crises in the region and the role U.S. policy played in their evolution. Sheldon L. Richman, "'Ancient History': U.S. Conduct in the Middle East since World War II and the Folly of Intervention," Cato Institute Policy Analysis no. 159, August 16, 1991, p. 2.

46. See Ze'ev Schiff and Ehud Ya'ari, *Milchement Sholal* (Hebrew) (Tel Aviv: Schocken, 1984).

47. See Ronald Reagan, "The Mideast: Into the Quagmire," *Time*, November 12, 1990, p. 66, excerpted from Ronald Reagan, *An American Life* (New York: Simon & Schuster, 1990).

48. See Jimmy Carter, *Keeping Faith: Memoirs of a President* (New York: Bantam Books, 1982), p. 491.

49. Yergin, p. 644. On American-Iranian relations, see also Jonathan Kwitny, *Endless Enemies: The Making of an Unfriendly World* (New York: Penguin Books, 1984), pp. 179–204.

50. Yergin, p. 643.

51. Ibid., p. 635.

52. Ibid., p. 634.

53. Ibid.

54. James Ridgeway, *The March to War* (New York: Four Walls Eight Windows, 1991), p. 10.

55. Ibid., p. 12.

56. Yergin, p. 758.

57. For a discussion of the Saudi role in Reagan's "secret wars," see Ridgeway, pp. 8–12; and Jonathan Marshall, "Saudi Arabia and the Reagan Doctrine," *MERIP Report*, November/December 1988, pp. 12–17. On the possible Israeli role in the October Surprise, see Richard H. Curtiss, "Reprise of the October Surprise," *Washington Report on Middle East Affairs*, May/June 1991, pp. 11–12. On Israel's role in the Iran-Contra affair and its blackmail power over Bush, see Giora Shamis, "Bush Approved and Participated in the Iran-Contra Affair," *Monitin* (Hebrew), May 2–16, 1991, pp. 8–10.

58. Ridgeway, pp. 12–15; and Murray Waas, "What We Gave Saddam for Christmas," *Village Voice*, December 18, 1990.

Chapter 4

1. For a discussion of the effects of the war on the Israeli-American relationship, see Leon T. Hadar, "U.S.-Israeli Relations: Coping with the Post–Cold War Blues and Surviving the Persian Gulf Hangover," *Middle East Insight* 7, no. 6 (May/June 1991): 40–46.

2. Thomas L. Friedman, "Baker Rebukes Israel on Peace Terms," *New York Times*, June 14, 1990.

3. On the irritation of the Bush administration with Shamir, see Thomas L. Friedman, "After Bush Puts PLO on Sidelines: Is Shamir the Man for U.S. to Press?" *New York Times*, June 22, 1990.

4. Andrew Rosenthal, "Bush and Shamir Show Solidarity," *New York Times*, December 12, 1990; and John M. Goshko, "Shamir Calls Bush Talks Reassuring," *Washington Post*, December 12, 1990.

5. Thomas L. Friedman, "Hard Times, Better Allies," *New York Times*, January 2, 1991.

6. Joel Brinkley, "Missiles Provoke Debate in Tel Aviv: Is It a Patriotic Duty to Stay in City?" *New York Times*, January 29, 1991.

7. See Peretz Kidron, "Israel and the U.S.: Heavy Bill for Forbearance," *Middle East International*, January 25, 1991, pp. 6–7.

8. See Peretz Kidron, "Shamir Gains from the Fallout," *Middle East International*, February 8, 1991, pp. 3–5.

9. Joel Brinkley, "Israel, Enduring Missiles, Expects a Political Victory," *New York Times*, January 27, 1991.

10. See Leon T. Hadar, "Israel Prepares for a Postwar Middle East," *World & I*, April 1991, pp. 38–39.

11. Leon T. Hadar, "Israel: Watching and Waiting," *World & I*, December 1990, pp. 44–45; and Kidron, pp. 6–7.

12. John E. Yang, "House Panel Approves $15.8 Billion to Help Cover Added Gulf War Costs," *Washington Post*, June 6, 1991.

13. Jackson Diehl, "Israel Said to Plan Settlement Buildup," *Washington Post*, February 14, 1991; and Jackson Diehl, "Israeli Housing Plan Faces U.S. Objections," *Washington Post*, April 5, 1991.

14. Thomas L. Friedman, "Baker Cites Israel for Settlements," *New York Times*, June 23, 1991.

15. David Hoffman, "U.S. Drawing Up Peace Plan for Post War Mideast," *Washington Post*, February 1, 1991.

16. Thomas L. Friedman, "Big-2 Horse Trade," *New York Times*, January 31, 1991.

17. President Bush, Text of address to Congress on the end of the gulf war, *New York Times*, March 7, 1991.

18. Haynes Johnson and Richard Morin, "Spoils of War: Victors Gain Public's Confidence," *Washington Post*, March 10, 1991.

19. See Leon T. Hadar, "Letter from Washington: Was It All Worth It?" *Journal of Palestine Studies* 20, no. 6 (Summer 1991): 124–32; and Gary Lee, "Pro-Israel Lobby Cold to Concessions," *Washington Post*, March 20, 1991.

20. Jackson Diehl and David Hoffman, "U.S. Miscalculated Readiness for Peace," *Washington Post*, May 17, 1991.

21. See Alan Cowell, "Israel and Arabs, Face to Face, Begin Quest for Middle East Peace," *New York Times*, October 31, 1991.

22. For a comprehensive analysis of the debate over the loan guarantee, see Leon T. Hadar, "High Noon in Washington: The Shootout over the Loan Guarantees," *Journal of Palestine Studies* 21, no. 2 (Winter 1992): 401–16.

23. See Michael McQueen, "Voters Support Bush's Hard Line on Israeli Aid: Issue May Add to a Backlash against the Nation," *Wall Street Journal*, September 26, 1991; and "Sentiment Swings against Israel" in "Washington Wire," *Wall Street Journal*, December 13, 1991.

24. See Jackson Diehl, "Shamir Approves New Military Site, Reaffirms Intent to Settle West Bank," *Washington Post*, December 4, 1991; and Jackson Diehl, "New Israeli Budget Funds Expansion of Settlements," *Washington Post*, January 3, 1992.

25. See Salah Khalaf (Abu Iyad), "Lowering the Sword," *Foreign Policy* 78 (Spring 1990): 91–112.

26. For a discussion of relations betweenn state and religion in Israel and the status of civil rights in the country, see Bernard Avishai, *The Tragedy of Zionism: Revolution and Democracy in the Land of Israel* (New York: Farrar, Straus, Giroux, 1985).

27. Quoted in Leon T. Hadar, "Perestroika in the Promised Land?" *Reason,* October 1991, p. 32.

28. For a history of the intellectual roots of Zionism, see Walter Laqueur, *A History of Zionism* (New York: Holt, Rinehart & Winston, 1972).

29. For a discussion of Israel's political economy from a free-market perspective, see Ezra Sohar, *Sodom or Helem?* (Hebrew) (Tel Aviv: Dvir, 1987), p. 321.

30. Alvin Rabushka, *Scorecard on the Israeli Economy: A Review of 1989* (Jerusalem: Institute for Advanced Strategic and Political Studies, February 1990), pp. 15–27.

31. Sohar, p. 321.

32. Ibid., p. 122.

33. Yifat Nevo in *Ha'aretz,* March 26, 1986; and Beni Barak in *Yediot Aharonot,* September 17, 1982.

34. Sohar, p. 122.

35. Alvin Rabushka et al., *Toward Growth: A Blueprint for Economic Rebirth in Israel* (Jerusalem: Institute for Advanced Strategic and Political Studies, December 6, 1988), cited in Warren Brookes, "Israel's Other Enemy: Its Own Socialism," *Washington Times,* December 4, 1988.

36. Sohar, p. 123.

37. Leon T. Hadar, "Israel and America: Is It Divorce Time?" *Washington Post,* January 21, 1991.

38. See Peter Grose, *Israel in the Mind of America* (New York: Alfred A. Knopf, 1983); and Clark Clifford (with Richard Holbrooke), "Serving the President: The Truman Years," *New Yorker,* March 25, 1991, pp. 40–71.

39. Paul Johnson, *Modern Times: The World from the Twenties to the Eighties* (New York: Harper & Row, 1983), p. 485.

40. See Uri Bialer, *Between East and West: Israel's Foreign Policy Orientation 1948–1956* (Cambridge: Cambridge University Press, 1990).

41. See Donald Neff, *Warriors at Suez: Eisenhower Takes America into the Middle East* (New York: Simon & Schuster, 1981). For background on the debates in Israel in the 1950s regarding its foreign policy orientation, see Michael Bar-Zohar, *Bridge over the Mediterranean* (Hebrew) (Tel Aviv: Am Hasefer, 1964); and Israel Be'er, *Israel's Security: Yesterday, Today, Tomorrow* (Hebrew) (Tel Aviv: Amikam, 1966). Be'er's controversial book criticizes Israeli leaders for aligning themselves with the West and missing an opportunity to adopt a more nonaligned policy.

42. For the development of Johnson's policies after the 1967 war, see Mitchell G. Bard, "The Turning Point in United States Relations with Israel: The 1968 Sale of Phantom Jets," *Middle East Review* 20, no. 4 (Summer 1988): 50–58.

43. For some of the domestic repercussions of the 1967 war, see Donald Neff, *Warriors for Jerusalem: The Six Days That Changed the Middle East* (New York: Simon & Schuster, 1984).

44. For U.S. policy in the Middle East during the Kissinger and Carter periods, see Milton Viorst, *Sands of Sorrow: Israel's Journey from Independence* (New York: Harper & Row, 1987); Seymour M. Hersh, *The Price of Power: Kissinger in the Nixon White House* (New York: Summit Books, 1983); and Jimmy Carter, *Keeping Faith: Memoirs of a President* (New York: Bantam Books, 1982).

45. See William Quandt, *Decade of Decision* (Berkeley: University of California Press, 1977).

46. Eric Rozenman, *United States–Israel Strategic Cooperations: Conversations and Comments* (Washington: Jewish Institute for National Security Affairs, 1989), pp. 3–5.

47. Ibid.

48. For a discussion of neoconservatism and its role in Reagan's Israeli policy, see Leon T. Hadar, "Camelot to Conservatism," *Jerusalem Post,* February 20, 1981.

49. Quoted in Joe Stork, "Israel As a Strategic Asset," *MERIP Report,* May 1982, p. 7.

50. Ze'ev Schiff, "The Green Light," *Foreign Policy* 50 (Spring 1983): 73–85.

51. See James Adams, *Israel and South Africa: The Unnatural Alliance* (New York: Quartet Books, 1984); and Benjamin Beit-Hallahmi, *The Israel Connection: Who Israel Arms and Why* (New York: Pantheon, 1987).

52. See Leon T. Hadar, "The Arab Gulf States," *Journal of Defense and Diplomacy,* January 1988, pp. 46–50.

53. See Anwar el-Sadat, *In Search of Identity: An Autobiography* (New York: Harper & Row, 1978).

54. Cited in Roli Rosen, "The Age of the Conventional War Has Ended: The Battlefield of the Future Is the Intifada," *Ha'aretz* (Hebrew), May 12, 1989, pp. 7–11.

55. Quoted in Alisa Solomon, "Cancelling Israel's Credit Card," *Village Voice,* August 14, 1990, pp. 27–32. See also Donald Neff, "Bob Dole Squares Up to Israel," *Middle East International,* April 27, 1990, pp. 3–5.

56. Andrew Meisels, "Israel Warned of Eroding U.S. Support," *Washington Times,* May 24, 1990.

57. Joe Stork and Rashid Khalidi, "Washington's Game in the Middle East," *Middle East Report* 20, nos. 3–4 (May/August 1990): 9–11, 16.

58. William E. Schmidt, "Americans' Support for Israel: Solid, but Not the Rock It Was," *New York Times,* July 9, 1990.

59. See Victor Ostrovsky, *By Way of Deception: The Making and Unmaking of a Mossad Officer* (New York: St. Martin's, 1980).

60. See Wolf Blitzer, *Territory of Lies* (New York: Harper & Row, 1989).

61. For a discussion of the tensions between supporters of Israel and black leaders caused by the Jackson presidential campaign, see Paul Findley, *They Dare to Speak Out: People and Institutions Confront Israel's Lobby* (Westport, Conn.: Lawrence Hill, 1985), pp. 136–38.

62. On Buchanan's views on the Middle East and the tensions between him and supporters of Israel, see Leon T. Hadar, "The 'Neocons': From the Cold War to the 'Global Intifada,'" *Washington Report on Middle East Affairs,* April 1991, pp. 27–28.

63. Stork and Khalidi.

64. Paul Eidelberg, "Towards a New Israeli Foreign Policy," *Washington Jewish Week,* July 19, 1990, p. 10.

65. See Nadav Safran, *Israel: The Embattled Ally* (Cambridge, Mass.: Harvard University Press, 1978), pp. 359–81.

66. Barry Rubin, "Reshaping the Middle East," *Foreign Affairs* 69, no. 3 (Summer 1990): 131–46.

67. Charles Krauthammer, "The New Crescent of Crisis: Global Intifada," *Washington Post,* February 16, 1990.

68. On the role *U.S. News & World Report* and other publications played in mobilizing public support for the war, see Jim Naureckas, "Media on the March," *Extra* 3, no. 8 (November/December 1990): 1–9.

69. Shimon Schiffer, "We Are Not a Strategic Asset?" *Yediot Aharonot*, August 10, 1990, p. 7.

70. Quoted in Jackson Diehl, "Israel Fears Sideline Role Jeopardizes Its Ties to U.S.," *Washington Post*, August 16, 1990.

71. On Israeli lobbying for war in Congress, see Rowland Evans and Robert Novak, "Israel's Call for Action," *Washington Post*, September 24, 1990. On AIPAC's lobbying, see "American Jews Are Divided over Wisdom of the Gulf War: Jewish Groups Lean to Force While Most Religious Bodies Urge Reliance on Sanctions and Diplomacy," *Special Interest Report*, American Council for Judaism, Alexandria, Va., January/February 1991, p. 1.

72. On the efforts by Solarz and Lantos, see *Israeli Foreign Affairs*, March 21, 1991, p. 8.

73. Charles Krauthammer, "The Ground War: Hold It Off," *Washington Post*, February 1, 1991.

74. Norman Podhoretz, "Unleash the Israelis," *New York Times*, February 1, 1991.

75. Jackson Diehl, "Levy Links Palestinian, Arab Talks," *Washington Post*, February 1, 1991.

76. See Stephen Solarz, "Get Involved: U.N. Must Oust Saddam," *Wall Street Journal*, April 17, 1991; and Charles Krauthammer, "Good Morning, Vietnam," *Washington Post*, April 19, 1991.

Chapter 5

1. Jackson Diehl, "Israel Said to Plan Settlement Buildup, *Washington Post*, February 14, 1991.

2. Clyde R. Mark, "Israel: U.S. Foreign Assistance Facts," Congressional Research Service Issue Brief, Washington, May 12, 1989, p. 4.

3. Keith Bradsher, "U.S. Aid to Israel: $77 Billion since 1967," *New York Times*, September 22, 1990.

4. Some parts of this chapter are based on Leon T. Hadar, "Reforming Israel—Before It's Too Late," *Foreign Policy* 81 (Winter 1990–91): 106–27.

5. Quoted in Allen Graubard, "From Commentary to Tikkun: The Past and Future of Progressive Jewish Intellectuals," *Middle East Report*, May/June 1980, p. 18.

6. See William Quandt, *Decade of Decision* (Berkeley: University of California Press, 1977); Donald Neff, *Warriors for Jerusalem: The Six Days That Changed the Middle East* (New York: Simon & Schuster, 1984); and Michael Bar Zohar, *Embassies in Crisis* (New York: Prentice Hall, 1970).

7. See Uri Bialer, *Between East and West: Israel's Foreign Policy Orientation 1948–1956* (Cambridge: Cambridge University Press, 1990).

8. Quoted in *Zionism: An Anthology of the History of the Zionist Movement and the Jewish Population in Israel*, ed. A. Gal (Hebrew) (Tel Aviv: University of Tel Aviv Press, 1981), p. 99.

9. Ibid., pp. 97–145.

10. Daniel Doron, quoted in Leon T. Hadar, "Perestroika in the Promised Land?" *Reason*, October 1990, p. 32.

11. For studies on the changes in Israeli foreign policy, see Nadav Safran, *Israel: The Embattled Ally* (Cambridge, Mass.: Harvard University Press, 1978); Michael Brecher, *The Foreign Policy System of Israel* (New Haven, Conn.: Yale University

Press, 1972); and Michael Brecher, *Decisions in Israel's Foreign Policy* (London: Oxford University Press, 1972).

12. For a review of the debate in Israel's foreign policy establishment and the fall of Sharett, see Livia Rokach, *Israel's Sacred Terrorism* (Washington: AAUG Press, 1980).

13. For the struggle in Labor on foreign policy issues, see Yossi Beilin, *The Price of a Union: The Labor Party until the Yom-Kippur War* (Hebrew) (Tel Aviv: Revivim, 1980).

14. On Peres's efforts to facilitate a solution with Jordan, see Yossi Melman and Daniel Raviv, *An Hostile Partnership: The Secret Relations between Israel and Jordan* (Hebrew) (Tel Aviv: Metam, 1987).

15. For an analysis of the demographic and political factors behind the fall of the Israeli Labor party, see Leon T. Hadar, "The Decline and Fall of the Israeli Labor Party," *World & I*, March 1990, pp. 598–615.

16. Quoted in Alisa Solomon, "Cancelling Israel's Credit Card," *Village Voice*, August 14, 1990.

17. Jackson Diehl, "New Israeli Budget Funds Expansion of Settlements," *Washington Post*, January 3, 1992.

18. See Benjamin Beit-Hallahmi, "A 'Miracle' Made in Moscow and Washington," *Middle East Report* 20, nos. 3–4 (May/June–July/August 1990): 46–48.

19. For a discussion of the impact of the Bush administration's recent tough stand on Israeli politics, see Amy Dockser Marcus, "Israel Begins Public Soul Searching about Extent of Dependence on U.S. Aid," *Wall Street Journal*, October 11, 1991; Amy Dockser Marcus, "Public Debate Emerges as Israel Seeks to Reduce Its Dependence on U.S. Aid," *Wall Street Journal*, December 12, 1991; Leon T. Hadar, "U.S. Pressure Places Israel at a Crossroads," *Atlanta Journal and Constitution*, September 22, 1991; and Leon T. Hadar, "Bush's Bombshell Is Shattering the Status Quo in Israel," *Washington Report on Middle East Affairs*, November 1991, pp. 9–10.

20. Joseph Pelzman, "Sweetheart Deal: The U.S.-Israel FTA Is Not a Model: It Was Mostly Geopolitical," *International Economy*, March/April 1989, pp. 53–56.

Chapter 6

1. *Crisis in the Persian Gulf Region: U.S. Policy Options and Implications*, Hearings before the U.S. Senate Committee on Armed Services (Washington: Government Printing Office, 1990), p. 278.

2. Ibid.

3. For a discussion of those issues, see Paul Kennedy, *The Rise and Fall of the Great Powers* (New York: Random House, 1987); Walter Russell Mead, *Mortal Splendor: The American Empire in Transition* (Boston: Houghton Mifflin, 1987); Robert Giplin, *War and Change in World Politics* (Cambridge: Cambridge University Press, 1981); Robert O. Keohane, *After Hegemony: Cooperation and Discord in the World Political Economy* (Princeton, N.J.: Princeton University Press, 1984); and *Collective Defense or Strategic Independence? Alternative Strategies for the Future*, ed. Ted Galen Carpenter (Lexington, Mass.: Lexington Books, 1989).

4. Patricia S. Schroeder, Foreword to *NATO at 40: Confronting a Changing World*, ed. Ted Galen Carpenter (Lexington, Mass.: Lexington Books, 1990), p. xii.

5. R. W. Apple, Jr., "Oil, Saddam Hussein and the Reemergence of America as the Superpower," *New York Times*, August 20, 1991.

6. *Le Monde,* December 6, 1991. On the French position and maneuvering, see also Robert Swann, "What Was Mitterrand Up To?" *Middle East International,* January 25, 1991, pp. 15–16; and Paul Lewis, "France and 3 Arab States Issue an Appeal to Hussein," *New York Times,* January 15, 1991.

7. Quoted in Alan Riding, "French Maneuvering: Taking the Lead for Europe," *New York Times,* January 6, 1991.

8. Alan Riding, "French Seem Willing to Work with U.S. in the Middle East," *New York Times,* March 14, 1991. See also William Drozdiak, "EC Leaving Diplomacy to U.S.," *Washington Post,* March 8, 1991.

9. Quoted in William Drozdiak, "Mitterrand and Bush to Nurture Rapport," *Washington Post,* March 14, 1991. On the changing French position, see also Dan Balz, "French Envoy Urges Israel to 'Engage,' " *Washington Post,* March 12, 1991.

10. Shada Islam, "European Community: Keeping Up the Pressure," *Middle East International,* March 22, 1991, pp. 8–9.

11. Lionel Barber, "New World Order: The View from America," *Europe,* March 1991, p. 8.

12. Daniel Singer, "Braving the New World Order," *Nation,* March 25, 1991, p. 368.

13. John M. Goshko, "Baker Told Europe Wants Role in Any Middle East Peace Talks," *Washington Post,* April 18, 1991.

14. Maxim Ghilan, "After the Storm," *Israel and Palestine Political Report,* March 1991, p. 7. On the reaction in the Arab world, especially in North Africa, see also Peter Hiett, "The Maghreb: Government and People," *Middle East International,* February 8, 1991, p. 14; and Howard LaFranchi, "France Tries to Reconcile Role in Gulf War with History of Strong Arab Ties," *Christian Science Monitor,* February 1, 1991.

15. Charles Krauthammer, "Bless Our Pax Americana," *Washington Post,* March 22, 1991. For a similar view, see Joshua Muravchik, "At Last, Pax Americana," *New York Times,* January 24, 1991.

16. Josef Joffe, "In the Gulf, Allies Are Doing Their Part," *New York Times,* October 9, 1990.

17. Thatcher made her remarks before an audience at the American Enterprise Institute in Washington. The quote is from David Broder, "The Thatcher View: America Must Lead," *Washington Post,* March 13, 1991. Thatcher also dismissed Europe's ability to form an independent military group, saying that "the Community is not a security organization. It has foreign policy cooperation, but when it comes to taking practical steps, you have to rely on the few countries that have been used to acting in that way."

18. On the transition to American domination in the Middle East after 1956, see Donald Neff, *Warriors at Suez: Eisenhower Takes America into the Middle East* (New York: Simon & Schuster, 1981).

19. For sources of American-European competition in the Middle East, see *Security in the Middle East: Regional Change and Great Power Strategies,* ed. Samuel F. Wells, Jr., and Mark Bruzonsky (Boulder, Colo.: Westview, 1987), especially chap. 11, Robert J. Lieber, "Middle East Oil and the Industrial Democracies: Conflict and Cooperation in the Aftermath," pp. 217–25.

20. See David D. Newsome, "America Engulfed," *Foreign Policy* 43 (Summer 1981): 26.

21. On the results of American-Israeli cooperation in the Reagan era, see Leon T. Hadar, "Reforming Israel—Before It's Too Late," *Foreign Policy* 81 (Winter 1990–91): 106–27.

22. On the decline of America's Middle Eastern paradigm and the reaction of the American foreign policy establishment, see Leon T. Hadar, "The Rise of the Middle Eastern Bogeyman: Sliding toward Post-Cold-War Interventionism," Cato Institute Foreign Policy Briefing no. 2, September 5, 1990. On the decline of the Soviet threat in the Middle East, see Avigdor Haselkorn, "Does Soviet 'New Thinking' Apply in the Mideast?" *World & I*, June 1989, pp. 122–29.

23. See Hobart Rowen, "Singing OPEC's Tune," *Washington Post*, August 2, 1990; and David R. Henderson, "Do We Need to Go to War for Oil?" Cato Institute Foreign Policy Briefing no. 4, October 24, 1990.

24. See Leon T. Hadar, "Israel and America: Is It Divorce Time?" *Washington Post*, January 21, 1990; and Leon T. Hadar, "Israel As a 'Strategic Asset,'" *Christian Science Monitor*, September 28, 1990.

25. See Paul E. Gallis, "U.S.–West European Affairs: Responding to a Changing Relationship," Congressional Research Service Issue Brief, Washington, April 3, 1991; and Paul E. Gallis and Steven J. Woehrel, "Germany after Unification: Implications for U.S. Interests," Congressional Research Service Issue Brief, Washington, March 22, 1991.

26. Michael T. Klare discussed the debate between the geoeconomic and the geostrategic schools of thought in "Policing the Gulf—And the World," *Nation*, October 15, 1990. Three months before the gulf crisis, James Blackwell, *Conventional Combat Priorities: An Approach for a New Strategic Era* (Washington: Center for Strategic and International Studies, May 1990), proposed focusing American strategic planning on involvement in conflicts in the Middle East, including possible war with Iraq.

27. See, for example, Anthony H. Cordesman, "America's New Combat Culture," *New York Times*, February 28, 1991.

28. Nicholas Henderson, former British ambassador to the United States, analyzed the benefits Great Britain drew from the gulf war, including the strengthened special relationship with Washington, in "The Special Relationship," *The Spectator*, January 19, 1991, pp. 11–12. For more analysis of the issue, see Walter Russell Mead, "Germany and Japan—Dragging Their Boots," *New York Times*, February 3, 1991; and Alexander MacLeod, "Britain Outlines a Plan for Mideast Peace," *Christian Science Monitor*, February 5, 1991.

29. See Leon T. Hadar, "U.S.–Israeli Relations: Coping with the Post–Cold War Blues and Surviving the Persian Gulf Hangover," *Middle East Insight* 7, no. 6 (May/June 1991): 40–46.

30. Quoted in Tomislav Sunic, "The Gulf Crisis in Europe," *Chronicles*, May 1991, p. 49.

31. Walter S. Mossberg, Urban C. Lehner, and Fredrick Kempe, "Some in U.S. Ask Why Germany, Japan Bear So Little of Gulf War," *Wall Street Journal*, January 11, 1991. For an analysis of the debate on burden sharing during the war, see Gary J. Pagliano, "Iraq/Kuwait Crisis: The International Response and Burdensharing Issues," Congressional Research Service Issue Brief, Washington, March 25, 1991. See also Hobart Rowen, "The Free-Lunch Countries," *Washington Post*, November 3, 1990.

32. See Doug Henwood, "After the Cold War—Economic War," *Middle East Report* 21, no. 2 (March/April 1991): 13–15.

33. For American reactions, see Michael Lind, "Surrealpolitik," *New York Times*, March 28, 1991; and Amy E. Schwartz, "Germany's 'Special Way,' " *Washington Post*, February 13, 1991.

34. Ian Buruma, "The Pax Axis from Japan to Germany," *New York Review of Books*, April 25, 1991, pp. 25–28, 38–39, points to the concern that the German position may reflect anti-Semitic attitudes.

35. Ignacio Ramonet, quoted in *Le Monde Diplomatique*, February 1991.

36. Robert Steuckers in *Diorama Letterario*, November 1990.

37. Alan Riding, "For the Europeans, Worry That War Could Hit Home," *New York Times*, January 13, 1991.

38. Quoted in "The Second Trajan's Empire," *The Economist*, September 29, 1990, p. 57.

39. See Steven Greenhouse, "Pro-Iraq Sentiment Is Increasing in North Africa," *New York Times*, January 29, 1991.

40. See Marc Fisher, "Germany's Outburst of Yankee-Bashing: What's Going On?" *Washington Post*, January 27, 1991.

41. See Andrew Rosenthal, "Bush in Germany, Finds Kohl Cool to Gulf Policy, Stressing Talks Instead," *New York Times*, November 19, 1990; and Marc Fisher, "Kohl Expected to Give No Excuses, No Troops," *Washington Post*, September 15, 1990.

42. Umberto Bossi in *Corriere della Sera*, January 20, 1991.

43. Quoted in Flora Lewis, "A Shabby French Sulk," *New York Times*, February 20, 1991. See also William Drozdiak, "French Defense Minister Resigns amid Dispute over Military Aims," *Washington Post*, January 30, 1991; and Robert Swann, "Chevenement Goes," *Middle East International*, February 8, 1991, pp. 17–18.

44. See Swann, "What Was Mitterrand Up To?"

45. Quoted in Sunic.

46. Chirac's argument is discussed in Flora Lewis.

47. Quoted in Hella Pick, "Europe 'Left Out of Gulf Decisions,' " *Guardian*, December 14, 1990. For a comprehensive discussion of the Europeans' perception that Washington was using the gulf war to reassert its global economic power, see Henwood.

48. Quoted in Craig R. Whitney, "Thatcher Warns Europe over Gulf," *New York Times*, August 31, 1990.

Chapter 7

1. Quoted in Charles Goldsmith, "New World Order: A View from Europe," *Europe*, March 1991, p. 10.

2. Ibid.

3. Jim Hoagland, "Saddam's Sand in the Gears," *Washington Post*, October 25, 1991.

4. Quoted in Goldsmith, p. 10.

5. Christopher Layne, "Ambivalent Past, Uncertain Future: America's Role in Post–Cold War Europe," in *NATO at 40: Confronting a Changing World*, ed. Ted Galen Carpenter (Lexington, Mass.: Lexington Books, 1990), p. 246.

6. Gerald Frost, "America and Her Friends," *National Review*, May 27, 1991, p. 30.

7. Ted Galen Carpenter, "U.S. Must Shake Its NATO Habit," *Christian Science Monitor*, June 19, 1991.

8. Goldsmith, p. 10.

9. See discussion in Glenn Frankel, "Europeans Rethinking National Security Policies," *Washington Post*, March 23, 1991.

10. The idea is recommended by Nicholas Henderson in "The Relationship under Fire," *The Spectator*, January 19, 1990, pp. 11–12. NATO's leaders adopted a decision along those lines at their meeting in Rome in November 1991. See Alan Cowell, "Bush Challenges Partners in NATO over Role of U.S.," *New York Times*, November 8, 1991.

11. Quoted in Goldsmith, p. 10.

12. Craig Whitney, "Europe Discovers the German Colossus Isn't So Big after All," *New York Times*, April 21, 1991.

13. William Drozdiak, "NATO Redefines Defense Role," *Washington Post*, August 8, 1990.

14. Thomas Goltz, "Dealing Turkey into the Power Game," *Washington Post*, September 23, 1990.

15. For a discussion of new Atlanticism and its application to the Middle East, see Brian Beedham, "A Survey of Defence and the Democracies: A New Flag," *The Economist*, September 1, 1990, Supplement, pp. 1–18.

16. Marc Fisher, "Bonn Takes First Steps to Quiet Allied Critics," *Washington Post*, April 27, 1991.

17. Quoted in "Europe's New Line on NATO: 'Yankee Don't Go Home,' " *Business Week*, April 1, 1991, p. 41.

18. Ibid.

19. Ibid.

20. "Europe's New Line on NATO."

21. Anthony de Jasay, "Lessons from the Gulf War," *National Review*, May 27, 1991, p. 28.

22. Ibid.

23. Jim Hoagland, "Europe—A Great Idea, Up to a Point," *Washington Post*, April 25, 1991.

24. Paul E. Gallis, "U.S.–West European Affairs: Responding to a Changing Relationship," *Congressional Research Service Issue Brief*, Washington, April 3, 1991, p. 11.

25. Ibid. There were also other indications of European independence in the security field. One example is the coordinated European efforts in the defense procurement area (which is currently excluded from EC responsibilities). The independent European Program Group (IEPG), to which 11 of the 12 EC states and 13 of the 14 European NATO states belong, has taken early steps to move into the gap. The IEPG's stated task is to eliminate wasteful duplication in weapon systems. However, two of its implied goals are to develop a defense industrial base competitive with that of the United States and to take over functions that are at present assigned to an American-controlled NATO body, the Conference of National Armaments Directors.

26. Whitney. More recently, Kohl and Mitterand have proposed giving the European Community a more significant role in European security, which until now has been within the exclusive purview of NATO. The Franco-German plan calls for the eventual creation of a "European army corps" that would bring army units of the

members of the European Community under joint command of the nine-nation Western European Union, the community's defense forum. Earlier, Britain and Italy called for gradual creation of an independent European pillar of NATO. See Mark M. Nelson and Martin du Bois, "France, Germany Initiate EC Plan for Defense Role," *Wall Street Journal*, October 17, 1991.

27. Hoagland, "Europe—A Great Idea."

28. Ibid.

29. See R. Jeffrey Smith, "Cheney to Take Up French Proposal for European Force outside NATO," *Washington Post*, May 27, 1991.

30. Charles Krauthammer, "Unipolar Moment," *Foreign Affairs* 70, no. 1 (1991): 23–33. For a critique of that reasoning, see Ted Galen Carpenter, "The New World Disorder," *Foreign Policy* 84 (Fall 1991): 24–39.

31. Beedham, pp. 5–7.

32. Quoted in Shada Islam, "European Community: Keeping Up the Pressure," *Middle East International*, March 22, 1991, pp. 8–9.

33. *Le Monde*, December 6, 1991.

34. A UN group used that term to describe the results of the American destruction of Iraq. Paul Lewis, "UN Survey Calls Iraq's War Damage Near-Apocalyptic," *New York Times*, March 22, 1991.

35. See Youssef M. Ibrahim, "Iraq Rejects European Plan for Kurdish Haven in North," *New York Times*, April 10, 1991.

36. See, for example, Bruce Stokes, "Scrapping over the Economic Spoils," *National Journal*, March 23, 1991, pp. 670–71.

37. I would like to thank officials at the Italian embassy in Washington, D.C., for providing me with information on the CSCM, including a draft of the proposal itself.

38. See Alan Riding, "Spain Seeks to Mend Europe's Ties with North Africa," *New York Times*, March 20, 1991.

39. For the history of the proposal, see Gianni de Michelis, "Global Viewpoint," *San Francisco Chronicle*, February 2, 1991.

40. See *CSCE: A Framework for Europe's Future* (Washington: U.S. Department of State, Bureau of Public Affairs, 1989).

41. "The Second Trajan's Empire," *The Economist*, September 29, 1990, p. 57.

42. For developments in the Maghreb, see Peter David, "A Survey of the Arab World: Squeezed," *The Economist*, May 12–18, 1990, Supplement, pp. 1–26.

43. William Drozdiak, "North Africans' War Stand Makes Europeans Uneasy," *Washington Post*, January 29, 1991.

44. Frankel.

45. Barry James, "De Michelis Urges 'Helsinki' Talks on War's Aftermath," *International Herald Tribune*, February 18, 1991.

46. De Michelis.

47. Quoted in Riding.

48. Ibid.

49. See Sam Cohen, "U.S., EC Rebuffs Force Turkey to Look Elsewhere," *Middle East Times*, July 24–30, 1990, p. 6; and Clyde Haberman, "Turks Claim Some of Victor's Spoils," *New York Times*, March 13, 1991.

50. Rashid Khalidi, "A Peace Strategy for the Persian Gulf," *New York Times*, December 26, 1990; and John M. Goshko, "Syria Rebuffs Baker on Peace Process," *Washington Post*, April 25, 1991.

51. James.

52. For ideas on reorienting Israeli foreign policy, see Leon T. Hadar, "Reforming Israel—Before It's Too Late," *Foreign Policy* 81 (Winter 1990–91): 106–27.

53. Raymond Cohen, "Twice Bitten? The European Community's 1987 Middle East Initiative," *Middle East Review* 20, no. 3 (Spring 1988): 33–44.

54. Ibid.

55. Ibid., p. 35.

56. Joel Bainerman, "The Economic Dimensions of the Palestinian-Israeli Conflict," *World & I*, December 1990, pp. 588–89.

57. Cohen, p. 37.

58. See Bainerman. See also Joel Brinkley, "Israeli Economy Is Keeping Many Jews in USSR," *New York Times*, May 5, 1991.

59. "EC Announces Aid to Israel, Kuwait, and Frontline Nations," *Europe*, March 1991, p. 32.

60. Edward A. Gargan, "Palestinians in Kuwait Waiting Sadly for the Stamp of Alien," *New York Times*, May 6, 1991.

61. Islam, "European Community: Keeping Up the Pressure," p. 10.

62. John M. Goshko, "Baker Told Europe Wants Role in Any Middle East Peace Talks," *Washington Post*, April 18, 1991.

63. Shada Islam, "European Community: Let Us In, or Else," *Middle East International*, April 19, 1991, p. 14.

64. Italian ambassador Gabriele Sarda in an address before the Middle East Institute, Washington, D.C., May 22, 1991.

65. Bonar Law, the late leader of the British Conservative party, quoted in David Fromkin, *A Peace to End All Peace: The Fall of the Ottoman Empire and the Creation of the Modern Middle East* (New York: Avon Books, 1989), p. 554.

66. For reflections of changes in thinking on the war, see Patrick E. Tyler, " 'Clean Win' in the War with Iraq Drifts into a Bloody Aftermath," *New York Times*, March 31, 1991; Flora Lewis, "Here We Go Again—Arming the Mideast," *New York Times*, March 21, 1991; and Anthony Lewis, "What We Have Wrought," *New York Times*, March 29, 1991. For a discussion of the problems that will confront the United States in the region, see Leon T. Hadar "When the War Stops: Chaos and Instability Await," *San Diego Union*, February 17, 1991; and Leon T. Hadar and Alan Tonelson, "What Happens Postwar," *Los Angeles Times*, January 27, 1991.

67. For a discussion of that scenario, see Leon T. Hadar, "U.S.-Israeli Relations: Coping with the Post–Cold War Blues and Surviving the Persian Gulf Hangover," *Middle East Insight* 7, no. 6 (May/June 1991): 40–46.

68. L. Carl Brown, *International Politics and the Middle East: Old Rules, Dangerous Game* (Princeton, N.J.: Princeton University Press, 1984), especially part 2.

69. For a discussion of the long-term prospects for American disengagement from the Middle East, see Leon T. Hadar, "Creating a U.S. Policy of Constructive Disengagement in the Middle East," Cato Institute Policy Analysis no. 123, December 29, 1989.

70. Denis Healey, "A Bloody Shambles in the Wake of War," *Guardian Weekly*, March 31, 1991, p. 11.

71. Theo Sommer, "A World beyond Order and Control," *Guardian Weekly*, April 28, 1991, p. 10.

72. For a discussion of those trends, see Richard Rosecrance, *The Rise of the Trading State: Commerce and Conquest in the Modern World* (New York: Basic Books, 1986).

73. Quoted in Sommer, p. 10.

74. Shibley Telhami, "Stay Out of Iraq's Civil War," *New York Times*, April 5, 1991.
75. Christine Helms, "Is Iraq Smashed beyond Repair?" *New York Times*, March 30, 1991.
76. President Wilson's adviser Colonel House, quoted in Fromkin, p. 257.

Chapter 8

1. For a standard history of Zionism, see Ben Halpern, *The Idea of a Jewish State* (Cambridge, Mass.: Harvard University Press, 1969). For a history of Arab nationalism, see George Antonius, *The Arab Awakening* (New York: G. P. Putman & Son, 1946).
2. The most recent study of post–World War I Middle Eastern diplomacy is David Fromkin, *A Peace To End All Peace: The Fall of the Ottoman Empire and the Creation of the Modern Middle East* (New York: Avon, 1989).
3. Leopold S. Amery, aide to British prime minister Lloyd George, quoted in Fromkin, p. 283.
4. Ibid.
5. On the agreement signed by Feisal and Weizman on January 3, 1919, see Avi Shlaim, *The Politics of Partition: King Abdullah, the Zionists and Palestine 1921–1951* (New York: Columbia University Press, 1990), pp. 40–41.
6. For an original and critical study of the early stages of the development of Zionism by an Israeli journalist and historian, see Boaz Evron, *A National Reckoning* (Hebrew) (Tel Aviv: DVIR Publishing House, 1988).
7. For the most recent extensive study of Arab history in the 20th century, see Albert Hourani, *The History of the Arabs* (Cambridge, Mass.: Harvard University Press, 1991).
8. For background on the Zionist and pro-Arab efforts in the United States during that period, see Peter Grose, *Israel on the Mind of America* (New York: Alfred A. Knopf, 1983); and Eliahu Elath, *The Struggle for Statehood* (Tel Aviv: Am Oved, 1979).
9. For background on the first Arab-Israeli war, see J. C. Hurewitz, *The Struggle for Palestine* (New York: Schocken, 1976).
10. See Shlaim.
11. On the integration of the Arab-Israeli conflict into the context of the Cold War, see Malcolm Kerr, *The Arab Cold War: Gamal 'Abd al-Nasir and His Rivals, 1950–1969* (New York: Oxford University Press, 1971); Israel Be'er, *Israel's Security: Yesterday, Today, Tomorrow* (Tel Aviv: Amikam, 1966); and Yair Evron, *The Middle East: Nations, Superpowers and Wars* (New York: Praeger, 1973).
12. On developments that followed the 1967 war, see Donald Neff, *Warriors for Jerusalem: The Six Days That Changed the Middle East* (New York: Linden Press/Simon & Schuster, 1984). On the effects of the war on Palestinian nationalism, see Aaron David Miller, *The PLO and the Politics of Survival* (New York: Praeger, 1983).
13. For a provocative Israeli analysis of the background of the *intifada*, see Ze'ev Schiff and Ehud Ya'ari, *The Intifada* (New York: Simon & Schuster, 1990).
14. For different perspectives on the post–Cold War era, see Francis Fukuyama, "The End of History?" *National Interest* 16 (Summer 1980): 4–5; Earl C. Ravenal, "The Case for Adjustment," *Foreign Policy* 81 (Winter 1990–91): 3–19; and Stanley Kober, "Idealpolitik," *Foreign Policy* 79 (Summer 1990): 3–24.
15. For a discussion of the role of the trading state in the international system, see Richard Rosecrance, *The Rise of the Trading State: Commerce and Conquest in the Modern World* (New York: Basic Books, 1986).

16. The optimistic view can be found in Fukuyama, pp. 3–18. More pessimistic assessments are found in Ravenal and Ted Galen Carpenter, "The New World Disorder," *Foreign Policy* 84 (Fall 1991): 24–39.

17. For an interesting discussion of that thesis, see William S. Lind, "Our Coming Alliance with Russia," *Policy Review* 49 (Summer 1989): 18–21.

18. See Hernando de Soto, *The Other Path: The Invisible Revolution in the Third World* (New York: Harper & Row, 1989).

19. For an interesting discussion of the competing political visions in Israel, see Amnon Rubinstein, *The Zionist Dream Revisited* (New York: Schocken, 1984).

20. Quoted in Avishai Margalit, "Israel's White Hope," *New York Review of Books,* June 27, 1991, p. 22.

21. Ibid.

22. On the political debate in the Arab world, see Fouad Ajami, *The Arab Predicament: Arab Political Thought and Practice Since 1967* (Cambridge: Cambridge University Press, 1981).

23. Peter David, "Squeezed: A Survey of the Arab World," *The Economist,* May 12, 1990, Supplement, p. 26.

24. Ibid., p. 3.

25. Quoted in Leon T. Hadar, "Perestroika in the Promised Land?" *Reason,* October 1990, p. 32.

26. Schiff and Ya'ari, p. 76.

27. Joel Bainerman, "The Economic Dimensions of the Palestinian-Israeli Conflict," *World & I,* December 1990, p. 593.

28. For a similar, canton-based libertarian solution to the South African conflict, see Frances Kendall and Leon Louw, *After Apartheid: The Solution for South Africa* (San Francisco: Institute for Contemporary Studies, 1987).

29. Ibid., p. 127.

30. Quoted in Hadar, "Perestroika in the Promised Land?" p. 32.

31. For development of the argument for Israeli nationalism, see Joseph Agassi, *Religion and Nationality: Towards an Israeli National Identity* (Tel Aviv: Papirus, 1984).

Chapter 9

1. Maureen Dowd, "Bush Proclaiming Victory, Seeks Wider Mideast Peace; Hints at Pressure on Israel," *New York Times,* March 7, 1991.

2. See, for example, Lisa Beyer, "The Future: Now, Winning the Peace," *Time,* March 11, 1991, pp. 46–49.

3. Quoted in Christine Helms, "Is Iraq Smashed beyond Repair?" *New York Times,* March 30, 1991.

4. James Gleick, *Chaos: Making a New Science* (New York: Viking, 1987).

5. Tareq Ismael from Calgary University used a model based on the chaos theory to explain Middle Eastern politics during a discussion, "The Post-War Persian Gulf: Political and Economic Issues," that took place in the Mayflower Hotel in Washington, D.C., June 13, 1991, under the auspices of the Middle East Institute.

6. For a discussion of the Butterfly Effect, see Gleick, pp. 20–23.

7. David Fromkin, *A Peace to End All Peace: The Fall of the Ottoman Empire and the Creation of the Modern Middle East* (New York: Avon Books, 1989), p. 564.

8. For a revealing analysis of the nature of the Kuwaiti ruling elite, see Christopher Dickey, "Kuwait, Inc.," *Vanity Fair,* November 1990, pp. 154–61, 238–39.

9. Examples include Ben Wattenberg, *The First Universal Nation* (New York: Free Press, 1991); and Joshua Muravchik, *Exporting Democracy* (Washington: American Enterprise Institute, 1991).

10. See Leon T. Hadar, "The Best Laid Plans of Global Dreamers Are No Match for the Realpolitik of the Middle East—So Resist Them," *Los Angeles Times,* January 27, 1991. The recent parliamentary elections in Algeria, which highlighted the power of the Moslem fundamentalist groups, accentuated the dilemma faced by the West. See, for example, Youssef M. Ibrahim, "The Arab World Comes to the End of Illusions," *New York Times,* January 5, 1992; and Gerald F. Seib, "U.S. Push for Democracy Doesn't Seem to Extend to Nations of Middle East," *Wall Street Journal,* November 4, 1991.

11. See, for example, *Restoring the Balance: U.S. Strategy and the Gulf Crisis* (Washington: Washington Institute on Near East Policy, Strategic Study Group, 1991); and Shireen T. Hunter, "Ingredients for Stability," *Middle East International,* February 22, 1991, pp. 18–19.

12. For the problems involved in assigning a security role in the gulf to the Egyptian military, see Leon T. Hadar, "The Egyptian Armed Forces," *Journal of Defense and Diplomacy* 6, no. 10 (October 1988): 40–47; and "Winning the Peace: A Stable Mideast Will Be Harder to Achieve Than Military Victory," *Business Week,* March 11, 1991, pp. 24–27. For a discussion of the economic problems confronting Saudi Arabia, see "The Prospects for the Saudi Arabian Economy in the Wake of the Gulf War," *Oxford Analytica Daily Brief,* March 25, 1991, pp. 2–5.

13. See Patrick E. Tyler, "U.S. and Bahrain Near Pact on Permanent Military Base," *New York Times,* March 25, 1991.

14. See Youssef M. Ibrahim, "Gulf Nations Said to Be Committed to U.S. Alliance," *New York Times,* October 25, 1991.

15. Ann Devroy, "President Proposes Mideast Arms Curb," *Washington Post,* May 30, 1991; and Andrew Rosenthal, "Bush Unveils Plan for Arms Control in the Middle East," *New York Times,* May 30, 1991.

16. R. Jeffrey Smith, "U.S. Now Stockpiling Arms in Israel," *Washington Post,* June 1, 1991.

17. Joel Brinkley, "U.S. Begins Storing Military Supplies in Israeli Bunkers," *New York Times,* June 1, 1991.

18. See "Shut Down the Mideast Arms Bazaar? Forget It," *Business Week,* March 11, 1991.

19. See R. Jeffrey Smith, "U.S. Faces Contradiction on Mideast Arms Control," *Washington Post,* March 7, 1991; and Patrick E. Tyler, "As the Dust Settles, Attention Turns to New Arms Sales," *New York Times,* March 24, 1991.

20. For an Israeli study proposing nuclear proliferation in the Middle East as a way of strengthening stability there, see Shai Feldman, *Israeli Nuclear Deterrence: A Strategy for the 1980's* (New York: Columbia University Press, 1982).

21. See, for example, Thomas L. Freedman, "A Missing Olive Branch," *New York Times,* October 20, 1991.

22. See, for example, Robert S. Greenberger, "Arab-Israeli Talks Recess with Delegates Puzzled That World Paid Little Attention," *Wall Street Journal,* December 19, 1991.

23. See Leon T. Hadar, "U.S.-Israeli Relations: Coping with the Post–Cold War Blues and Surviving the Persian Gulf Hangover," *Middle East Insight* 7, no. 6 (May/June 1991): 40–46.

24. For an example of the sense of triumph among members of the military-industrial complex, see Anthony H. Cordesman, "America's New Combat Culture," *New York Times*, February 28, 1991.

25. On the Israeli lobby's strategy, see Gary Lee, "Pro-Israel Lobby Cold to Concessions," *Washington Post*, March 20, 1991.

26. On changing Iranian attitudes, see Alan Cowell, "Iran's View of U.S. Seems to Soften," *New York Times*, May 26, 1991. On America's reaction, see Elaine Sciolino, "U.S. Responds Cooly to Overture from Iran," *New York Times*, May 29, 1991. On the recent rise in the political power of Islamic fundamentalism in the Arab world, see Jonathan C. Randal, "Algerian Army Given Powers to Curb Islamic Fundamentalists," *Washington Post*, June 6, 1991; and Jonathan C. Randal, "Tunisia Appears to Have Defused Its Militant Fundamentalist Surge," *Washington Post*, June 6, 1991.

Index

Arafat, Yasir, 130
Aramco, 43
Armenia (in Commonwealth of
Independent States), 82
Arms control, Middle East, 173,
184–86
Arms race, Middle East
post war, 141, 185–86
Soviet concern about, 12–13
Arms sales
expanding business of, 185–86
to Iran by United States, 55
petrodollars used in, 56
by U.S. to Iraq, 59
Ashkenazim, 91, 94–95
Assad, Hafez al-, 90, 174
Assyrians, 150

Baghdad Treaty, 49
Baker, James A., III, 10, 18
at end of Cold War, 6
on European role in Middle East,
139–40
post–gulf war shuttle diplomacy of,
66
relations with Shamir, 61
Balance of power
internal requirement for Middle
East, 184
Soviet and U.S. policy for Middle
East, 49
U.S. policy to maintain Middle East,
25–27, 60, 181–83
Balance of terror, 16
Balfour Declaration (1917), 29, 40, 41
Bandar bin-Sultan, 20
Begin, Menachem, 52
Ben-Gurion, David
foreign policy of, 93–94, 95
position on Israel's security, 73
role in Mapai party of, 73, 96
Biermann, Wolf, 116–17
Boren, David L., 115
Bossi, Umberto, 117
Brandeis, Louis, 94
British Royal Dutch-Shell Company, 43
Brown, L. Carl, 49, 51, 175
Brzezinski, Zbigniew, 9
Buchanan, James M., 31
Buchanan, Patrick, 4, 81
Burden sharing
in gulf war, 142
proposed European, 123–26

Thatcher on, 119, 140
Bureaucracy, Israel. *See* Public sector,
Israel
Bush, George, 2
European perception of, 108
goals for postwar Middle East, 141
meets Mitterrand, 108–9
on need for strong America, 2
plan for Middle East arms control,
184–85
policy toward Saddam, 11
position on U.S. military power, 6–7
post–Cold War goal, 6
post–gulf war Middle East
proposals, 64–65, 173, 184
relations with Shamir, 61
strategy for Persian Gulf military
action, 23–24
Bush administration
on European defense plan
alternative, 126–27
geostrategic perspective, 11
New Atlanticism concept of, 123
plan for Middle East arms control,
173, 184–85
position on CSCM plan, 140
position on financial aid to Eastern
Europe, 92
pro-Saudi trend of, 141
on threats to security, 6, 11
Butterfly Effect (chaos theory), 176–77

Camp David, 50
Camp David accords, 111–12
Carlucci, Frank, 20
Carter, Jimmy, 19
Carter Doctrine (1980), 36, 112
Center for International and Strategic
Studies report (1990), 9
Central Treaty Organization, 49
Chaos theory, 175–76
Cheney, Richard, 184–85
Chevènement, Jean-Pierre, 117–18
Cheysson, Claude, 118
Chirac, Jacques
relations with Levy, 136
on U.S. control of oil suply, 118–19
Coalition for America at Risk, 21
Cold War
effect of end of, 15, 16, 37, 112–14,
154, 162
effect on Arab-Israeli conflict, 152
influence on Arab regimes of, 161

inequalities in, 95
needed reform for, 104
progressive and reactionary
  elements in, 159–60
recommendation to encourage
  changes, 101, 104
U.S. should encourage reform of,
  101
in West Bank and Gaza, 137–38
Egypt
  Copts in, 150
  fear of Saddam, 60
  in perspective of Arab nationalists,
    147–48
  Soviet arms agreement with, 49–50
  U.S. aid to, 34
Egyptian-Czech arms agreement, 49
Egyptian-Israeli peace process, 46, 49,
  50
  See also Camp David accords
  effect of, 34, 52, 111–12
  role of political elites in, 52
  U.S. Cold War policy for Middle
    East in, 10–11
  use for, 35
Eidelberg, Paul, 82
Eisenhower, Dwight D., 73, 102
Eisenhower Doctrine (1957), 36, 47, 49,
  111
Elath, Eliahu (Epstein), 29
Eldar, Akiva, 85
Emigration, 160
  See also Refugees
Eretz Israel, 147
Eshkol, Levi, 96, 102
Euro-Arab Conference (1989), 132
Europe
  economic role in Middle East,
    136–39
  as independent force in Middle East,
    131–32
  as new global power, 112–13
  policy with proposed CSCM in
    place, 132
  proposal to restructure NATO, 2
  role as new power center, 15
  role in gulf war, 108–10, 114–18
  role in redefined NATO structure,
    123
European Community (EC)
  associate membership for Israel,
    Jordan, and a Palestinian state,
    138–39
  Middle East policy of, 136–37

policy toward Palestinian
  population, 137–38
predicted shift of responsibility to,
  110
proposals for security role for, 127
rejects Turkey as member, 22
relations with Israel, 137–38
stance in gulf war of, 114–15
European nationalism, 146, 150
European nations
  position on U.S. role in gulf war
    and Middle East, 119
  subsidy argument in GATT, 115
Europe for the Europeans, 126–28

Faisal el Husseini, 168
Federation
  of Israel and proposed Palestinian
    state, 104
  proposal to organize Iraq as, 164
  in a proposed Palestinian state,
    167–69
Feisal (emir), 40, 41
Fernández Ordóñez, Francisco, 116
Foreign aid, U.S.
  See also Economic aid, U.S.; Military
    aid, U.S.
  effect of Egyptian-Israeli peace
    agreement on, 52
  to Iraq, 25
  to Israel, 77–78, 80, 90–91, 94, 97–98
  proposal to cut all, 80
  recommendation to cut Israeli,
    100–101
Foreign intervention
  See also Intervention policy, U.S.
  effect of military, 180
  in Middle East, 47–54, 176–78
  role of Middle Eastern elite in, 51–52
Foreign policy, Israel
  Arabists and pro-Iranian segments
    in, 26
  debate on reorientation of, 82
Foreign policy, Soviet Union
  strategy in Middle East, 48
  toward Middle East, 12–13
Foreign policy, U.S.
  See also Cold War policy, U.S.;
    Intervention policy, U.S.;
    Neoconservatives, American;
    Strategic asset paradox
  balance-of-power in gulf region,
    25–27

basis for Middle East, 47–51
Cold War and post–Cold War
  paradigms for Middle East, 10–11
effect on Israel's incentives to
  change, 98–100
economic aid as component of,
  36–37
geoeconomist group influence on,
  81–82, 83
for gradual disengagement from
  Israel, 90–91, 100–101
Iran-Iraq balancing act, 25–26
Israeli and Saudi manipulation of,
  58–59
in Middle East: post–World War I,
  40–41
Middle East twin pillar policy, 55
of paleoconservatives and
  libertarians, 4–5
role of foreign policy iron triangles
  in, 32
role of oil interests in, 42–44
shaping of Middle Eastern, 42
toward Israel and Middle East:
  post–Cold War, 17–18
toward Israel as strategic asset,
  15–16, 21, 53, 72–75
Zionism enters, 45
Foreign policy elite
  See also Foreign policy triangles
  investments to obtain benefits,
  31–32
  perpetuating activities of, 31–32
Foreign policy elite, U.S., 3–5
  See also Geoeconomic group;
  Geostrategic group
Foreign policy triangles
  composition and role of, 32
  effect of wars and crises on, 35–36
  information networks for, 34–37, 54
  Middle Eastern iron triangle, 32–38,
  190
  in Middle East issue, 32–38
Four Plus Five Forum for Regional
  Cooperation in the Mediterranean,
  135
Fourth World countries, 56
France
  conditions for renewed power of,
  139
  independence for Syria and
  Lebanon, 42
  Moslem population in, 116
  position on gulf war, 117–19

position on reform in Middle East,
  130, 131
proposed Franco-German security
  alliance, 127–28
relations with Iraq, 118
relations with Israel, 83
relations with United States (1991),
  108–9
role in idea of CSCM, 132
support for European defense plan,
  126
territories held under Sykes-Picot
  agreement, 39–40
France-Iraq Friendship Association,
  118
Franco-German security arrangement,
  127
Free-riders
  European nations as, 115
  European proposal to eliminate, 119
  new powers as, 107–8
  U.S. criticism of Europe's, 115, 119,
  121
Free-trade area, U.S.-Israeli, 104
Friedman, Milton, 97
Fukuyama, Francis, 1

Galilee, 138
Gaza Strip
  economy of, 137, 138
  Israeli invasion of (1967), 153
  Israeli policy for settlements in, 79
  Israel's forced withdrawal from, 102
  support for Palestinian homeland in,
  81
Genscher, Hans-Dietrich, 117
Geoeconomic group, 3–4, 6–7, 11, 115
Georgia (in Commonwealth of
  Independent States), 82
Geostrategic group, 4–6, 9–10
  See also Neoconservatives, American
Germany
  under new Atlanticism, 124
  response to gulf war, 116–17
  support for European defense plan,
  126
  U.S. concerns about, 128
Glaspie, April C., 24–25
Gorbachev, Mikhail
  meets Kohl (1990), 2
  statements after Helsinki summit
  (1990), 23
  transforms Middle East policy, 12–13

Government control, Israel, 69–70, 90
  See also Economic system, Israel;
    Political system, Israel
Great Britain
  as dominant Middle East power, 39
  economic condition, post–World
    War II, 44
  impact of gulf war on, 114
  overthrow of Iraqi government
    (1942), 42
  perception of position on Jewish
    homeland, 29
  position on European defense plan,
    126
  post–World War I relations with
    Jewish and Arab nationalists, 148
  relations with Kuwait, 114
  relations with U.S., 114, 119
  urges U.S. military intervention in
    Middle East, 22
  U.S. concerns about, 128
Greece, 44
Gulf Cooperation Council, 162, 182

Halter, Marek, 118
Hashemite dynasty, 40
Hassan bin Talal, 19
Hegel, G. W. F., 69
Hegemony, U.S.
  See also Burden sharing; Economic
    integration; European Community
  decline of, 107, 110, 114
  European resentment of, 121
  in Middle East, 108–9, 113
  neoconservative vision of, 129
  U.S. insistence on, 140
Helsinki process. *See* Conference on
  Security and Cooperation in Europe
  (CSCE)
Helsinki summit (1990), 23
Herzl, Theodore, 146, 147
Higgs, Robert, 34, 35
Himmelfarb, Gertrude, 92
Histadrut, 94
Holocaust, the, 45, 92, 95, 151
Houston, meeting in (1990), 2
Human rights
  Helsinki Accords, standards for, 133
  violation in Iraq, 25
  violation in Turkey, 22
Hungary, 157
Hussein Ali-Sherif, 149
Hussein bin Ali (emir), 40

Hussein (king of Jordan), 96, 179

Ickes, Harold, 44
Ideologies
  See also Cold War; Cold War policy,
    U.S.; Moral commitment to Israel,
    U.S.; Neoconservatives, American
  to activate information networks,
    35–36
  use for maintaining foreign policy
    commitment, 37
Immigrants
  to Palestine (late 1800s), 149
  value to Israel of, 13, 90
  See also Refugees
Immigration
  conditions for southern European,
    133
  effect of massive Israeli, 101, 137–38
  estimates to Israel of Eastern
    European, 89–90
Immigration law, U.S., 101
Independence
  of Algeria, 111
  of Arab states, post–World War II,
    151, 160
  goals for Palestine, 111–12
Information networks
  conditions for erosion of Middle
    Eastern, 37
  for foreign policy triangles, 34–35,
    54
  ideologies to activate, 35–36
  Middle Eastern, 35, 190
Interest groups
  See also Geoeconomic group;
    Geostrategic group; Lobbies;
    Neoconservatives, American
  activities of Arab and Israeli, 19
  coalition of American Jewish
    organizations, 32
  coalition of Arab-Israeli, 20, 21–22,
    30–31
  foreign policy benefits to, 31
  pressure for U.S. Middle East
    involvement, 18–24, 30–31
  use of Cold War as leverage by,
    45–47
Intergovernmental Conference on
  European Union, 127
International system
  See also Core region; Middle states
    and regions; Peripheral states and
    regions

interests of, 34, 37–38
in Middle East foreign policy
  triangle, 32–33
Italy
  on gulf war, 117
  Moslem population in, 116
  role in independent CSCM, 132

Jackson, Jesse, 24, 81
Japan, 113, 119, 155, 157
Jewish community, American
  eroded support for Israel in, 82
  factors to neutralize support of, 102
  financial and political support from,
    95
  influence of Arab-Israeli wars on, 36
  in Middle East information network,
    35
  political power of, 41, 45, 72–73
  position on Israel, 91
  position on Israeli policy in occupied
    territories, 80
  support for Israel, 151, 152
  support open immigration, 101–2
  U.S. policy toward Israel to court, 46
Jewish nationalism
  See also Arab-Israeli conflict
  after World War II, 150–53
  conflict with Arab nationalism, 145
  historic broadening of, 146–47
  U.S. support for, 152
Jobert, Michel, 118
Johnson, Lyndon B., 73–74, 102
Johnson, Paul, 45
Johnson, Samuel, 27
Jordan
  democratic trend in, 163
  failed economy of, 137
  response to CSCM proposal, 136
  West Bank annexed (1948), 151
Joxe, Pierre, 125
Judaism
  See also Religion in Israel
  interpretation with nationalist base,
    146
  in Israel today, 68–69, 158, 160

Kendall, Frances, 168
Kennan, George, 48
Kennedy, John F., 73, 96
Kennedy, Paul, 3
Khomeini, Ayatollah, 7

King-Crane report, 41
Kirkpatrick, Jeane, 5, 20, 25, 75–76
Kissinger, Henry, 46
  on gulf war, 143
  as player in U.S. foreign policy, 74
  prediction of shift of U.S.
    responsibility, 110
  prediction of U.S. Middle East
    involvement, 107
  on rationale for higher oil prices, 55
  shuttle diplomacy (1973), 50, 96
Kitchener, Horatio H., 38
Klare, Michael, 4
Kohl, Helmut
  meets Gorbachev, 2
  meets Mitterrand (1991), 127
  policies of, 92
Korea, 157
Krauthammer, Charles, 83–84, 86
Kristol, Irving, 5
Kurdistan, 41
Kurds
  failure of Arab nationalism for, 161
  German relief efforts for, 124
  Iraq policy toward, 25
  as non-Arab national group, 150
  postwar problems of, 141, 174
  as potential political force, 163
Kuwait
  British relations with, 114
  effect of Iraqi invasion of, 60,
    113–14, 116
  Iraqi invasion of, 54
  postwar situation of, 141, 181

Labor party, Israel
  decline of, 98
  effect of U.S. policy on, 96–97
  political elite of, 95
  post–Cold War and gulf war, 136
Lahat, Shlomo, 62
Lantos, Tom, 20, 86
Lawrence, T. E., 38
Lebanon
  creation of, 41
  effect of Arab nationalism on, 161
  Israeli invasion of (1982), 50, 76, 79,
    81
  Maronites in, 150
  proposed division of, 164
  U.S. peacekeeping role in, 76
Lebanon war (1982), 35, 153
Ledeen, Michael, 27

227

competition of U.S. and British, 110
role after World War II of U.S., 44
Oil interests
  See also Arab oil lobby
  British-American Middle East
    competition, 43–44
  higher prices serve, 55–56
  post–World War I U.S., 42–43
  predicted role in formation of Israel,
    29–30
  U.S. commitment to Arab oil states,
    33
Oil price shocks
  effect on Europe of, 112
  effect on Fourth World countries of,
    56
OPEC. *See* Organization of Petroleum
  Exporting Countries (OPEC)
Operation Desert Storm, 173–75
Organization of Petroleum Exporting
  Countries (OPEC)
  Iraq's interest in, 59–60
  U.S. role in price rise of, 55–56
Ostrovsky, Victor, 81
Ottoman Empire, 39
Ozal, Turgut, 22

Paleoconservatives, American, 4–5
Palestine
  British commitment to Jewish
    homeland in, 29
  Jews in, 150
  problem of Arabs in, 149–50
  proposal for independent federation
    of, 167–69
  as proposed Jewish homeland, 147
  under Sykes-Picot agreement, 39–40
  UN partition plan for, 45
Palestine Liberation Organization
  (PLO)
  creation of, 153
  dialogue with U.S., 14, 17
  recognizes Israel (1988), 13, 153
  war with Israel (1982), 50
Palestinian-Israeli conflict
  economic aspects of, 166–67
  effect of end of Cold and Persian
    Gulf Wars on, 153–54
  Iraq-Israel proposed agreement, 16,
    26
  lack of solution for, 158–59
  Lebanon war (1982) as outcome of,
    50

proposal of Palestinian state to end,
  167–68
result of circumventing, 77
role of United States in solving,
  187–89
Palestinian-Israeli war (1982), 49, 50
Palestinians
  See also Intifada
  American support for homeland,
    80–81
  catalyst for nationalism, 153
  in Cold War alignment, 152
  European Community policy
    toward, 137
  European support for solving
    problem of, 116
  Israel diverts attention from problem
    of, 113
  post–gulf war problems of, 174
  response to CSCM proposal, 136
  in state of Israel, 78, 151–52, 166–67
Pan-Arabism
  See also Nationalism, Arab; Islamic
    fundamentalism
  after World War II, 150–51
  British help in creation of, 39
  conditions for emergence of, 146
  in conflict with Zionism, 145–46
  effect of hypothetical decline, 166
  French confrontation with, 83
  identification with Islam, 161
  replacement by national identities,
    165
  Saddam's fading commitment to, 26
Pan-Islam. *See* Islamic fundamentalism
Pax Americana
  failure in Middle East to impose, 49
  problems with imposition of, 141–42
  Soviet strategy to prevent Middle
    Eastern, 23–24
  world view of, 129
Pax Britannica
  costs of managing Middle East, 42
  plan in Middle East for, 38–39
Pelzman, Joseph, 104
Peres, Shimon
  diplomatic initiative of, 97
  relations with Mitterrand, 136
Peripheral states and regions, 156
Persia, 150
  See also Iran
Persian Gulf region, 112
Persian Gulf War (1991)
  See also Operation Desert Storm

Sykes-Picot agreement (1916), 39, 40
Syria
  after Israeli-Palestinian war, 49
  independence of (1945), 42
  Kurds in, 150
  postwar economy of, 143
  proposed division of, 164
  public relations campaign against,
    190–91
  relations with Soviet Union, 12–13
  response to CSCM proposal, 136
  under Sykes-Picot agreement, 39–40

Taiwan, 157
Terrorism
  as consequence of U.S.-Israeli
    policies, 112
  effect of Palestinian, 37
  as form of reaction, 191
  motives in Lebanon for anti-
    American, 76
Texaco, 43, 44
Thatcher, Margaret
  on burden sharing and U.S.
    protection, 119
  position on American hegemony, 3,
    131
  position on Saddam, 114
  Reagan preference for policies of, 92
  support of United States in gulf war,
    122
  on united Europe, 109–10
Thies, Joachim, 125
Trade policy. See Free-trade area, U.S.-
  Israeli
Transjordan, 41
Treaty of Lausanne (1923), 40
Treitschke, Heinrich, 69
Truman, Harry S, 43, 45
Truman Doctrine, 36, 44, 110
  See also Greece; Turkey
Tullock, Gordon, 31
Tunisia
  democratic trend in, 163
  Islamic fundamentalism in, 133
  response to CSCM proposal, 135
Turkey
  American post–World War II aid for,
    44
  British World War I victory over, 148
  as non-Arab entity, 150
  response to CSCM proposal, 135
  role as strategic asset, 22

role in gulf war, 124
urges war in Middle East, 22

Uganda, 147
Union of American Hebrew
  Congregations, 82
United Jewish Appeal, 95
United Nations
  gulf war Security Council action,
    23–24
  role of, 12
U.S.-PLO talks (1989), 82

van Creveld, Martin, 79
Venice Declaration (1980), 111–12

Wahhabi dynasty, 40
Weinberger, Caspar, 57, 75
Weizman, Ezer, 26
Weizmann, Chaim, 149
Welfare system, Israel, 70–71, 97
  See also Public sector, Israel
Welles, Sumner, 29–31, 34
West Bank
  economy of, 137
  extreme Zionist wing in, 158
  Israeli invasion (1967), 153
  Israeli settlements in, 78, 79, 97, 141
  support for Palestinian homeland in,
    81
Western European Union (WEU), 123,
  127
WEU. See Western European Union
  (WEU)
Wilson, Woodrow, 40–41, 42
World Bank policies, 56
Wörner, Manfred, 123

Ya'ari, Ehud, 167
Yergin, Daniel, 55
Yom Kippur War (1973), 35, 46, 50, 74,
  111
  See also Egyptian-Israeli peace
    process
  effect of, 78–79, 152–53
  as illustration of U.S. Middle East
    policy, 10–11
Young, Andrew, 54
Yugoslavia, 157

Zaire, 76
Zionism
  See also Anti-Zionism; Palestine
  after World War II, 38
  British perception of, 38–39, 41
  conditions for emergence of, 146
  in conflict with Pan-Arabism and
    Arab nationalism, 17, 145–46
  effect of hypothetical decline, 166

financial support for, 94
influence of Palestine immigrants
  on, 149
support in U.S. for, 29
in U.S. foreign policy, 45
Zionists
  British post–World War I relations
    with, 148–49
  in United States, 32

About the Author

Leon T. Hadar teaches in the School of International Service of the American University and is an adjunct scholar in foreign policy studies of the Cato Institute. He has been a New York and Washington correspondent for several foreign newspapers and UN bureau chief for the *Jerusalem Post*. He has also been affiliated with the Institute of East-West Security Studies and the Center for International Development and Conflict Management as a research fellow in foreign policy.

Hadar's articles on Middle Eastern issues have appeared in journals such as *Foreign Policy, Columbia Journalism Review,* and *World Policy Journal* and in U.S. and foreign newspapers including the *New York Times*, the *Washington Post*, the *Los Angeles Times*, the *Atlanta Journal & Constitution*, and the *San Diego Union*. He appears frequently on radio and television and has been interviewed by CNN, ABC News, BBC, ITN, Voice of America, Monitor Radio and Television, and German television.

Hadar is a graduate of the Schools of Journalism and International Affairs and the Middle East Institute of Columbia University. He earned his Ph.D. in international relations from the American University.

Cato Institute

Founded in 1977, the Cato Institute is a public policy research foundation dedicated to broadening the parameters of policy debate to allow consideration of more options that are consistent with the traditional American principles of limited government, individual liberty, and peace. To that end, the Institute strives to achieve greater involvement of the intelligent, concerned lay public in questions of policy and the proper role of government.

The Institute is named for *Cato's Letters*, libertarian pamphlets that were widely read in the American Colonies in the early 18th century and played a major role in laying the philosophical foundation for the American Revolution.

Despite the achievement of the nation's Founders, today virtually no aspect of life is free from government encroachment. A pervasive intolerance for individual rights is shown by government's arbitrary intrusions into private economic transactions and its disregard for civil liberties.

To counter that trend, the Cato Institute undertakes an extensive publications program that addresses the complete spectrum of policy issues. Books, monographs, and shorter studies are commissioned to examine the federal budget, Social Security, regulation, military spending, international trade, and myriad other issues. Major policy conferences are held throughout the year, from which papers are published thrice yearly in the *Cato Journal*. The Institute also publishes the quarterly magazine *Regulation* and produces a monthly audiotape series, "Perspectives on Policy."

In order to maintain its independence, the Cato Institute accepts no government funding. Contributions are received from foundations, corporations, and individuals, and other revenue is generated from the sale of publications. The Institute is a nonprofit, tax-exempt, educational foundation under Section 501(c)3 of the Internal Revenue Code.

CATO INSTITUTE
224 Second St., S.E.
Washington, D.C. 20003